At Freedom's Crossroads: Making Sense of Modern Slavery

David Lohan

Published by Frederick Douglass Anti Slavery Press, Cork, Ireland. Web: www.fdouglasspress.com. Email: endslavery@fdouglasspress.com.

Printed in Ireland, the UK, and the European Union by Carraig Print Litho Press, Cork, Ireland. Web: www.cprint.ie. Email: info@cprint.ie. Printed on demand internationally by IngramSpark and Amazon. Available in eBook format from Amazon.

Subject Areas

Slavery • Slaves • Human Trafficking • Sex Trafficking
Prostitution • Sex Trade
Human Rights
Economics • Labor • Labor Rights • Migrants
Psychology • Psychological Effects of Violence
Sociology • Social Justice • Gender Studies • Gender Based Violence
History • U.S. History • African-American History • Antebellum
• U.S. Civil War
America • Africa • Europe • Asia
Women • Women's Rights • Feminism • Radical Feminism
Children • Children's Rights
African Witchcraft • Juju • Voodoo
Environment • Environmental Degradation • Sustainability • Corporate
Social Responsibility
Politics • Government • International Relations • Policy • Crime
Equality Model • Nordic Model • Swedish Model
Abolition • Legalization • Decriminalization

But what needs tell the story, told too oft,—every day told,—of heart-strings rent and broken,—the weak broken and torn for the profit and convenience of the strong! It needs not to be told;—every day is telling it,—telling it, too, in the ear of One who is not deaf, though he be long silent.

Harriet Beecher Stowe, *Uncle Tom's Cabin*

To my wife Lorna,
and
in loving memory of Tom, Bernadette, Willie, Ina & Ciara.

Disclaimer

Every precaution has been taken to verify the accuracy of the information contained herein. The author and publisher assume no responsibility for any errors or omissions. No liability is assumed for damage that may result from the use of information contained within. This publication is intended for informational purposes only.

Reviews

An exceptional book which helps the reader make valuable connections between the wrongs of the past and what is currently happening in the world today. Connections which must be made visible and acknowledged in order for things to change. The forensic research exposes the heart wrenching existence of many, at times even hard to imagine but we must go there for those who are suffering now are dependent on us applying the logic and reasoning which the author has done impeccably. As a survivor of the sex trade who has experienced and witnessed the trauma inflicted upon us, it should not still be the case where women & girls need to 'prove their humanity' in order for states to protect us from all who exploit.

Mia de Faoite LLM, Coordinator of the Beyond Exploitation Campaign, Ireland

This is a must-read for all who want to gain a deeper understanding of modern slavery, its root causes and the conditions under which it thrives, how and why perpetrators benefit from it. Importantly, it offers a convincing explanation on why human trafficking for sexual exploitation continues to flourish in an environment where prostitution is legalized – and why the Swedish (or Equality) model might be a better alternative. David Lohan's book is a very comprehensive work and by providing a thorough introduction into the history of slavery in the United States, the author sheds new light on the mechanisms of today's modern slavery. At SOLWODI, we support several hundred victims of human trafficking each year – women who have suffered severe physical and mental abuse, who are deeply traumatized. May the insights shared in this book contribute to ending this de-humanizing practice.

Dr. Maria Decker, Chairwoman, SOLWODI Deutschland e.V..

With this new book, David Lohan once again proves his gift for exploring the historical and philosophical depths of significant constructs that have been often overlooked due to their frequent and sometimes inaccurate use. By employing logical parallels to colonial slavery and by exposing its inhuman 'economic rationale' and unfathomable violence, the author presents his innovative perspective on human trafficking. The trafficking of women and children into prostitution is unpacked in an informed factual way with compelling analysis. An exceptional read for those working on human trafficking and all people interested in this phenomenon.

Dr. Nusha Yonkova, a well-recognized expert in human trafficking, migration, and gender-based violence at Irish and European Union (EU) levels.

The author's holistic approach to the subject provides a good foundation for anyone looking to gain insight into the concept of human trafficking in general, a form of slavery which continues through new labels. The book is structured into sections that take the reader on a journey through the history of slavery, setting the scene for the recognition of new patterns and differing characteristics of "modern slavery". The underlying themes of profiteering, culpable governance, and dehumanization amid race relations echo throughout the book reflecting the presence of such themes in the capitalist world of yesterday, today, and potentially tomorrow. This book serves as an important tool that should be used to educate, inform, and raise awareness.

Dr. Salome Mbugua, Head of Operations & Strategy, AkiDwa.

The issue of slavery and its exploitative nature is not something we can explore as an exclusively historical phenomenon. Slavery is alive in the world today and the slaves live amongst many of our own communities, including here in Ireland. David Lohan presents us with an excellent overview of our past, our present and our engagement with slavery. An insightful and incredibly well researched book, At

Freedom's Crossroads is highly recommended to anyone wishing to learn more about slavery, its construct and the worlds around us which profiteer from it, facilitate it and governments who choose to ignore it.

JP O'Sullivan B.Soc.Sc, MSW, Network & Communications Manager, MECPATHS.

Contents

Acknowledgements

Some years ago, I was introduced to the good work of a small charity with a big heart. The mission of the charity, called Cois Tine (which simply means *by the fireside* in the Irish language), was to provide a place of welcome, warmth and refuge to African migrants living in Ireland. Through the life of its mission, the charity encountered the reality of the lives of those who visited. One of those realities was modern slavery, otherwise known as human trafficking. I am eternally grateful to Angelo Lafferty SMA of Cois Tine for a great many things, but not least for the opportunity to learn about the harsh realities of modern slavery, and for starting me upon this path.

A special word of thanks is owed to Mr. Thomas E. Griffith of the U.S. State Department who, through his support and efforts, made an immense contribution to this work. In every undertaking there are hurdles that simply cannot be overcome alone, and this undertaking was no exception. I am eternally grateful for your encouragement, for your support of my work, and for your willingness to go the extra mile when it was needed most. Thank you!

For more than five years Ambassador Luis CdeBaca, as Ambassador-at-Large to Monitor and Combat Trafficking in Persons, led the United States' response to the plight of millions across the globe. I wish to express my gratitude for his leadership during his tenure, and for the immense contribution made to this work in the form of the interview provided, for the many insights generously shared and for the hospitality warmly extended.

I wish to express my thanks to Ms. Mai Shiozaki and Ms. Sara E. Gilmer of the Office to Monitor & Combat Trafficking in Persons at the U.S.

State Department in Washington D.C. for facilitating the interview with Ambassador CdeBaca.

To others at the U.S. State Department, I also wish to express my thanks. Over the years you have continued to shed a light upon the darkness that is modern slavery. Your contributions to global efforts to alleviate the suffering of slaves are too many to be counted. You have made other important contributions too, diligently encouraging and facilitating the efforts of partners. I convey a special word of thanks to Mr. Peter Glennon at the U.S. Embassy in Ireland and to Ms. Lynne Gadkowski at the State Department.

My gratitude to Ms. Corrine Dettmeijer, Dutch National Rapporteur on Trafficking in Human Beings and Sexual Violence against Children, for the contribution made to this work in the form of the interview provided, and for the sharing of insights on so complex an issue.

To Ms. Linda Watson, founder of Linda's House of Hope in Australia, my many thanks for your contribution to this work.

To Ms. Wendy Barnes, my heartfelt thanks for sharing the experience of so difficult an issue as human trafficking and for your willingness to be a voice for survivors through the medium of this work.

To Ms. Sarah Benson, CEO of Women's Aid in Ireland, and to Ms. Nusha Yonkova, Principal Officer at the Irish Human Rights and Equality Commission, my many thanks for your assistance extended in pursuit of the completion of this work.

To Detective Sergeant Jonas Henriksson of the Polismyndigheten, the Swedish Police Authority, thank you for sharing the lessons learned from Sweden.

To Mr. Mike Davis, Asia Director of Global Witness, my sincerest thanks for your reflections on the *Kimberley Process* and the challenges faced in regulating conflict diamonds and conflict minerals.

To Ms. Sarah Scott-Webb of Hagar International, thank you for the contribution made to this work, and for shedding light upon the human trafficking situation in New Zealand, as well as the cultural norms it challenges.

To Mr. Nivit Kumar Yadav of India's Centre for Science and Environment, my thanks for the insights provided on brick kilns in India.

I wish to offer my sincerest gratitude to Dr. David Fitzgerald of the School of History at University College Cork in Ireland. This work has its origins in a thesis supervised by Dr. Fitzgerald and submitted to University College Cork in Ireland as part of my studies for an M.A. in Politics.

To Dr. Lawrence Dooley of the Management and Marketing Department, and Dr. Vittorio Bufacchi of the Department of Philosophy, both at University College Cork in Ireland, I express my gratitude for the contributions made to the original thesis upon which this work is based.

To Dr. Jason Dockstader of the Department of Philosophy at University College Cork in Ireland, I am similarly grateful for the many insights, both philosophical and historical, imparted during my time at the University.

To Ms. Roslyn Phillips, National Research Officer at FamilyVoice Australia, my sincerest thanks for your assistance as facilitator, and for the contribution made as a result.

To Ms. Mia De Faoite, my thanks for your steadfast advocacy, for sharing your insights and for your assistance with making this work a reality.

To Ms. Catherine O'Brien and Sr. Mary Anne O'Brien, my thanks for all your support and for your many recommendations.

To Francis Rozario SMA, Advisor at the Society of African Missions, my sincerest thanks for your assistance.

To Mr. Brian O'Kane of Oak Tree Press in Ireland, my thanks for your meticulousness.

To Ms. Lucy Huddlestone, Publisher Account Manager at Neilson Book Services Limited, thank you for your guidance.

I wish to express my thanks to the University of North Carolina at Chapel Hill, for permitting the use of its electronic edition of *Recollections of My Slavery Days* by William Henry Singleton, and to East Carolina University which holds the original work, subsequently digitized and presented online by the University of North Carolina at Chapel Hill. To this end I acknowledge the assistance of Mr. Jason E. Tomberlin and Mr. Tyler Gilmore of the Research & Instructional Services Department at the University of North Carolina's Louis Round Wilson Special Collections Library, and Mr. Dale Sauter, Manuscripts and Rare Books Department, at the Joyner Library of East Carolina University.

My thanks too to Mr. Kyle Buetzow, Director of Campaigns at Made In A Free World, for information provided in relation to the Slavery Footprint online survey.

My thanks to Mr. Hal Jespersen of CWMaps.com, who not only for allowed his wonderful Civil War map of Charleston Harbor to be used, but who also assisted in making it available.

My thanks to Ms. Petra Lent McCarron and Mr. Len Morris, both of Media Voices For Children, who kindly provided their organization's photographs of a young girl working in a brick kiln, and a boy aboard a wooden structure sieving small fish.

To Detective Niall Stack of An Garda Siochána and to Mr. Barra McGrory, Queen's Counsel, thank you for the interest you both took in human trafficking and for the impetus it provided in making this work a reality.

To Orla Kelly, of Orla Kelly Publishing, my many thanks.

I gratefully acknowledge the permission granted to reproduce copyrighted material in this book and I wish to thank the following for granting permission or for facilitating it being granted: Mary Andrews of The Independent newspaper; Dr. Mary Garner of The Child And Woman Abuse Studies Unit; Professor James Nickel of the University of Miami, Thea Tjeerdema at the office of The Procurator General of the Supreme Court of the Netherlands; Dr. Robert Bunker of C/O Futures, LLC; Dayna Nicole of Engage Books in Vancouver; Johanna Carlson of the Swedish Economic Crime Authority; Nadia Jaber at Sweden's national police media center; Kristina Radford at The Swedish Institute; Alison Irvine-Moget at the International Labour Organization (ILO); Koert Debeuf at EUObserver.com; Roxanne Koenis at the Dutch National Rapporteur's office; Ron Gluckman; Olivier Sprée at the International Organization for Migration (IOM); Dr. Connie Lester at Florida Historical Quarterly; Jörg Rehder at Der Spiegel; Judith Forman at New Zealand's Ministry of Justice; all the team at Walk Free who produce the *Global Slavery Index*; Claire Roberts of the Environmental Justice Foundation (EJF); Thorbjorn Tellefsen of the Associated Foreign Press (AFP); all at Yale's Gilder Lehrman Center for the Study of Slavery, Resistance, and Abolition and to Joseph Opala; Craig Myles and Claire Louise Hooper of Sage Publishing; Ashleigh Harding of New Zealand Media and Entertainment (NZME); Amy Moss of The Economist; Ben Kennedy of Oxford University Press; Rheian Shannon of Canada's House of Commons; Dr. Isabelle Guérin of Institut de Recherche pour la Dévelopment; Suzanne Hoff of La Strada International; Sanja Ćopić of *Temida*; Alexandra Donskova-Huber, Evan Karr, and Lisa Villard at the Organization for Security and Co-operation in Europe (OSCE); Brian P. Moss at Thomson Reuters; Yi Deng and Justine Evans at Columbia University Press; Professor

Kathleen Scalise at the University of Oregon; Jessica Follini and David Yokoyama at the University of California Press; Sam Anselmo at Louisiana State University Press; Katie Konrad and Victoria Nordell at Save The Children; Olubiyi Olusayo at National Agency for Prohibition of Trafficking in Persons (NAPTIP); Honorary Consul of Uganda to Ireland Dr. Sylvia Gavigan; Yessenia Santos and Mabel Mante Taveras of Simon & Schuster; the rights management team at Taylor & Francis Group; Kenechukwu Esom at the United Nations Development Programme (UNDP); Professor Phil Hubbard of King's College London and Professor Jane Scoular of the University of Strathclyde Glasgow; and Professor Richard HJM Staring of the University of Rotterdam.

Every effort has been made to contact copyright holders of material reproduced in this book. Any omissions will be gladly rectified in subsequent editions upon notification.

Preface

Across the world, more than 40.3 million people are held in modern slavery today. If every single man, woman and child in the U.S. states or territories of Alaska, Colorado, Delaware, Guam, Hawaii, Idaho, Kansas, Kentucky, Louisiana, Maine, Montana, New Hampshire, New Mexico, North Dakota, Oklahoma, Rhode Island, South Dakota, U.S. Virgin Islands, Vermont, Virginia, Wyoming, and Mississippi was held in slavery their combined number would be slightly less than the present global reality. Add in the population of Washington D.C. and now the picture is about right. This book is about modern slavery, about slaves, about the reasons why slavery existed in the past, about why it exists today, and what might be done to end it. In using the term *modern slavery*, I mean the slavery not belonging to the ancient world, or more specifically slavery encompassing both the present-day practice of *human trafficking* and slavery's historical practice during the modern era. In researching this book, I wanted first to make sense of slavery and its slaves, and to understand too what others have understood these to mean. I also wanted to form this understanding free of the influence of present-day political debate so that, through the past, I could assess the merits of the claims of the present. In this way I also wanted to make sense of the politics of slavery.

My fascination with slavery, and with modern slaves, began over a decade ago when I first undertook advocacy work for a charity working with African migrants. I encountered the issue of slavery not as a phantom of the past, but as a living breathing entity of the present, and not as a faraway thing, but as something close to home. The plight of human trafficking's victims has ensnared my heart and my mind ever since. As part of my advocacy work at Cois Tine (*by the fireside* in the Irish language), I co-authored a book entitled *Open Secrets: An Irish Perspective on Trafficking & Witchcraft*. The book scrutinized the use of Juju and Voodoo in human trafficking. My Master of Arts thesis, *Sex Trafficking, Legalization and Abolition: The end of the affair*, examined the policy approaches of Sweden and the Netherlands on prostitution. When legislative change was being sought on Ireland's prostitution policy, I actively supported the *Turn Off The Red Light (TORL)* campaign and the efforts of the survivor activists who led the campaign. During 2018, the Society of African Missions published *Mission, Migration and the ministry of exorcism* in Rome, a book to which I contributed my insights on human trafficking. During 2020, I submitted my views to the Irish government's review of the *Criminal Law (Sexual Offences) Act 2017*. At www.DavidLohan.com I share my thoughts on various aspect of human trafficking and news of the latest human trafficking happenings globally. As a result of my work, I have been a frequent invitee to anti-trafficking events hosted by the U.S. Department of State. Ireland's national police service, An Garda Siochána, and Northern Ireland's Public Prosecution Service have sought opinion on matters relating to human trafficking and the use of African Witchcraft to carry it out.

Many contributed to making this work possible, and those contributions were made in a variety of ways. Key contributions were made in the form of interviews given by those working in government positions, in policing, in the charity sector, and by those who are survivors of modern slavery. Those contributions were made at various times. Some were made nearly 10 years ago at the outset of the journey that made this book possible. Others were given during the years intervening. The research informing this work extends to tens of thousands of pages of material reviewed. It draws upon accounts from hundreds of survivors of slavery past and present. The research is predominantly qualitative in nature, and it uses a variety of methods. The book itself consists of three sections. The first of these addresses the practice of chattel slavery, the practice where one human being legally holds another as property, as it existed once in the antebellum United States. The second section addresses contemporary slave practices. It includes an extensive walk-through and a reflection of modern slavery as viewed by America's (now-former) Ambassador-at-Large to Monitor and Combat Trafficking in Persons. The third, and final, section explores three policy approaches to sex trafficking and the results those approaches have yielded in the years since they were instituted.

The book is written as a testament to those who once suffered through the slavery of the past, and in service to those who suffer through it today. It seeks to share the memories of the past, with the contemporary reader, in a bid to assuage present suffering. It is written for citizen and legislator alike. It is written for those who are students and for those who are teachers. It will be of assistance to those who find themselves struggling amidst the debate over modern slavery, trying to reconcile seemingly irreconcilable claims. In as much as it poses challenging questions, it seeks to challenge ideas about slaves and their slavery, and to challenge some of the conditions that give rise to them. In as much too as it aims to make sense of slavery it strives to empower the reader, and through empowerment it hopes the reader will come to find their own role in efforts to end it.

There was no shortage of candidates to consider as starting points for this research. Over the 350 years of slavery's existence in Brazil, for example, many millions were brought to that country's shores to toil in a life of bondage. As time passed one generation gave way to the next. Many more were born into slavery, sharing in the inescapable inheritance of their forefathers, never knowing for even one day what it meant to be free. Eventually however I was drawn to the United States and to the years preceding the start of the U.S. Civil War and for good reason. During those years many wrote about slavery from a variety of perspectives. Abolitionists wrote about it to convey its horrors and its realities. With slavery so deeply ingrained in the

South those abolitionists needed to evoke passion in the North for their cause among brethren detached from it, so that they might rally political support against it. Former slaves wrote about slavery too, recounting their first-hand experiences. They added their voices to those of the abolitionists in cries to end the cruel trade. Surprisingly perhaps, some slaveholders also wrote about slavery. Their writings reveal a different perspective. Their motivation was itself different, for through their writings they advocated for slavery, and for the need for slaves. It is an intriguing question whether common ground could be found in the writings of all three (slaves, slaveholders, and abolitionists) and, if indeed this common ground could be found, just how informative might it be in presenting a holistic picture of slavery and of the slaves it traded.

There were other intriguing questions too, ones whose answers are gravely important to improving the fate of modern slaves. Having navigated the past, how many similarities might be found between the modern-day practice of human trafficking and the slavery of the recent past? What lessons might be learned from the past and applied to the present? Furthermore, having answered these questions, I wanted to evaluate the merits of some responses to one of the largest contributors to slavery in the world today, specifically sex trafficking. This is an important consideration as in the United States and in Europe, increased awareness of human trafficking is leading to a governmental reassessment of policy and legislative change.

Section 1

Chapter 1:

"The People"?

Early in the stillness and darkness of an April morning, the fate of a nation, in the shape of a simple lanyard, rested in the hands of a young lieutenant by the name of Farley. To the lieutenant's right stood Captain James, anxiously scrutinizing his pocket watch as the appointed time approached. There was nothing left now to do. There was nothing one could now do. All preparations had been made. With diligence the lieutenant had sighted the mortar himself.[1] The final few seconds ticked by. With a sharp tug of the lanyard the 10-inch mortar flashed, roared, and recoiled, sending its round screaming out into the dark emptiness of the early morning sky, soaring high across the harbor. Higher and higher the round climbed. Faster and faster, it sped. In an instant it was at the halfway point of its fateful journey. With the fatigue of its breathless pace gradually slowing its ascent, it arced over the waters below and, as it did so, it was increasingly fixed on the fast-approaching small island fort floating in the dark moonlit waters below. Finally, it plummeted from the darkness onto the target the lieutenant had so carefully chosen for it only minutes before. Within moments it was accompanied by flashes and the thunderous rumble of artillery fire from the many other batteries along the shore as they sent their rounds aloft. Soon these rounds were plummeting upon the small fort, lashing at her back with bitter blows, their trails scarring the night's sky in their wake. From the fort there was no response. It bore each mighty blow, for now at least, with quiet resignation. Precisely where his round fell, the lieutenant could not say. Precisely what he had just done, Farley was quite certain. The wolf, long restrained, had been unleashed. The time was precisely 4:30am; the day April 12, 1861; the war "of the people, by the people," upon the people, the U.S. Civil War, had begun.[2]

At the heart of the conflict between the two sides were several questions: who precisely were "the people," what did their freedom endow them to practice, and what was the very meaning of freedom itself? Not 100 years before this moment The Declaration of Independence clearly and carefully set out a vision of freedom. The Declaration emphatically asserts how those who wrote it, and those on whose behalf it was written, held certain truths "to be self-evident." Central to their assertion was the truth that "all men are created equal, that they are endowed by their Creator with certain unalienable Rights, that among these are Life, Liberty and the pursuit of Happiness." However, even before quill pen was put to parchment slavery was part of the fabric of American life, and slavery did not cease once the Declaration was made. Some years later, in 1787, the United States Constitution followed in a similar manner declaring:

> We the People of the United States, in Order to form a more perfect Union, establish Justice, insure domestic Tranquility, provide for the common defence, promote the general Welfare, and secure the Blessings of Liberty to ourselves and our Posterity, do ordain and establish this Constitution for the United States of America.

Side-by-side with these gallant words of freedom was something else, something surprisingly unworthy of them, something that left some delegates to the Constitution's convention unwilling to sign the document because it "codified and protected slavery and the slave trade."[3]

How could a nation proclaim freedom on one hand and practice slavery, which is so repugnant to freedom, on the other? How could "the People," described in the United States Constitution, establish a constitution to "secure the Blessings of Liberty" for themselves and how could some be slaves still in the aftermath of its establishment? How could a nation, so passionately committed to the freedom of "all men" who, it accepted, were "created equal" and still find itself at war between two parties, one of which fought to end slavery and the other to preserve it? Yet by 1861 when hostilities broke out, chattel slavery (the legally instituted form of slavery by which one person may hold another as property) and freedom had co-existed in the United States for over 70 years. The co-existence was uneasy, however. Before Lieutenant Farley sent the civil war's first shot arcing over Charleston's harbor on that April morning, the conflict between them meant his deed had long been anticipated and thought even to be inevitable. To answer these questions, a journey is begun of the more than three decades of politics which culminated in the events at Charleston. It is to the making sense of slavery, and to its politics, that this work is dedicated, not to the battle, or to the war, which are offered only as a starting point. More importantly the politics of that time are offered as a starting point for questioning whether and how those same politics bring about untold misery today for tens of thousands in America, and for millions around the world, in their new guise as *modern slavery*, or *human trafficking*.

The city of Charleston, South Carolina, sits on a peninsula on the westward side of a harbor whose mouth opens to the east. The water of the Ashley River flows down the western side of the peninsula, and that of the Copper River down the eastern side, where the two converge at the peninsula's apex, and merge in the harbor. These waters are divided again briefly as they flow eastward where they meet a small island fort, compelling them to flow north and south of it, before they merge once more and flow into the Atlantic Ocean beyond. Despite appearances this small island, just 2.5 acres in size, is not naturally occurring. Between the years 1829 and 1845 some 109,000 tons of rock and stone were manhandled to a location just offshore of the southern point of the harbor's mouth to create it. Once this gargantuan first phase of the work had been completed the second phase, the construction of the brick fort, commenced. Its architects, appreciating the strategic importance of the newly created island, gave the fort five sides, each armed with several artillery pieces on several tiers. The pentagonal structure enabled occupants to survey and barrage, if necessary, a seaborne threat navigating from any of the possible approaches to the fort or harbor. By assuring the security of the harbor, the security of the City of Charleston, a few short miles to the north-west, and the security of the city's inhabitants were assured against any who would assault it from the sea. Inspired by the memory of Brigadier General Thomas Sumter, a hero of South Carolina's militia during the Revolutionary War, its creators named the stronghold Fort Sumter.[4]

The term *secession* has become equated with the events of the Civil War and with the actions of the Southern states. It means to depart from an entity, and more particularly to depart from a political one. Secession has become equated with something else too, with the motivations underpinning the Civil War, with the very issue of slavery. Charleston was a bastion of slavery. During the time when slaves were imported into the South from Africa 40%, or 150,000, of the importees arrived through Charleston.[5] The city continued to be important to slavery even when those importations ceased. Now the question of slavery was at the very heart of a debate, as to whether it was better to stay in or to depart the Union. The Northern states wished to end slavery. The South was determined to preserve it, and not only that, but to assert the primacy of the rights of the States, over those of the Union, on this issue.

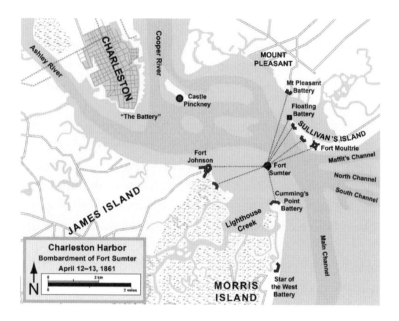

Figure: "Charleston Harbor. Bombardment of Fort Sumter. April 12-13, 1861"
by Hal Jespersen, www.cwmaps.com,
used under CC BY 3.0 / Converted to monochrome.

It was here, at Charleston, in December of 1860, that the decision was finally taken to secede from the political community of the United States, and by seceding to reshape a distinct community, one in favor of slavery. In early January Mississippi followed South Carolina's lead when it too seceded, and before long they were joined by Florida, Alabama, Georgia, Louisiana, and Texas. Some slave states opted not to secede. In February, the seceding states convened and formed the Confederate States of America. As secession spread, Fort Sumter became a symbol of the predicament overall.[6] Once the decision was taken to secede the presence of Union troops effectively became that of a foreign entity, one whose presence within South Carolina's territory was increasingly intolerable. From South Carolina's vantage it had seceded and would accept no external contentions to the contrary, however they might be asserted. Conversely, for the Union to abandon military installations in South Carolina was itself intolerable, for to do so would be to recognize the legitimacy of secessionist South Carolina. It was clear that, if war came, Fort Sumter was where it would start.

Some months before South Carolina's attempt at secession, Major Robert Anderson, a soldier in the service of the Union, a veteran of three wars and a graduate of West Point, was beginning to feel he could no longer depend upon southern hospitality. He was made certain of it when hostilities commenced. For nearly 36 hours the fort sustained bombardment. One of Anderson's officers, Captain Doubleday, later wrote: "I heard afterward that the enemy loudly cheered Anderson for his persistency under such adverse circumstances."[7]

One of those likely not cheering Anderson, his men, or the Union they represented, was Edmund Ruffin. As the hours passed, Ruffin was to be found at one of the batteries on Cummings Point where he was busy hacking away at Fort Sumter, at the Union for which she stood, and relishing the spectacle of seeing them burn. Ruffin was an aged, wealthy plantation owner, a slaveholder, and a volunteer fighting for the Confederacy. He was described as possessing an unconventional intellect, which he had used to rescue Virginia's depleted soil using special fertilizers.[8] For many years he produced his own journal, the *Farmers' Register*, as part of his commitment to the cause of Southern agriculture and to its advancement through reform.[9] Ruffin's interests extended further, however. Though initially moderate, he was an avid advocate of secession and of states' rights. He was also an avid defender of slavery. His contributions to the cause of slavery were many and included his authorship of several works on the subject, including *The Political Economy of Slavery* and *Slavery and Free Labor, Described and Compared.* Though separated from Sumter and its forces by a body of water and by a body of politics, his reputation transcended both. His hatred of the North, and that for which she stood, was passionate to the point of being white hot. Captain

Doubleday later wrote of Ruffin how his "love of slavery amounted to fanaticism," and he credited him even as a worthy contender for the title of "father of secession."[10] Indeed for a long time after these events it was Ruffin, and not Farley, who was credited with the dubious honor of firing the Civil War's first shot.

Figure: Edmund Ruffin (National Archives and Records Administration 1861).

Long before it was fired, in fact 40 years before, some foresaw its coming. In a letter, in April of 1820, Thomas Jefferson writes prophetically of a "momentous question, like a fire bell in the night" that "awakened and filled" him "with terror."[11] So terrifying was his prophecy he considered it "at once as the knell of the Union."[12] Jefferson's mood darkened further when he conceded to believing the sons of the revolutionary "generation of 76", through their "unwise and unworthy passions", would "perpetrate this act of suicide on themselves and of treason against the hopes of the world."[13] At the core of his foreboding question was a conundrum, and an apparent contradiction, at whose very heart was the issue of slavery and whose conflict was created by the politics of slavery. Southern states vehemently wanted to retain slavery. Northern states passionately wanted it abolished. Neither side was content to accede to the other. Jefferson summed it up thus:

> We have the wolf by the ear, and we can neither hold him, nor safely let him go. Justice is in one scale, and self-preservation in the other.[14]

In contrast to Jefferson's farsightedness years before, nobody saw the small boat coming from Charleston's shore to Fort Sumter. In it was Senator Wigfall and some men. Even when the boat landed at the island's shore it remained undetected. It was only when Wigfall emerged from the boat, took up a white flag and made his way to the fort that he was eventually seen. He brought with him the offer of generous terms for the surrender of Fort Sumter. After some deliberation, negotiation, and reconsideration these were duly accepted. Remarkably the honor of being first into the fort went to none other than pro-slavery firebrand Edmund Ruffin.[15] Major Anderson's trial, and that of his men, was over.

In 1846 Dred Scott started a trial of his own. He was not seeking to tear himself away from the whole, for as a black person he belonged to a group of people already long set apart. He was not fighting to preserve his freedom, for as a slave he had none to preserve. He was not seeking power, but escape from it, and he was not seeking to maintain a union but to be granted, as an equal in the union of humanity, his proper place in one. The defendant was one John F.A. Sanford. Owing to a clerical error in the spelling of the defendant's name the case came to be known as *Scott vs. Sandford* although it is more popularly referred to as the *Dred Scott Decision*. Mr. Scott petitioned the Supreme Court for his freedom, and in effect for that of his wife Harriet, on the basis that their travels with Dr. John Emerson, who had been his legal owner at the time, to parts of the United States where slavery was illegal, had endowed them with their freedom.[16] Mr. Sanford, who had inherited Mr. & Mrs. Scott following the death of Dr. Emerson, contested the matter.

In 1857 Chief Justice Taney delivered the opinion of the Supreme Court:

> The words "people of the United States" and "citizens" are synonymous terms, and mean the same thing. They both describe the political body who, according to our republican institutions, form the sovereignty and who hold the power and conduct the Government through their representatives.[17]

The opinion continues, ruling on the rights of slaves:

> The question before us is whether the class of persons described in the plea … compose a portion of this people, and are constituent members of this sovereignty? We think they are not, and that they are not included, and were not intended to be included, under the word "citizens" in the Constitution, and can therefore claim none of the rights and privileges which that instrument provides for and secures to citizens of the United States. On the contrary, they were at that time considered as a subordinate and inferior class of

10

beings who had been subjugated by the dominant race, and, whether emancipated or not, yet remained subject to their authority, and had no rights or privileges but such as those who held the power and the Government might choose to grant them.[18]

The Court then addressed the meaning of the language used in America's founding instruments:

In the opinion of the court, the legislation and histories of the times, and the language used in the Declaration of Independence, show, that neither the class of persons who had been imported as slaves, nor their descendants, whether they had become free or not, were then acknowledged as a part of the people, nor intended to be included in the general words used in that memorable instrument.[19]

Far from asserting the equality of black persons the Court asserted their inequality. They were, according to the Court, "a subordinate and inferior class of beings," a race "excluded from civilized Governments and the family of nations, and doomed to slavery."[20] The black man or woman had "no rights which the white man was bound to respect," it added.[21] In light of the judgement, Dredd Scott might have been minded years later to consider the sentiment of an advertising campaign by the Colt Manufacturing Company. The slogan, used by the company to promote its famed Colt .45 handgun stated: "God made man, but Samuel Colt made them equal."

It was power that made men equal by bestowing upon some a pivotal minimal standard of political equality. In the absence of this minimal standard, which confers the recognition of a common humanity upon all of Mankind, the black person was not an end in him or herself.

Rather she or he was a person degraded, a person measured by a lower standard. It was, of course, a standard by which people should not be measured, for it treated human beings as means to an end, rather than as ends in themselves. Robbed of humanity, and the moral and legal protections that recognition granted, America's slaves were in effect little more than mere property, or a foreign entity, or worse again, both. Power alone would dictate the slave's fate. If the opinion was welcomed as a vindication of the practice of the slavery of its own time, it served the purpose of being a vindication of its historical practice in the United States too. The opinion served a further purpose. It shed light on how slavery's advocates saw their black slaves at the time of the ruling, but also how their ancestors saw their slaves in their own time, as something cast apart from the main, an island unto themselves.

The opinion of the case conjures Jefferson's words, standing as it does in such stark contrast to them. It stands in stark contrast to their generosity, to their courage, and to their faith too. The Declaration says:

> We hold these truths to be self-evident, that all men are created equal, that they are endowed by their Creator with certain unalienable Rights, that among these are Life, Liberty and the pursuit of Happiness.

Interestingly Jefferson does not say it is self-evident that all men are equal; the wording used is more nuanced. Instead he says how he, and others, *hold it to be self-evident* that all men are created equal. Can it be proven, as a matter of fact, all men are indeed equal? Difficulty arises, of course, when the challenge is put to some to prove equality and when the security of their rights is contingent on their being able to prove it. There is more. Proof requires acceptance, so those who must prove their equality are at the mercy of those whose role it is to grant approval. Does equality then stem from proof, or from presumption? Consequently, does inequality stem from the actual inequality of men, or from the inequality of treatment that compels some to prove their equality, while holding it as proven for others? One can certainly make a declaration that man's equality with man is self-evident, but even Jefferson's declaration makes not so bold a statement.

Governor Hammond of South Carolina was an advocate of slavery, believing it to be "not only an inexorable necessity … but a moral and humane institution, productive of great political and social advantages."[22] He contests "as ridiculously absurd, that much-lauded but nowhere accredited dogma of Mr. Jefferson, that 'all men are born equal.'"[23] William Harper too, a social and political theorist, an advocate of slavery and a politician of the South, disclosed his exertions in having to repeatedly point out how self-assuredly Jefferson's words were uttered and how readily they may be countered with claims of one's own. "It is not the first time I have had occasion to observe that men may repeat with the utmost confidence, some maxim or sentimental phrase, as self-evident or admitted truth, which is either palpably false, or to which, upon examination, it will be found that they attach no definite idea," Harper shares.[24] He believed any part of the Declaration of Independence that served to be "its ornament [rather] than its substance," should not be shielded by the high regard for it.[25] Anything "false, sophistical or unmeaning" should be questioned.[26] He laid down the gauntlet to those who espoused the view that "All men are born free and equal. Is it not palpably nearer the truth to say that no man was ever born free, and that no two men were ever born equal?"[27] Harper's ideas of freedom allowed for human beings to be enslaved but, unusually, they allowed for him to be enslaved too. He thought it nonsense that human beings had inalienable rights. If conditions became so dire as to warrant it persons might choose to sell themselves into slavery for their own preservation, Harper contended.[28]

In *The Political Economy of Slavery* Edmund Ruffin sets out his case for the defense of slavery. His attempts to justify it rest on economic grounds. He starts by claiming how no country, even in the most ancient of times, has found itself capable of making significant industrial advances without the benefit of slavery.[29] He argues that, whether among civilized or uncivilized societies, "the lower that individuals are degraded by poverty and want" the more the individuals in those societies "magnify and dread the efforts and labors" beyond what is actually necessary to save them from hardship.[30] He proposes a "good and proper remedy ... if it could be applied, would be the enslaving of these reckless, wretched drones" for the comfort of the community and for "the comfort of the enslaved class."[31] Whatever the difference in justification, ultimately it amounts to the same thing, with one group of beings designated superior to another. Ruffin's defense of slavery continues in much the same way, as meeting community needs by harnessing for the community, and even for those enslaved, the supposed benefits secured through slavery. The *Dred Scott Decision* echoed the same rationale, noting how those who were the focus of slavery "might justly and lawfully be reduced to slavery" for their own "benefit."[32]

William Henry Singleton, a slave, experienced for himself the reality that flowed from the consequences of these opinions. He observes:

> In the country of the Declaration of Independence I was born a slave, for I was a black man. And because I was black it was believed I had no soul. I had no rights that anybody was bound to respect. For in the eyes of the law I was but a thing. ... But nothing could be done about it, for the law said we were only things and so we had no more rights under the law than animals.[33]

Another person who experienced the realities of slavery was Solomon Northup. He grew up, and lived most of his life, as a free man. As a black man living in the free states of the North his value was one of a fellow human being. To slave traders he had, as a free black person, an altogether different value. Such a person might become a commodity, one easily acquired and sold in the South for a handsome profit. This was the fate that befell Northup, who was deceived, drugged, kidnapped, and shipped south to be sold. It was in the South that he first encountered the realities of the predicament of one's humanity being refuted first-hand. Years later he recorded his misfortunes in his book *Twelve Years A Slave*. At a plantation on Bayou Boeuf, just west of New Orleans, where he was enslaved, Northup observed how his master's son:

> ... possessed some noble qualities, yet no process of reasoning could lead him to comprehend, that in the eye of the Almighty there is no distinction of color. He looked upon the black man simply as an animal, differing in no respect from any other animal, save in the gift of speech and the possession of somewhat higher instincts, and, therefore, the more valuable. ... Brought up with such ideas – in the notion that we stand without the pale of humanity – no wonder the oppressors of my people are a pitiless and unrelenting race.[34]

These traits were even more profound in the boy's father, a brutish man by the name of Epps.

Northup had the opportunity to confirm through Epps' own words what he had observed in Epps' son. While working alongside a Canadian laborer by the name of Bass, who was no friend of slavery, a debate broke out between Bass and Epps. Northup's recollection of this debate is important. Slavery was a sensitive topic, and it was made even more so when discussed with outsiders. Debates of this nature were unlikely to occur. When they did, they promised to be ill-tempered and consequently short-lived. Astutely Northup records of Bass how he:

> ... was that kind of person whose peculiarity of manner was such that nothing he uttered ever gave offence. What would be intolerable, coming from the lips of another, could be said by him with impunity. There was not a man on Red River, perhaps, that agreed with him on the subject of politics or religion, and not a man, I venture to say, who discussed either of those subjects half as much. It seemed to be taken for granted that he would espouse the unpopular side of every local question, and it always created amusement rather than displeasure among his auditors, to listen to the ingenious and original manner in which he maintained the controversy.[35]

Bass, it seems, possessed unique qualities that made the debate possible. Fate ordained that Northup was able to be present to overhear it and that he was able to share his recollection of it. The language is harsh and profoundly offensive. Nonetheless Northup conveys it as he heard it, in part because it expresses the sincere, albeit startling, perspective of Master Epps, and that of his compatriots who supported slavery. Northup writes:

> They were discussing the subject of Slavery. "I tell you what it is Epps," said Bass, "it's all wrong – all wrong, sir – there's no justice nor righteousness in it. ... what right have you to your n*****s when you come down to the point?" "What right!" said Epps, laughing; "why,

I bought 'em, and paid for 'em." "Of course you did; the law says you have the right to hold a n*****, but begging the law's pardon, it lies. Yes, Epps, when the law says that it's a liar, and the truth is not in it. Is every thing right because the law allows it? Suppose they'd pass a law taking away your liberty and making you a slave?" "Oh, that ain't a supposable case," said Epps, still laughing; "hope you don't compare me to a n*****, Bass." ... "Now, in the sight of God, what is the difference, Epps, between a white man and a black one?" "All the difference in the world," replied Epps. "You might as well ask what the difference is between a white man and a baboon. Now, I've seen one of them critters in Orleans that knowed just as much as any n***** I've got. You'd call them feller citizens, I s'pose?" – and Epps indulged in a loud laugh at his own wit. "Look here, Epps," continued his companion; "you can't laugh me down in that way. Some men are witty, and some ain't so witty as they think they are. Now let me ask you a question. Are all men created free and equal as the Declaration of Independence holds they are?" "Yes," responded Epps, "but all men, n*****s, and monkeys ain't;" and hereupon he broke forth into a more boisterous laugh than before. "There are monkeys among white people as well as black, when you come to that," coolly remarked Bass. "I know some white men that use arguments no sensible monkey would. But let that pass. These n*****s are human beings. If they don't know as much as their masters, whose fault is it? ... There's a sin, a fearful sin, resting on this nation, that will not go unpunished forever. There will be a reckoning yet – yes, Epps, there's a day coming

> that will burn as an oven. It may be sooner or it may be
> later, but it's a coming as sure as the Lord is just."[36]

Surprisingly, there is one element in which Epps is quite correct. It wasn't likely somebody was going to take away his liberty and consign him to slavery. His equality was taken for granted. The game of questioning the humanity of others applied only to black persons.

The text *American Slavery As It Is: Testimony of a Thousand Witnesses* observes the wording used in one section of a prospectus of the South Carolina Medical College at Charleston. The college points to one of the benefits bestowed upon it by slavery, noting how no "place in the United States offers as great opportunities for the acquisition of anatomical knowledge, subjects being obtained from among the colored population in sufficient number for every purpose, and proper dissections carried on without offending any individuals in the community"[37] Though the text contains the voluminous details of unfathomable suffering its authors, Weld *et al.*, temporarily free themselves of all restraint at this moment declaring: "*Without offending any individuals in the community!* More than half the population of Charleston, we believe, is 'colored,' their graves may be ravaged, their dead may be dug up, dragged into the dissecting room, exposed to the gaze, and heartless gibes, and experimenting knives, of a crowd of inexperienced operators, ... and as to the fathers, mothers, husbands, wives, brothers, and sisters, of those whom they cut to pieces from day to day, why, they are not 'individuals in the community,' but 'property,' and however *their* feelings may be tortured the 'public opinion' of the slaveholders is entirely too 'chivalrous' to degrade itself by caring for them."[38]

One former slave recalls a minister who began preaching to a group of slaves. She writes how many who previously had no experience of church "now gladly went to hear the gospel preached. The sermons were simple, and they understood them. Moreover, it was the first time they had ever been addressed as human beings. It was not long before his white parishioners began to be dissatisfied."[39] Misfortune struck a short time after. The minister's wife passed away and the minister decided he would leave the vicinity. The slave recalls many tears were shed on the news of his departure. Some years went later the minister returned briefly. In an address to those he had left behind he declared: "My friends ... it affords me great happiness to have an opportunity of speaking to you again. ... Your skin is darker than mine; but God judges men by their hearts, not by the color of their skins."[40] The slave who later recorded these events wrote how this "was strange doctrine from a southern pulpit. It was very offensive to slaveholders."[41]

Harriet Beecher Stowe understood the politics behind the debate and the impossible situation of compelling one section of humanity to prove their humanity, and thereby their rights, while at the same time holding it as self-evidently so for the remainder. In *Uncle Tom's Cabin*, one of her fictitious characters, George, is left in just this situation and fully appreciates his predicament: "'See here, now, Mr. Wilson,' said George, coming up and sitting himself determinately down in front of him; 'look at me, now. Don't I sit before you, every way, just as much a man as you are? Look at my face,—look at my hands,—look at my body.'"[42] George's protestations that he is "as much a man" as anybody else, like those protestations of generations of slaves who toiled in America at that time and elsewhere, are to no avail, however.[43] George's predicament is not that he lacks humanity, or either the logic or ability to communicate his case. The politics of George's predicament are that he is compelled to make it.

That the states would tolerate slavery, given the history of their own people, was a most bitter irony not lost on the Founding Fathers. A rough draft of the Declaration of Independence had included a charge against Britain's king accusing him of enslaving the people of the colonies. It was removed from the final version because South Carolina and Georgia comprehended how they could not denounce slavery on one hand and then proceed to institute it for their own benefit on the other.[44] Later when the Convention of 1787 was convened to draft the Constitution most of the 55 delegates anticipated the immediate abolition of slavery. They despaired when it became apparent how slavery would continue to be an institution after the Constitution had been drafted. One report from the Convention makes for particularly grim reading:

> It was said, that we had just assumed a place among independent nations, in consequence of our opposition to the attempts of Great Britain to enslave us; that this opposition was grounded upon the preservation of those rights to which God and nature had entitled us, not in particular, but in common with all the rest of mankind; that we had appealed to the Supreme Being for his assistance, as the God of freedom, who could not but approve our efforts to preserve the rights which he had thus imparted to his creatures; that now, when we scarcely had risen from our knees, from supplicating his aid and protection, in forming our government over a free people, a government formed pretendedly on the principles of liberty and for its preservation, — in that government, to have a provision not only putting it out of its power to restrain and prevent the slave-trade, but even encouraging that most infamous traffic, by giving the States power and influence in the Union, in proportion as they cruelly and wantonly sport with the rights of their fellow creatures, ought to be considered as a solemn mockery of, and insult to that God whose protection we had then implored, and could not fail to

> hold us up in detestation, and render us contemptible to every true friend of liberty in the world. It was said, it ought to be considered that national crimes can only be, and frequently are punished in this world, by national punishments; and that the continuance of the slave-trade, and thus giving it a national sanction and encouragement, ought to be considered as justly exposing us to the dis-pleasure and vengeance of Him, who is equally Lord of all, and who views with equal eye the poor African slave and his American master.[45]

When it was done, some of the delegates, having capitulated to the demands of Georgia and South Carolina, consoled themselves with the belief that slavery would die out of its own accord in its own time. Ultimately it was agreed the transatlantic importation of slaves would be allowed for 20 years, after which this element of the slave trade would cease. Some of the states would choose to practice slavery, while others would not. However, as there was no provision in the Constitution to prohibit slavery there was no basis for enforcing a prohibition. Problematically a measure was required to address fugitive slaves escaping from states where slavery was permitted, to those states where it was not. Loathe however to mention slavery in the Constitution, Northerners agreed to the wording of Article IV, Section 2 to address the problem of fugitive slaves:

> No Person held to Service or Labour in one State, under the Laws thereof, escaping into another, shall, in Consequence of any Law or Regulation therein, be discharged from such Service or Labour, but shall be delivered up on Claim of the Party to whom such Service or Labour may be due.

Having agreed to institute slavery in the fledgling United States the Convention next encountered the issue of the relationship between population and public representation. Those who had been opposed to slavery did not want slaves to factor for the purpose in calculating representation at the House of Representatives. Those who had championed the vile trade wanted their slaves to count for the purpose. In testament to the harsh reality of the politics of slavery, which at each step diminishes the intrinsic value of human beings while retaining, or even increasing, their utility, a compromise that did just this was reached. The "Three-Fifths Compromise," expressed in Article I, Section 2, Clause 3 states:

> Representatives and direct Taxes shall be apportioned among the several States which may be included within this Union, according to their respective Numbers, which shall be determined by adding to the whole Number of free Persons, including those bound to Service for a Term of Years, and excluding Indians not taxed, three fifths of all other Persons.

The last group, the one so innocuously referred to as "all other Persons," were America's slaves. For the states practicing slavery, each slave would bring three-fifths of a vote, giving the slave states an edge in obtaining representatives in the House. In return for conceding on the issue of slavery the North received its own benefits in the form of commercial concessions from the South. On this point one commentator, writing many years later in 1848, wrote how the North had in effect taken "the boon, and winked at the 'infernal traffic'" when it acceded to the South on the issue of slavery.[46]

Compromise often makes for good politics and especially for good democratic politics but bowing to the demands of slavery did not bring harmony. Extraordinary for its time the United States put the People center-stage through a commitment to the freedom of the People, and to government of the People, by the People. Having concluded the Constitutional Convention and having agreed to permit the individual states to determine for themselves whether slavery ought to be practiced, the Union appeared secure. For the free states, the People are simply those of the state. For the slave states, the People are those people of the state who are not slaves, and more particularly those people who are not black. This was, in effect, recognized in the Supreme Court's 1857 opinion on the *Dred Scott Decision*, when it declared how those held in slavery were "altogether unfit to associate with the white race, either in social or political relations."[47] The Court further noted how by the "common consent" of the framers of the Declaration of Independence black persons were excluded.[48] White and black races belonged to different domains. The ability to consent; equality with one's fellow man; and the freedom this equality bestowed; belonged to the domain of the white person. Slavery; inequality with the white person; and the horrors these conferred; all belonged to a domain that was entirely different, one occupied by the black person. The two domains were separate with the first superior to the second.

There were other divisions too. Foremost among these was the division between the free states and the slave states. With their differing comprehensions of who constituted the People and what counted as freedom, each side could claim the People of their state were free. In the South the existence of slavery was no impediment to such a claim because those enslaved were not classed as people. Each side could also claim to uphold the right of the People to choose their own government, in keeping with the principles of freedom they espoused. In the South the fact slaves could not vote was no impediment to this claim either, as slaves were not part of the People. Both sides could express their positions in wording that would appear to be compatible with the other's position and yet their positions were diametrically opposed. Slavery could never have been a criterion for success in the North. In the South it could never have been a criterion for failure because the portion of the population to whom it applied could be siphoned off and allocated to a domain where the curtailment of their freedom did not pose a problem for constitutional rights. While it was possible for both sides to make an apparently common declaration about their values, they could nonetheless look to one another as cases where those values were not upheld. Consequently, though they espoused a common good life, their ideas of what that meant in practice were incompatible. A tidy solution, or so it seemed, was found then in compartmentalizing the interests of each party. Within the Union, North was separated from South. Within the South, there were two domains: white was separated from black; those who were free were separated from those who were slaves; and those who could consent were separated from those who could not consent. Within the confines of these borders each section of the Union would now pursue its own conception of the good life, privately and free of the other competing conception.

Among those who were free there were some who celebrated the South in language akin to what one would expect of the Promised Land. For Southerners it was truly paradise. One prominent politician describes the South as being "helped by a kind Providence with a genial sun and prolific soil, from which spring the richest products."[49] On Southern agriculture he says it is "our ancient and favourite pursuit, to which our soil, climate, habits and peculiar labor are adapted."[50] That form of labor peculiar to the South's ways was, of course, slavery, and it was at the very heart of Southern identity. As an entity legal only in the South it became known as its *peculiar institution*. So important was slavery to its identity William J. Cooper, in *The South and the Politics of Slavery, 1828-1856*, observes how by "the hundreds and even the thousands, books, speeches, pamphlets, editorials, and sermons" the "joy and value of slavery" was conveyed across Southern society.[51] The institution of slavery was unassailable. How starkly slavery was loved, above even any consideration of those who suffered because of it. Such talk would not be tolerated! An attack on slavery was nothing short of an attack on the freedom of the South, upon its very identity, upon its way of life, upon its people, and consequently upon the South itself. The occupants of this Promised Land:

... thought of themselves, not the state, as lawmakers and enforcers. An individual handled his own affairs without calling for help from any legal body, especially when his personal reputation was involved. And many southerners proclaimed slander a worse crime than murder. To them slander meant any implication that a person lacked honor either as an individual or in the community.[52]

Among the slaves, matters could hardly have been more different. The people who resided in their domain suffered profusely. Here there was no protection or right of any sort. The slaves were mere property for their owners to deal with as they so wished. Critique the presentation for a moment. Did the problems reside with those who were free or with those who were slaves? Though both were apparently separate one must bear in mind how it was the conception of the good life that existed among the free Southerners, and not among the enslaved, that separated them. This false separation served the purpose of diminishing one domain, while elevating the other, so the bountiful rewards of the separation could flow freely from black to white. It was the slaves who bore all the burdens of these rewards. Weld *et al.* record:

> What is the master's gain is the slave's loss, a loss wrested from him by the master, for the express purpose of making it his own gain; this is the master's constant employment ... This daily practice of forcibly robbing others, and habitually living on the plunder, cannot but beget in the mind the *habit* of regarding the interests and happiness of those whom it robs, as of no sort of consequence in the comparison with its own; consequently whenever those interests and this happiness are in the way of its own gratification, they will be sacrificed without scruple. He who cannot see this would be unable to feel it, if it were seen.[53]

Eugene Genovese appreciated this point. In The *Political Economy of Slavery: Studies in the Economy & Society of the Slave South* Genovese discloses how, though the slave's master appeared to be independent of the slave, and it was so important to the master to be seen as independent, the act of slavery that brought about the master's independence was also the weak point in the master's armor. For the master always attained what he wanted, not by working for it, but by having someone else, his slave, work for it. Hence the object of his desire was always attained through his slave. The politics of his situation meant that, in effect, the apparently self-sufficient master was dependent on his slaves.[54] Thus separation was merely a vehicle for the sectional interests of one to preside over the more fundamental interest of the other. Testimony in favor of this assessment comes from a most unexpected quarter.

In 1829 Andrew Jackson was elected seventh President of the United States. Jackson's credentials, as far as the South was concerned, were impeccable. First, he was a Southerner: he was born in South Carolina and grew to manhood in Tennessee. Second, he was a hero: aged just 13, he joined his local militia to fight the British during the War of Independence. During the war he fought both British regulars and native Indian braves, earning the nickname "Old Hickory." It was his defense of New Orleans, during the battle for that city, which earned Jackson his fame and more importantly his standing in the South. Last, Jackson was a slaveholder and a landowner, both of which endeared him to the community of which he was part. True to the sentiments of the South the Jacksonian, or Democratic, party was committed to the sovereignty of the people and to being the party of the people. All white men, irrespective of their landholding status, should be entitled to vote, it contested.

Of grave concern to the South was the issue of tariff reform. In 1828 Congress introduced a protective tariff, known as the *Tariff of 1828*, with the intention of protecting Northern industry from cheaper foreign imports. Necessarily the tariff applied for the benefit of one portion of the Union came at the expense of another. In this case, the benefit was extended to New England's cloth manufacturers, and the expense was borne by the South's economy. The tariff acted as it was intended it should, boosting the price of some British imports, making them less competitive against comparable goods made at home in the United States.

Jackson's Vice President was John C. Calhoun, a southerner, an advocate of free trade and an advocate of states' rights. In 1828 he penned two publications anonymously, one called *The South Carolina Exposition*, sometimes known as *Calhoun's Exposition*, and another called *Protest*. That same year both publications were introduced to South Carolina's state legislature, and they shed light on how the South perceived its place within the Union. Calhoun proclaims the United States:

> … have a community of interests, which can only be justly and fairly supervised by concentrating the will and authority of the several States in the General Government; while, at the same time, the States have distinct and separate interests, over which no supervision can be exercised by the general power without injustice and oppression.[55]

More importantly both publications express the intense opposition of the South to the tariff. The argument Calhoun makes for the rights of the South, for the primacy of states' rights and the respect that should be afforded to its interests will appear familiar. The facts, he claims, "are few and simple."[56] The tariff, he states, is "[s]o partial … that its burdens are exclusively on one side and its benefits on the other."[57] He notes how the "true spirit of justice" entails only ever imposing burdens "on those who were to be benefited."[58] As the tariff only benefitted New England, it should have been applied to New England alone. To propose anything else was to propose something of sectional interest and this something was only ever achieved through the application of sectional language, he contends. Calhoun points to the conduct of the manufacturing states. In looking for an increase in the tariff they had provided proof of where their interests lay, or at the very least proof of where they believed their interests lay. That a tariff increase would benefit these states was certain. Why? It was certain because they were looking for it.[59] In looking for a tariff, which would apply to all imports made by all States, and not for export taxes, which would have applied only to the products they themselves manufactured, New England's producers had chosen the argument that best suited their cause, as it shared the burden with all, and the benefits with themselves alone.[60] Calhoun knew the game they played. He says, "they consider every addition as a blessing" and "every failure to obtain one [as being something else entirely,] as a curse" and this "is the strongest confession that, whatever burden it imposes, in reality falls, not on them, but on others."[61] "Men ask not for burdens, but benefits," he adds.[62] They had treated benefits and costs as though they belonged to different domains, with all the benefits of New England's cloth manufacturers belonging to them exclusively, and all of the costs paid for by the imposition of a tariff on all the States, most of whom were not its beneficiaries. For Calhoun, and for the South, the success of New England's industry was being paid for by the prospect of failure of Southern industry. This was a situation neither Calhoun, nor the South, would abide.

There were consequences for government and for the Union. In making the tariff for the protection of New England's cloth manufacturers, government had failed to recognize how "the protection of one branch of industry at the expense of others – is unconstitutional, unequal and oppressive."[63] He says Congress had been granted power by the Constitution, but to use that power so as to foster the "industry of one section of the country" at the expense of another entails an abuse of power.[64] He adds how it is "a violation by perversion – the most dangerous of all, because the most insidious, and difficult to resist."[65]

Why is it the most insidious? It is because "courts cannot look into the motives of legislators. They are obliged to take acts by their titles and professed objects," to accept the wording before them and, even if legislators have manipulated the meaning of words "and if these be constitutional, they cannot interpose their power, however grossly the acts may, in reality, violate the Constitution."[66] Calhoun identifies "the abuse of delegated power, and the tyranny of the stronger over the weaker interests, … [as] the two dangers, and the only two to be guarded against; and if this be done effectually, liberty must be eternal."[67] The economic situation was now so dire, he cautioned, it threatened the future of the South and the system that brought this about "if not arrested, must bring the country to this hazardous extremity."[68] Portentously for the Union, he commenced one element of his arguments with the words: "[i]f we were entirely separated, without political or commercial connection …."[69]

The South, it seems, had become a slave to the needs of other states and to the demands of the Union. The strong had come to dominate the weak by virtue of their power over the weak. This was not justice. For Calhoun and for the South it was the very embodiment of injustice. The language he used illustrates that this was indeed how he comprehended the predicament. However, one could scarcely have found a more damning indictment of slavery than in the words by which Calhoun, one of slavery's defenders, sought to advance the cause of the primacy of states' rights and through those rights the right to hold slaves:

> It is by this … price, which must be paid by their fellow-citizens … that their industry is affected, and the fruits of our toil and labor, which, on any principle of justice, ought to belong to ourselves, are transferred from us to them. … This unequal lot is ours. We are the serfs of the system. … Our complaint is, that we are not permitted to consume the fruits of our labor; but that, through an

artful and complex system, in violation of every principle of justice, they are transferred from us to others. It is, indeed, wonderful that those who profit by our loss, blinded as they are by self-interest, ... never thought to inquire what became of the immense amount of the products of our industry, which are annually sent out in exchange with the rest of the world; and if we did not consume its proceeds, who did – and by what means. If, in the ardent pursuit of gain, such a thought had occurred, it would seem impossible, that all the sophistry of self-interest, deceiving as it is, could have disguised from their view our deep oppression, under the operation of the system.[70]

In 1832 Jackson was re-elected and the tariff was lowered. Jackson called for further reductions. Many greeted the lowering of the tariff as a step in the right direction. Others were not convinced and perceived the reduction as reticence on the part of Jackson in dealing with the issue. Extremists in South Carolina were not to be placated and, acting unilaterally, they nullified the applicability of the tariff to the State, provoking a crisis that threatened the very fabric of the Union, one which came to be known as the *Nullification Crisis*. Jackson, the champion of the South, found himself defending the Union. He rejected nullification, but not only that, he also rejected the idea states had a right to secede. Through proclamation and legislation, Jackson and Congress responded. The President was given executive power to use whatever force he deemed necessary to enforce federal tariffs. South Carolinians mooted the possibility of nullifying this too. Eventually a *Compromise Tariff* was introduced, and the crisis ended. In provoking the crisis, the case for states' rights was arguably worse off than it had been before even if the advocacy for them went undiminished.

Some may have been able, with exceptional foresight, to see how, in a nation committed to the sovereignty of the People, to the principles of freedom, and to the Union, the separations created by slavery might prove troublesome. Most others, though, showed no such foresight. Article IV, Section 2 of the Constitution ordained that the "Citizens of each State shall be entitled to all Privileges and Immunities of Citizens in the several States." Slavery, of course, was one of the privileges to which some citizens were entitled. When Chief Justice Taney delivered the opinion of the U.S. Supreme Court in the *Dred Scott Decision* the tidy compartmentalization of the Union into different sections with their own interpretations of who constituted the People, and consequently corresponding interpretations of freedom, which had existed since the Constitutional Convention, was undone. In *The Slave Power: Its Character, Career, and Probable Designs* the economist John Elliot Cairnes writes:

> Chief Justice Taney ... laid down two principles which went the full length of the views of the Slave party. He declared, first, that in contemplation of law there was no difference between a slave and any other kind of property; and secondly, that all American citizens might settle with their property in any part of the Union in which they pleased.[71]

The policy made ostensibly for the few, was really one made for all. With the fallacy of the separation revealed came confirmation of what some had long suspected: the North's complicity in Southern slavery. Even so, the supposedly private interests of one section, those of the South, its conception of freedom, and its conception of the good life, now threatened to engulf the whole. "The Union, if this doctrine were to be accepted, was henceforth a single slaveholding domain," Cairnes explains.[72] In 1858, a year after the *Dred Scott Decision*, Abraham Lincoln, at that time the Illinois Republican Party's nominee for the role of United States senator, delivered a speech in which he declared a "house divided against itself cannot stand."[73] America's two domains would indeed become one, though which one they would become he could not yet say. "I believe this government cannot endure, permanently, half slave and half free. I do not expect the Union to be dissolved — I do not expect the house to fall — but I do expect it will cease to be divided. It will become all one thing or all the other," he added.[74] Only time would tell for sure.

Many in the North wished to bring about slavery's demise. Not all of them had virtuous motives. Some in the North wanted to end slavery for purely selfish reasons. The practice of slavery necessitated sharing their communal lives with black persons, and, for some, this was intolerable. One former slave could find little good with the Northerners who visited the South when she recalled how even "the slaves despise 'a northern man with southern principles;' and that is the class they generally see. When northerners go to the south to reside, they prove very apt scholars. They soon imbibe the sentiments and disposition of their neighbors, and generally go beyond their teachers."[75] Others had different reasons for their opposition to slavery. Some of these were grounded in economic justifications, such as a fear of being unable to compete with a workforce constituted of slaves. A great many, though, opposed slavery for the profound injustice it was, for the cruelty it imposed, for the price it exacted, for the motivations that underpinned it and for the violation of human dignity it perpetrated. The South cared little about the opinions of the North. It cared even less about those of abolitionists. It had its own interests, which it viewed as legitimate, and it was prepared to defend them vigorously and unapologetically.

What is evident is how the origins of these problems stem from issues of identity. Having agreed to permit slavery as a choice for individual States, slavery nonetheless became a wedge between North and South for it fashioned their comprehension of themselves and that of their neighbors. That wedge existed not only at the level of individual commitment to slavery on the part of Southerners, but as a political and societal commitment to slavery as an institution in the South, differentiating it from the politics and society of the North. That they could live alongside one another appeared initially plausible. By recognizing the equality of states, and enjoying the security afforded by association with these other states, all states could repel foreign threats and secure freedom on the world stage, but by insisting on the primacy of the sovereignty of the people of a state, Southern states could also repel domestic threats and secure freedom from a voting majority of states at home. While each was content with their respective identities, it nonetheless raised immense questions for the identity they supposedly held in common. This in turn led to tension and even to the threat of violence. The Union was suffering from a profound crisis of identity. It was to this matter that the newly elected Lincoln referred in his first inaugural address, as to whether the United States was "not a government proper, but an association of States."[76]

What is evident too is how a great many of the problems with identity were firmly rooted in definition. This was the crux of the situation. The People, who were sovereign, were divided on exactly who constituted the People. It was a question of *who was in* and *who was out*. To accept the premise that whites-only constituted the People could never be the starting point for arguing against the premise. It was fallacious to start on that path in the first place, for having started upon it, one had already acceded to it. For Jefferson, the only proof required was acceptance in the form of presumption. Slavery's advocates, whose own rights were assured, who enjoyed the presumption of humanity, demanded the one thing of their slaves that their slaves, and that they themselves, could not give. They demanded proof of humanity. The conclusions one reached were a direct consequence of the definition one accepted. Therein lay the politics of the problem. Therein lay part of the politics of slavery, a politics that fashioned a segregated society one that existed conceptually and as reality. Two households were raised: one utopian and one dystopian. One embodied success and one embodied failure. The two were compellingly independent and apparently unrelated. That the South was fully prepared to fight, in the name of all that was right with the first of these households, for all that was wrong with them both, was not in doubt. The injustice of this situation may best be expressed in Jefferson's writings when he declares how "we lay it down as a fundamental, that laws, to be just, must give a reciprocation of right: that, without this, they are mere arbitrary rules of conduct, founded in force, and not in conscience."[77]

Chapter 2:

Violence

Crudely fashioned, cumbersome, and cold, chains are one of slavery's most potent visible manifestations. A whole variety of restraints were used in the acquisition, transfer, sale, maintenance, and punishment of slaves. They were sometimes made to wear handcuffs, bars, enclosures about their heads, iron gags in their mouths, collars around their necks, iron clogs about their feet, and a whole assortment of other restraints. Such was the variety of these items by type, and such was the variety within each of those types, that it almost defies description. Equally defiant is the torture they were capable of inflicting. An iron collar, for example, was sometimes fashioned with long prongs, known as horns, protruding outwards and upwards. Bells were sometimes attached to these.[1] A Reverend John Dudley testified to seeing a slave held by an iron fetter. It was a half an inch thick, three inches wide and a full foot long. Reverend Dudley estimated it must have been difficult for any person to have to carry such a burden, but in this instance the slave had to work while at the same carrying it about his ankles as he moved timber logs. The fetter was equipped with a piece of string attached to its center. The slave held this string in his hand so that he could lift the center of the fetter prior to walking, but as he did so the fetter came to rest upon his ankle, creating discomfort. He was now left with only one hand to carry out the heavy work. Occasionally the poor man would fall, and the fetter would inflict even greater pain upon him. Day after day, night after night the slave carried this burden. The effect of the burden on the slave was such that the Reverend describes him as a "dejected, heart-broken creature."[2]

A letter recounts the experience of one Mr. Curtis from Marietta, Ohio, who witnessed the treatment of one slave along the Mississippi River. He saw an overseer, a contractor who worked slaves on behalf of their owner, in the company of a slave who had an iron band around his head. This band was locked with a padlock so the slave could not remove it. At the place where it passed by the slave's mouth, part of the band projected inwards to about an inch and a half, effectively creating a gag. The slave was being punished for repeatedly trying to escape. Any further attempts would mean escaping with the band locked securely in place, ultimately resulting in the death by starvation of the slave. Mr. Curtis heard the slave ask for something to drink. In response the overseer subjected this tortured soul to yet more abuse. The slave was made to lie on his back and water was poured over his mouth, though he could drink none of it. Exasperated the slave asked permission to go to the river, which was allowed, and there he plunged his head under its waters, finally quenching his thirst. Mr. Curtis learned how little reprieve was afforded the slave, as it was only when the slave ate that this instrument of barbarity was taken off, and immediately when the slave was done, it was put back on.[3]

Indeed, not all the equipment of slavery was visible. One of its most potent tools was entirely invisible. Deception played a role, and none are more easily deceived than those who are held in perpetual ignorance. Some may have been tempted to educate their slaves. An educated worker will in all probability complete tasks to a superior standard and show more adaptability but, as the economist John Elliot Cairnes notes, whatever case might have been made for educating slaves "there are always very weighty reasons against conferring this boon."[4] Depriving slaves of education was not just a requirement imposed by the slaveholder. It was strictly taboo and formally imposed through the enactment of law to prohibit it by the slaveholding States. The law made transgressions a serious offence for both those who were taught and for those who taught them. The repercussions of being deprived of an education were as weighty as the shackles slaves bore. The eminent abolitionist and former slave Frederick Douglass outlined the moment of his epiphany. It occurred shortly after his mistress started to teach him the rudiments of reading. Her husband soon learned she was educating a slave. Douglass describes the unhappy scene:

> To use his own words ... he said, "If you give a n***** an inch, he will take an ell. A n***** should know nothing but to obey his master—to do as he is told to do. Learning would spoil the best n***** in the world. Now," said he, "if you teach that n***** (speaking of myself) how to read, there would be no keeping him. It would forever unfit him to be a slave. He would at once become unmanageable, and of no value to his master. As to himself, it could do him no good, but a great deal of harm. It would make him discontented and unhappy." These words sank deep into my heart, stirred up sentiments within that lay slumbering, and called into existence an entirely new train of thought. It was a new and special revelation, explaining dark and mysterious things, with which my youthful understanding had struggled, but struggled in vain. I now understood what had been to me a most perplexing difficulty—to wit, the white man's power to enslave the black man.[5]

Thereafter Douglass knew freedom was attained through education, and he strove hard to attain both freedom and education.

Another tool, also invisible, was the withdrawal of food, leading to slow starvation of the slave. The food fed to slaves was meager at best. Its quality was poor and there was little in the way of variety. Some may have been able to secure some additional nourishment for themselves. Others may have access to a little meat. Few, it seems, could have been considered well-nourished. Nevertheless, matters could be made worse for the slave as most were dependent on the slaveholder for their continued nourishment. The slaveholders were content to use this dependence for their own advantage. Misbehaving slaves could be starved as a form of punishment, some of them until they were dead.

There is one element of the violence that is striking, even cringeworthy, yet it uses no physical blows, and it withdraws no vital support necessary for the welfare of the person. It is the way in which language is used to address the slaves directly and indirectly. When Douglass' new master berates his wife for teaching the young Frederick, he speaks of him as though he were not even in the room. There is no sense in either the words or the sentiments of Douglass' master that young Frederick is a human being. Imagine what it must have felt like to stand before one's master day-after-day and to be spoken about as if just a thing. Any sense of dignity or self-worth is obliterated. It demonstrates how there was no reprieve for the slave. Even in the use of language one could be demeaned and degraded. As a type of assault upon the person it takes its place among others of its kind as a form of verbal abuse.

The mental imagery of the hapless slave bound to a post as she or he is whipped is another matter entirely. The image is a potent one, readily conjured when contemplating slavery of the time. Slaves were whipped, sometimes in public and at other times in private. The hands were first bound at the wrist. The cord used to restrain the slave's hands was then thrown over the branch of a tree or over a beam in a building. The slave was then hoisted up until he was outstretched with his feet still on the ground, sometimes just barely. Then the whipping begins:

In this distorted posture the monster flies at them, sometimes in great rage, with his implements of torture, and cuts on with all his might, over the shoulders, under the arms, and sometimes over the head and ears, or on parts of the body where he can inflict the greatest torment. Occasionally the whipper, especially if his victim does not beg him enough to suit him, while under the lash, will fly into a passion, uttering the most horrid oaths; while the victim of his rage is crying, at very stroke, "Lord have mercy! Lord have mercy!" The scenes exhibited at the whipping post are awfully terrific and frightful to one whose heart has not turned to stone; I never could look on but a moment. While under the lash, the bleeding victim writhes in agony, convulsed with torture. Thirty-nine lashes on the bare back, which tear the skin at almost every stroke, is what the South calls a very moderate punishment![6]

One man recorded how, when in his youth he worked for a short time on a plantation as an overseer of slaves, he had one slave whipped for refusing to work. The slave was newly arrived from Africa. His hands were duly bound, and he was whipped. There was never a problem with the poor fellow ever again in all the time the overseer supervised him. Though the abused in this case was male, women and children were shown no quarter with a great many suffering this punishment. The overseer understood how slaves were not just commodities acquired: slaves were a thing fashioned; fashioned and maintained, through violence. He writes, "it is hard work for the masters to whip them into brutes, ... to subdue their noble spirit."[7]

Whipping it seems was indeed hard work. Many of the masters would "whip until they ... [were] tired – until the back ... [was] a gore of blood – then rest upon it: after a short cessation, get up and go at it again."[8]

If indeed it proved to be hard work to whip one's fellows, there were solutions at hand. The deed could be outsourced. Slaves could be sent to places of punishment or constables could be employed to do the job. One observer gives testimony of a woman who was the owner of slaves but, having no husband, was unable to mete out punishment.[9] She would consequently send her misbehaving slaves to jail for several days, along with the particulars of the punishment they were to receive. Having arrived, the slaves perhaps once, perhaps twice, daily in accordance with her wishes received their lesson. At times they would be locked up for a time after being whipped and deprived of light and food. Sometimes slaves died in those dark places. That whipping could be outsourced attests to the fact there must have been ample demand for it as a service. The tendency to associate slavery in the South with the use of the whip is so potent that it might lead to the conclusion it has been overplayed, but even in its own time the impression was the "lash is always at hand; if a slave disobeys, – the whip; if he is idle, – the whip; does he murmur, – the whip; is he sullen and silent, – the whip; is the female coy and reluctant, – the whip."[10] Scenes of slaves being whipped were so common in places, it seems, they attracted little attention.

In a letter a Reverend William Dickey recounts the extraordinary events at Livingston, Kentucky, close to the mouth of the Cumberland River where two brothers, Lilburn and Isham Lewis, lived along with their slaves. These brothers were nephews, through their mother, of Thomas Jefferson. It was written of Lilburn that he was "the wealthy owner of a considerable gang of negroes, whom he drove constantly, fed sparingly, and lashed severely."[11] As a result of this harsh treatment Lilburn's slaves would often run away. One of them, George, a youth of just 17 years of age, had just returned of his own accord when he was sent upon an errand. He was given an elegant pitcher and instructed to fill it with water from a nearby spring. He proceeded to fulfill the task he had been assigned but, on the way home, misfortune struck and he dropped the valuable pitcher, which was immediately dashed into a multitude of pieces. Reverend Dickey records how this "was made the occasion for reckoning with him."[12] When night came Lilburn put his plan into action. All the slaves were gathered in the largest of the slave houses. A large fire was lit. It was only when the doors were secured so none might escape that the ever-increasing anxiety of the slaves was confirmed as well-founded. Poor unfortunate George was brought into the room and bound by Lilburn, with the assistance of Isham. Having bound George tightly they laid him on a bench. This, though, was no ordinary bench. It was the meat-block. The Reverend describes what Lilburn did next:

> He then proceeded to hack off George at the ankles! It was with the broad axe! In vain did the unhappy victim scream and roar! for he was completely in his master's power; not a hand among so many durst interfere: casting the feet into the fire, he lectured them at some length. He next chopped him off below the knees! George roaring out and praying his master to begin at the other end! ... throwing the legs into the fire – then, above the knees, tossing the joints into the fire – the next stroke severed the thighs from the body; these were also committed to the flames – and so it may be said of the arms, head, and trunk, until all was in the fire! ... Nothing now remained but to consume the flesh and bones; and for this purpose the fire was brightly stirred until two hours after midnight.[13]

When the murderous and barbaric deed was complete the slaves were permitted to leave the room and given strict instruction never to speak of what they had witnessed, with the assurance that if they did speak then they too would meet a similar end.

Despite all that had been done to conceal the act it became known and when neighbors found what remained of poor George, they seized Lilburn and his brother. Bringing them before a court of law, the neighbors testified against the brothers but were dumbfounded when the brothers were granted the right to bail themselves. Lilburn escaped judgment by the court when he died by his own hand. Isham was convicted of the murder of George and sentenced to death. He was found to be missing by means unknown, though some suspicion must fall upon the white inhabitants of the area who must have been unwilling to see a white man face the gallows, however grievous his crime against a black man may have been. It seems certain Isham went to Natchez where he married, and he subsequently joined Jackson's army in defense of New Orleans. There, he fell in battle.[14]

To the uninitiated in the horrors of slavery, George's horrific fate appears to have served no purpose at all. This was not the case, at least not in the minds of Lilburn and Isham. Reverend Dickey notes how when the slaves were all assembled in the room Lilburn disclosed to them the purpose of what they were about to witness, "namely, that they be effectively advised to stay at home and obey his orders."[15] There would be no more running off. The violence of George's murder was planned by his master with a purpose in mind. The depravity of George's death was designed to breathe such absolute fear into Lilburn's slaves as to have the effect of imposing upon them his absolute will. There was room for many slaves, but room only for Lilburn's goals.

One contributor, writing in 1833, stated how were "there nothing else to prove it a system of monstrous cruelty, the fact that FEAR is the only motive with which the slave is plied during his whole existence, would be sufficient to brand it with the execration as the grand tormentor of man."[16] Fear then was the motivator; pain the fulcrum through which the slave was moved, the commentator adds. Armed with this knowledge it "plants all its stings; here it sinks its hot irons; cuts its deep gashes; flings its burning embers, and dashes its boiling brine and liquid fire; into this it strikes its cold flesh hooks, grappling irons, and instruments of nameless torture; and by it drags him shrieking to the end of his pilgrimage," he adds.[17] Tellingly Harriet Beecher Stowe describes the slavery of her time as "the essence of all abuse."[18]

Figure: Harriet Beecher Stowe (National Archives and Records Administration 1942 - 1945)

How heart-wrenching it must have been for children to stand by helplessly and for them to look upon their fathers and mothers tortured and degraded so; for wives to see their husbands whipped; for husbands to see their wives so brutally scarred; for parents to see their tender children suffer. Harriet Ann Jacobs, writing under her *nom de plume*, Linda Brent, poignantly acknowledges: "When I lay down beside my child, I felt how much easier it would be to see her die than to see her master beat her about, as I daily saw him beat other little ones. The spirit of the mothers was so crushed by the lash that they stood by, without courage to remonstrate."[19] All these tortures of the heart, the spirit and the mind worked in favor of the slaveholder, for as one former overseer acknowledged the purpose of whipping slaves in the front of other slaves was "to strike them with terror."[20] It all serves to illustrate how violence could be used not only on those who suffered its blows but also on those who were compelled to witness it, knowing how they too might suffer the same fate. Violence was an opportunity; it was an opportunity for a spectacle; it was an opportunity for theatre.

There were other grave indignities to be suffered. It was clear some of these fell most harshly on women. As each new black generation was born it was clear how some among them were less identifiable as black, owing to the intermingling of blacks and whites. Mulattos, born to one black parent and one white parent, possessed half-African ancestry. Quadroons followed with their quarter-African ancestry, and after them octoroons with their one-eighth-African ancestry, and so on. In *A Letter to the People of the United States Touching the Matter of Slavery* Theodore Parker records, the South was "full of mulattoes; its 'best blood flows in the veins of the slaves' … Girls, the children of mulattoes, are sold at great price, as food for private licentiousness."[21] Jacobs concurs, wondering whether it could be possible to "measure the amount of Anglo-Saxon blood coursing in the veins of American slaves?"[22] Beecher Stowe's character, George, admits, with distress: "I've had a sister sold in that New Orleans market. I know what they are sold for."[23] Jacobs adds that a young woman, if she is even scarcely that, who is a slave, will soon "learn to tremble when she hears her master's footfall. She will be compelled to realize that she is no longer a child. If God has bestowed beauty upon her, it will prove her greatest curse. That which commands admiration in the white woman only hastens the degradation of the female slave."[24] For those who doubt her testimony she adds, "You may believe what I say; for I write only that whereof I know. I was twenty-one years in that cage."[25]

The sexual abuse of slaves was one of its daily realities. As in all other areas of the slavery to which they were subjected there was little a slave could do about the situation. That is not to say, however, they were held blameless for their victimhood. In time the master's and mistress' white children would hear their parents argue. The subject of the conflict was not always known to them, though they may have overheard some mention of the name of a female slave. "Jealousy and hatred enter[ed] the flowery home, and … ravaged [it] of its loveliness," Jacobs assures.[26] Life in the household was never quite the same again. The slave girl or woman now became the focus of her mistress' wrath. The other slaves of the household knew why the changes came, and how they came as inevitably as night follows day.

In time too, the children of the house might come to comprehend the nature of their parent's quarrel, especially if the slave whose name they had heard mentioned bore a child. This is how it was for the slave Singleton who shares that "although I was born black and a slave, I was not all black. My mother was a colored woman but my father was the brother of my master. I did not learn this until some years later. It caused me much trouble."[27]

Socially, it was practically "a crime for a slave to tell who was the father of her child."[28] Southern women often knew the man they married was the father of a great many children. It did not always trouble them as they regarded "such children as property, as marketable as the pigs on the plantation; and it [was] ... seldom that they ... [did] not make them aware of this by passing them into the slave-trader's hands as soon as possible, and thus getting them out of their sight."[29] Sometimes both mother and child were sold, forever banished from the house and from the vicinity. At other times the newborn infant was murdered. In many instances the master's children by his slave grew up alongside those by his wife. Jacobs recalls how she once "saw a letter from a member of Congress to a slave, who was the mother of six of his children. He wrote to request that she would send her children away from the great house before his return, as he expected to be accompanied by friends. The woman could not read, and she was obliged to employ another to read the letter. The existence of the colored children did not trouble this gentleman, it was only the fear that friends might recognize in their features a resemblance to him."[30]

It is untenable to presume all the perpetrators were male. Testimony can be found to verify the sexual exploitation of male slaves by their mistresses.[31] It can be presumed men, women and children were abused. However, it would be untenable, and inaccurate, to presume the burden of these abuses fell on males to anywhere near the extent that it did on females. Jacobs perceived this reality, and she felt its burden. She knew it to be so through her own experience and she feared her own daughter might one day encounter these abuses. The picture she paints through her words is harrowing and it asserts the tendency for females particularly to suffer. Jacobs confides how when "they told me my new-born babe was a girl, my heart was heavier than it had ever been before. Slavery is terrible for men; but it is far more terrible for women. Superadded to the burden common to all, they have wrongs, and sufferings, and mortifications peculiarly their own."[32]

Sexual abuse is a grievous violation of human beings. For slaves, the prospect of its occurrence was real. It presented a slave with an element of fear for their own safety but also for that of their womenfolk. Imagine the angst of a multitude of hearts perpetually on the lookout for the welfare of its womenfolk. Aside from the violation, sexual abuse imposes an enormous psychological, spiritual, and physical burden upon the abused. Abuse of this nature is sufficient of itself to break any human being. For those abused in slavery there was the added assurance that once abused there was every likelihood it would occur again. There was quite simply nothing to protect the slave from it. The power the slaveholders held over their slaves afforded ample opportunities for their slaves to be subjected to all sorts of abuses, including sexual abuse, but the abuse also served to underline the power of the master, the powerlessness of his victim, and the powerlessness of his victim's community to stop it.

In *American Slavery as It Is: Testimony of a Thousand Witnesses*, Weld and his co-authors considered a horde of objections to their portrayal of slavery as exploitative and cruel. One of these objections was how Northerners visiting the South would have opportunities to see for themselves the realities of slavery and to enquire of slaves as to their daily lives. Not so, contend Weld and his co-authors, who describe the "folly of arguing the good treatment of slaves from their own declarations, while in the power of their masters."[33] Weld gives as proof of this the words of Chief Justice Henderson of North Carolina, a man who was no stranger to slavery as he was himself a slaveholder. The Chief Justice refused a slaveholder permission for his slave to be a source of corroboration for the slaveholder's evidence. The Chief Justice argued:

> The master has an almost absolute control over the body and mind of his slave. The master's will is the slave's will. All his acts, all his sayings, are made with a view to propitiate his master. His confessions are made, not from a love of truth, not from a sense of duty, not to speak a falsehood, but to *please his master* – and it is in vain that his master tells him to speak the truth, and conceals from him how he wishes the question answered. The slave will ascertain or, which is the same thing, think that he has ascertained the wishes of the master, and MOULD HIS ANSWER ACCORDINGLY. We therefore more often get the wishes of the master, or the slave's belief of his wishes, than the truth.[34]

This serves to illustrate how there is an element of what might be called *slave luck*. Knowing the eternal tendency of the die to fall in favor of slavery, and to fall in disservice to the slave, Jacobs once pondered whether her brother could truly entrust his fate "to a slave's chances."[35]

Figure: Theodore Dwight Weld (Library of Congress 1885)

It was indeed contested that slavery was cruel. During one part of his long journey through the Southern states the journalist Frederick Law Olmsted struck up a conversation with a fellow passenger on a riverboat as they travelled along Louisiana's Red River. The passenger was a merchant and a plantation owner. The conversation turned to the issue of slavery and to Beecher Stowe's *Uncle Tom's Cabin*. The passenger was vehemently opposed to the portrayal of slavery as cruel. He thought no man who was cruel to his slaves could possibly be respected by his fellows in the South. He thought it likely slavery was cruelly practiced in some instances but these, he thought, were the exceptions rather than the rule.[36] For him, Beecher Stowe's work reflected these exceptions and not the norm. Ruffin too thought cruelty in slavery was exceptional. In making a comparison between England's poor laborers and Virginia's slaves he claims, "there is as much and as rigid coercion of the paupers [in England], as painful to endure, ... as in the exceptional cases of the few negro slaves in Virginia who are, indeed, hardly and cruelly treated."[37] He goes so far even to say, "the general condition of our ... slaves is one of comfort, ease and happiness."[38] This being so, one might ask why so many fled and why the Southern states so fervently pursued the enactment of a law permitting their seizure from the supposed refuge in the North?

Slavery's violence was naked in slave trading. Without slave trading there could have been no slaves. States such as Virginia, Kentucky and Tennessee became slave-breeding states, catering to the demands of customers in other slave states. Between those who bred slaves for sale and those who acquired them for work, there stood an intermediary. The slave trader purchased slaves from the breeders, before bringing them to market where they could be sold at auction. It was at the auction block where children were wrested from parents, spouses from one another, brother from brother, sister from sister, and sister from brother. The indignity of the sale must have been small indeed in comparison to the darkness of the abyss into which they had just been thrown. Parker states how, even 1,500 years before his time, the Roman Emperor had prohibited the separation of families of slaves. "Who can bear, ... that children should be separated from their parents, sisters from their brothers, wives from their husbands?" the Emperor had implored.[39] In 1835 an address by the Presbyterian Synod of Kentucky to the churches under its care made a similar plea:

> Brothers and sisters, parents and children, husbands and wives are *torn assunder*, and permitted to see each other no more. These acts are DAILY occurring in the midst of us. The *shrieks* and the *agony*, *often* witnessed on such occasions, proclaim, with a trumpet tongue, the inquity of our system. *There is not a neighbourhood* where these heart-rending scenes are not displayed. *There is not a village or road* that does not behold the

sad procession of manacled outcasts, whose mournful countenances tell that they are exiled by *force* from ALL THAT THEIR HEARTS HOLD DEAR.[40]

To give some depth to the fathomless evil of these transactions the following is offered. Reverend C.S. Renshaw, originally of Quincy, Illinois, resided for a time in Kentucky. He testifies:

> Just before the steamboat put off for the lower country, two negro women were offered for sale, each of them having a young child at the breast. The traders bought them, took their babes from their arms, and offered ... [the babes] to the highest bidder; and they were sold for one dollar apiece, whilst the stricken parents were driven on board the boat, and in an hour were on their way to the New Orleans market.[41]

Jacobs provides another startling instance of a sale:

> On one of these sale days, I saw a mother lead seven children to the auction-block. She knew that some of them would be taken from her; but they took all. The children were sold to a slave-trader, and their mother was brought [sic] by a man in her own town. Before night her children were all far away. She begged the trader to tell her where he intended to take them; this he refused to do. How could he, when he knew he would sell them, one by one, wherever he could command the highest price? I met that mother in the street, and her wild, haggard face lives to-day in my mind. She wrung her hands in anguish, and exclaimed, "Gone! All gone! Why don't God kill me?" I had no words wherewith to comfort her. Instances of this kind are of daily, yea, of hourly occurrence.[42]

It is enough for Jacobs to ask why "does the slave ever love? Why allow the tendrils of the heart to twine around objects which may at any moment be wrenched away by the hand of violence?"[43]

The threat of being sold at auction cast a long shadow over the fate of generations of slaves. What little surety slaves enjoyed in life could be torn asunder in the space of just a few hours. The very business of slavery assured there was nothing, no matter what its value, that could not be sold. The violence this prospect promised, if it occurred, was a source of immense power for the slaveholder, who could threaten a slave's entire existence, threaten his or her family, and consign that slave to a future likely worse than death itself.

A gentleman by the name of Silas Stone, a native of New York, testifies how in 1807 he witnessed a sale at Charleston, South Carolina. He likens the events to what one would expect to see at a horse market. In this instance the mother stood alongside her eight children. Each child was sold separately and taken away each in turn. The scene, he says, "beggars description; suffice it to say, it was sufficient to cause tears from one at least 'whose skin was not colored like their own,' and I was not ashamed to give vent to them."[44]

Surprisingly, perhaps because of the nakedness of the violence that occurred at auctions, or because of the crude character of the traders who transacted the business, or both, slave traders were utterly reviled by slaveholders. In *The Progress of Slavery in the United States,* George M. Weston reveals how in "all parts of the South, the occupation of slave trader is positively disreputable. Vast numbers of men, who hold slaves, would disdain the idea of selling them, without some reference to the character of the purchaser."[45] Solomon Northup says of "James H. Burch [that he] was a slave-trader – buying men, women and children at low prices, and selling them at an advance. He was a speculator in human flesh – a disreputable calling – and so considered at the South."[46] The business of slave trading brought contempt for its traders in other ways too, for it not only exposed the violence of slavery, but it exposed the disparity between what those who bred slaves stated as being their honorable intention, and how they subsequently acted. Weston noted how, in the slave-breeding states, men would often claim not to be rearing their slaves for sale. Weston observed, however, that of "the men who deny for themselves individually the fact of raising slaves for the purpose of selling them, too many make no scruple in insisting upon markets to keep up the price of slaves."[47] It was surely of great consolation to the slave traders that those who held them in low esteem, proved to be good customers nonetheless.

Can it be supported then that slavery was not cruel? That some claimed it was not cruel, or that they reasoned cruelty to be at odds with the interests of slavery, is evidentially insufficient. Testimony of the truth of the matter comes from establishing that their words were at odds with their deeds. However, this in turn raises the question of whether the activity of trading in slaves was the exception rather than the norm? In 1832 the Honorable Thomas Jefferson Randolph, a former governor of the state of Virginia denounced the practice of slave trading in the following manner:

> The exportation [from Virginia] has averaged EIGHT THOUSAND FIVE HUNDRED for the last twenty years. Forty years ago, the whites exceed the colored 25,000, the colored now exceed the whites 81,000; and these results too during an exportation of near 260,000 slaves since the year 1790 now perhaps the fruitful progenitors of half million in other states. It is a practice and an increasing practice, in parts of Virginia, to rear slaves for market. How can an honorable mind, a patriot and a lover of his country, bear to see this ancient dominion converted into one grand menagerie, where men are to be reared for market like oxen for the shambles.[48]

The presentation of slavery as a benevolent institution is contradicted elsewhere too. Look at how the slaveholders spoke of their slaves and for the race from which the slaves were drawn. The utter contempt for the person of the slave, the sheer revile for their demeanor and for their race, and the bitter hatred for the manner in which they conducted their work, are apparent. Specific words of hatred, usually race-based, were concocted and used at every turn in discourse between master and slave, and in discourse between fellow slaveholders. These words became part of the daily way of talking about slaves and could only have served to reinforce social norms. If it is extraordinarily difficult to conceive how human beings could be so cruel to one another is it more, or less, difficult to conceive of slaveholders going about their business in the South, engaging with their white compatriots and declaring to them what wonderful fellows were their slaves, and how great were their virtues in the conduct of work? That the slaveholder loved the act of slavery is beyond doubt: that most of them showed compassion for the person of the slave is unconvincing. Through the slaveholders' own words, the nature of the relationship between master and slave is revealed. It is a palpable realization, yet it is one hidden in plain sight.

Nowhere was this language more evident; nowhere was it so publicly offered or more widely distributed; nowhere was it so damning; and nowhere was the self-proclaimed compassion of slaveholders so contradicted, than in the advertisements slaveholders routinely placed in the hope of recovering escaped slaves. It occurred to the slaveholders that their slaves might try to escape. One problem this created for the slaveholders was how they might alert the wider public as to the identity of an escaped slave. One approach was to brand a mark into the flesh of the slave, as one would brand a mark into the flesh of a beast. Another approach is known as *cropping*. The principle is akin to branding. Its purpose was to leave some permanently identifiable feature on the body of the slave, one that distinguishes the slave from others. Some slaveholders cropped a slave by cutting off an ear, or part of an ear, or by cutting a notch in the ear. Others would break the slave's teeth, especially the front teeth.

Once an escape attempt was made an advertisement was placed in the local press, or in the press of the locality to which the slave was known to have escaped. One such advertisement read: "10 DOLLARS REWARD, for Mary, one or two upper teeth out, about 25 years old."[49] Another describes a boy named Peter who "had an *iron round his neck* when he went away."[50] Another describes a man by the name of Hambleton who "limps on his left foot where he was shot a few weeks ago, while [sic] runaway."[51] Another still describes a mulatto who "had on when he left, *a pair of handcuffs and a pair of drawing chains.*"[52] Fifty dollars were offered for "Jim Blake – has a *piece cut out of each ear*, and the middle finger of the left hand *cut off* to the second joint."[53] A slave named Fountain, it seems, had not fared much better in regard to his treatment as the advertisement advises he had "holes in his ears, a scar on the right side of his forehead – has been shot in the hind parts of his legs – is marked on the back with the whip."[54] Little Mary too had suffered unspeakably. She was described in the advertisement seeking her return as having "a small scar over her eye, a good many teeth missing, the letter A is branded over her cheek and forehead."[55] That Mark could have absconded beggars belief considering "his left arm has been broken, right leg also."[56] One slaveholder was doubtlessly relieved to learn his slave, Tom, had been recovered and was now in jail where arrangements could be made for him to be returned to his rightful owner. Of course, there were likely a great many slaves by the name of Tom but the fact this one had "a scar over his right cheek and appears to have been burned with powder on his face" made identifying him all that much easier.[57]

Would a system abhorrent of cruelty have required the branding of flesh, the cropping of ears, the breaking of teeth and sometimes that of bones, the scarring of the face with knives, the disfigurement of the flesh by whipping, the amputation of fingers, the shooting of persons unarmed and their physical restraint using chains? If slavery was not reputed to be cruel among those who practiced it, how could practitioners nonetheless disclose to their neighbors in public advertisements the marks made on the persons of their slaves? How would the significance of those marks be understood? Moreover, could advertisements publicly declare a slave was wanted *dead or alive*? Why too was it so important for slaveholders to wish for a law allowing for the return of their slaves once these slaves had made their way to the free states? Yet still, why did so many slaves seek escape if slavery in the South was not cruel?

There was certainly good cause for slaves to want to escape slavery. By the time of the Civil War slavery had existed in the United States since its inception some 80 years before. It was already old in the Americas prior to the establishment of the United States. It was older still in the world before then. The ability to own slaves and to do with them as their owner wished was synonymous with doing what one wished to do with one's property. In her book, one of Beecher Stowe's fictitious but brutish characters puts it thus: "It's a free country, sir; the man's mine, and I do what I please with him – that's it!"[58] Jacobs' real-life master once asked of her menacingly: "Do you know that I have a right to do as I like with you – that I can kill you, if I please?"[59] In 1828 in Charleston a slaveholder flogged a young girl of just 13 years of age. When he was done, he put her feet in restraints, left her upon a table, and then he left her alone in a locked room. When he returned later, she was found to have fallen from the table and to have died as a result. This testimony was given by one who later enquired whether the slaveholder would be indicted for the girl's murder. The enquirer was, he records, "coolly" told by "a prominent lawyer" of the state how the slave was her master's property and if her master "chose to suffer the loss, no one else had anything to do with it."[60] With the legitimization of slavery, and the corresponding legitimization of the right to hold slaves as property, came a right not to be scrutinized. What a slaveholder did with his slave was nobody's business but his own. Legitimization resulted not in transparency, but absolute privacy.

In defiance of both its longevity and its institution in law, some important elements of the practice of slavery remain obscure. Satisfactory answers to key questions are difficult to find and, in some cases, may never be found. Some slaveholders may have been more astute, knowing the value of discretion, unlike their colleagues who were guided only by what their property rights permitted. Jacobs, for example, appreciated just how easily people could be hidden from plain sight and sometimes hidden in plain sight when she says, "often did I rejoice that I lived in a town where all the inhabitants knew each other! If I had been on a remote plantation, or lost among the multitude of a crowded city, I should not be a living woman at this day."[61] She identifies remoteness and anonymity among crowds of people as two characteristics lending themselves to obscurity and the concealment of cruel violations.

There is some irony here, for if the slaveholders understood how violence was used as a tool in fashioning slaves, it was the slaves who understood how violence also shaped the slaveholder. Beecher Stowe again shows remarkable insight when one of her fictitious characters, a reluctant slaveholder by the name of St. Clare, declares how, when he became an owner of slaves, he soon realized the role violence played in their maintenance. He knew how the slaves would adjust in time to the punishment he doled out, and how in time he would have to escalate the dose in accordance with their increasing immunity to it. Instead, he retorts: "I resolved never to begin, because I did not know when I should stop, —and I resolved, at least, to protect my own moral nature. The consequence is, that my servants act like spoiled children; but I think that better than for us both to be brutalized together."[62] Northup says slavery "has a tendency to brutalize the humane and finer feelings" as a result of daily witnessing "human suffering – listening to the agonizing screeches of the slave – beholding him writhing beneath the merciless lash – bitten and torn by dogs – dying without attention, and buried without shroud or coffin – it cannot otherwise be expected, than that … [those who engage in slavery] should become brutified and reckless of human life."[63] Jacobs concurs: "I said to myself, 'Surely there must be some justice in man;' then I remembered, with a sigh, how slavery perverted all the natural feelings of the human heart."[64] Northup applies his analysis:

> The effect of these exhibitions of brutality on the household of the slave-holder, is apparent. Epps' oldest son is an intelligent lad of ten or twelve years of age. ... Mounted on his pony, he often rides into the field with his whip, playing the overseer, greatly to his father's delight. Without discrimination, at such times, he applies the rawhide, urging the slaves forward with shouts, and occasional expressions of profanity, while the old man laughs, and commends him as a thorough-going boy. ... on arriving at maturity, the sufferings and miseries of the slave will be looked upon with entire indifference. The influence of the iniquitous system necessarily fosters an unfeeling and cruel spirit, even in the bosoms of those who, among, their equals, are regarded as humane and generous.[65]

Douglass evidenced it for himself when he saw, at first, how his new mistress' "face was made of heavenly smiles, and her voice of tranquil music. But, alas! this kind heart had but a short time to remain such. The fatal poison of irresponsible power was already in her hands, and soon commenced its infernal work. That cheerful eye, under the influence of slavery, soon became red with rage; that voice, made all of sweet accord, changed to one of harsh and horrid discord; and that angelic face gave place to that of a demon."[66] Jacobs summarizes these effects saying, "slavery is a curse to the whites as well as to the blacks. It makes white fathers cruel and sensual; the sons violent and licentious; it contaminates the daughters, and makes the wives wretched."[67] Slavery's violence is then double-edged. While the daily dispensing of it served the purpose of dehumanizing the slave, those who dispensed it were themselves dehumanized through the violence they dispensed.

This was not the limit of slavery's transformative effect. Beecher Stowe thinly veils the significance of one of her fictional character's parentage, in such a way as to suggest it was of no significance at all. However, she is fully aware of the significance of the politics of the point she makes when she mentions "*en passant*, that George was, by his father's side, of white descent. His mother was one of those unfortunates of her race, marked out by personal beauty to be the slave of the passions of her possessor, and the mother of children who may never know a father. From one of the proudest families in Kentucky he had inherited a set of fine European features, and a high, indomitable spirit. From his mother he had received only a slight mulatto tinge amply compensated by its accompanying rich, dark eye."[68] For a brief time the refined George, on the run from his master, masquerades upon his arrival at a village as a foreign gentleman. His genteel ways distinguish him from the village's crass and crude inhabitants, the same inhabitants who would consider George to be an inferior being. Yet George's disguise involves nothing more than a "slight change in the tint of the skin and the color of his hair" and he is "metamorphosed" into a "Spanish-looking fellow."[69] What was once black was less black, what was once not white was becoming white, but what was once a slave was a slave still. Parker notes how this gave rise to situations of "masters owning children [as] white as themselves."[70] Slavery in America was changing. Through its violence generations of slaves and slaveholders were transformed. Slowly, but steadily, it was becoming no longer exclusively the domain of the black man, woman, or child. Slavery in America was becoming white.

Other transformations were underway too. Amidst all the violence, generations of slaves grew to adulthood. The only home they ever knew was the place where they were brutalized. The only tongue they spoke was that of their tormentor. The songs they sang, the society they knew, its customs, sentiments, manners, culture, and even the God they worshipped were no longer those of a foreign people. The people enslaved were not as they once were. As time passed the slaveholders could look less and less to the justifications once offered for slavery. Even so, the slaves remained enslaved. The ideologically neat compartmentalization that segregated black from white, the free from the enslaved, some of the People from all the People, and success from failure was beginning to fracture under the weight of its innumerable violations. In laying the foundation by which some could be enslaved, the foundations by which all could be enslaved had also been laid. Slavery's advocates had truly fashioned a rod for their own backs and for those of future generations.

That slaveholders used physical restraints, such as chains, fetters, handcuffs, and others, is clearly the case. These were the visible elements of slavery of the time. Nonetheless the slave existed in a condition of slavery whether these things were put on or taken off. So, while one can associate the tangible, and obvious, equipment of slavery with the practice, it is only part of it, and likely an optional part of it at that. It is why Beecher Stowe writes: "On the lower part of a small, mean boat, on the Red River, Tom sat, — chains on his wrists, chains on his feet, and a weight heavier than chains lay on his heart."[71] The slave William Henry Singleton realized the ulterior motives behind slavery's violence when he noted how some "slave owners used to have a custom of whipping their slaves frequently to keep them afraid. They thought it made them more obedient."[72] The economist Cairnes writes how the "only means by which the ancients maintained … [slavery] were fetters and death; the Americans of the South of the Union have discovered more intellectual securities for the duration of their power. They have employed their despotism and their violence against the human mind."[73] Some, it was said, became so "debased that the man is mainly silenced … [with] the animal [in him] alone surviving."[74] Jacobs implores:

> Pity me, and pardon me, O virtuous reader! You never
> knew what it is to be a slave; to be entirely unprotected
> by law or custom; to have the laws reduce you to the

condition of a chattel, entirely subject to the will of another. You never exhausted your ingenuity in avoiding the snares, and eluding the power of a hated tyrant; you never shuddered at the sound of his footsteps, and trembled within hearing of his voice.[75]

Through violence the will of the master becomes the will of the slave. Whether slaveholders knew these things innately *via* their nature, or whether it was learned by observation and passed down over time, or both, is hard to say. What one can say, and what can be supported, is how the violence intrinsic to slavery was entirely compatible with it. That violence served a role beyond the immediately discernible is certainly the case. It was, however, much more than mere contempt for the person of the slave. It was a tool by which the person was transformed from the state of being an autonomous individual to the state of being a slave. Parker asserts the idea "of Slavery is to use a man as a thing, against his nature and in opposition to his interests."[76] Parker goes further, stressing the "relation of master and slave begins in violence; it must be sustained by violence ... There is no other mode of conquering and subjugating a man."[77] Those who lived in the South came to understand these things. Daily, they saw it with their own eyes, and they exerted violence in the knowledge of the effects it produced. Where slavery is concerned, much is often not as it first appears, the apparently trivial becomes significant as the nature of acts reveal new depths each time they are visited. Any effort to make sense of slavery must entail an understanding of the role of violence.

Chapter 3:

What is Slavery?

A distinction can be made between slave and slavery. One example illustrating this distinction is the passionate embrace of the South for the institution of slavery and its utter contempt for the slave who was necessarily part of it. Paradoxically one can find similar sentiments among some of those who wished to abolish slavery, not out of compassion for the person of the slave, but from an abhorrence of the institution. The words of a Mr. Marshall, who addressed the Virginia State Legislature in 1832, shed light on the distinction:

> It is not for the sake of the slave, nor to ameliorate his condition, that abolition is desirable. Wherefore, then object to slavery? Because it is ruinous to whites – retards improvement – roots out an industrious population – banishes the yeomanry of the country – deprives the spinner, the weaver, the smith, the shoemaker, the carpenter, of employment and support. There is no diversity of occupation, no incentive to enterprise. Labor of every species is disreputable, because performed mostly by slaves. Our towns are stationary, our villages almost everywhere declining, and the general aspect of the country marks the curse of a wasteful, idle, and reckless population.[1]

Marshall's abolitionism then is wholly and unapologetically one of self-interest. Slavery was bad for the South, he contends. It was catastrophic to its white workers who associated vast tracts of manual labor with acts of slavery, thereby making those acts unworthy of them. It curtailed industry and development, stifling the economic prosperity of the South, ruining its people, and its prospects for the future. In the North too there were people who objected to slavery based on how it shaped the relationship between the North and the South. The slave was not party to this relationship. His or her relationship was solely with the Southern slaveholder. The fact that the abolition of slavery would be of major benefit to the slave is not a consequence with which Marshall wishes to be associated. He specifically shies away from it. With this distinction in mind, between the person of the slave and the practice of slavery, one cannot understand one by virtue of the other. So, what then is slavery?

In *Slavery and Free Labor, Described and Compared* Ruffin seeks to define slavery. It is a challenging task, one he apologetically acknowledges by saying, "I cannot expect to succeed in attempting what so many other and more able writers on the subject have failed to accomplish."[2] Ruffin is quite correct. Slavery is difficult to define and, without an accurate definition, the first step towards understanding cannot be taken. Undaunted, Ruffin proceeds to the task at hand:

> What I understand as the general condition that constitutes slavery is the subjection of one individual, or class, to the authority and direction of another individual or class, so that the subjected party is compelled (no matter by what means) to labor, serve, or act, at the will and command, and for the benefit or objects, of the ruling individual or class.[3]

His definition comprises three parts: an act or acts of subjugation, by whatever means, for the purpose of another or others. The person of the slave is but part of the definition, not the whole of it. Slavery then is a system of which the slave is but a component part.

In *A Letter to the People of the United States Touching the Matter of Slavery* Parker lays out three specific conditions as requirements for a system of slavery to establish its foothold and for it to maintain itself thereafter. First, Parker states how the population of an area in which slavery is to be practiced must be sparse. He elaborates on this, stating how this means there cannot be sufficient free labor to allow for a division of labor in the chosen activity.

One famous example concerning the fruits of dividing labor is given by the political economist Adam Smith, in An *Inquiry into the Nature and Causes of the Wealth of Nations*. Smith addresses the manufacture of pins. He says a tradesperson unacquainted with the trade of pin-making, and without any of its machinery, could scarcely manage to make one pin over the course of a day. To be certain, Smith adds how there is absolutely no way such a person could make as many as 20 pins in a day. Such were the developments in manufacturing of his time, the task could be divided into different parts. These parts became trades in their own right:

> One man draws out the wire; another straights it; a third cuts it; a fourth points it; a fifth grinds it at the top for receiving the head; to make the head requires two or three distinct operations; to put it on is a peculiar business; to whiten the pins is another; it is even a trade by itself to put them into the paper; and the important business of making a pin is, in this manner, divided into about eighteen distinct operations, which, in some manufactories, are all performed by distinct hands, though in others the same man will sometimes perform two or three of them.[4]

The process typically requires about 10 persons, who over the course of the day can produce between them a total of 12 pounds of pins. Each pound consists of an average of 4,000 pins, resulting in a total of about 48,000 pins per day, or 4,800 pins per worker per day. This compares to the 20 pins Smith asserts there is absolutely no possibility of a single worker producing in a day had the labor not been divided and had machinery particular to that division not been employed.

Technological advancement had allowed pin-making to become a manufacturing process. The product was no longer the work of one person but of a series of skilled people working in tandem. Thus, the kind of labor that had existed prior to these advances was destroyed and with its demise went the prospect of slavery being employed in it. Unskilled slaves, producing just 20 pins per day, cannot compete with a manufacturing process employing free laborers who produce 4,800 pins per worker per day. Logically one might expect slavery to effect a similar transformation to make it competitive with these developments. Cairnes, however, believed slavery "has never been, and can never be, employed with success in manufacturing industry," precluding any possibility of slaves then being used to compete.[5] The reason he gives for his conclusion is how the condition of the slave, particularly the tendency of the time to keep the slave in perpetual ignorance, precluded any possibility of him or her being suitable for manufacturing operations. In fact, Cairnes also believed the North's manufacturers in New England were not so moral as to exclude the option of slave labor, had it been suitable to their ends. On the contrary it was not their morals that excluded slavery from being used by them, he contends, but rather the fact that slavery excluded itself from being so used.[6]

Technological advancement reduced the applicability of slavery in other activities too. It was written how when:

> ... corn was ground by hand, and mines were drained by
> the bucket, slaves ... had a value which they no longer
> possess. And the marked tendency of the age is, still
> further to curtail the requirement for them, and the
> uses to which they can be economically applied.[7]

Not all technological advancement resulted in a division of labor. Some tasks no longer required the interaction of man and machine, or required them only minimally, once they were mechanized. In *Civil War* Ken Burns declares that at the time of the nation's founding slavery was in its death throes in the North. That changed in 1793, Burns asserts, when Northerner Eli Whitney showed the South how slavery could pay.[8] That slavery was actually dying out is probably untenable. The claim concerning the contribution of Whitney's "Engine", or gin, however, is not. The gin made it possible for cotton to be separated from its seeds. Until the moment of its arrival the work of separating cotton from its seeds was slow, tedious, manual work. Slaves were employed to carry it out. Production averaged only one pound per slave per day. With the introduction of the gin the work of separating cotton by hand was destroyed. There was no longer any need to have slaves for the task. Sometimes a small number were engaged, albeit peripherally, in the operation of the gin. A single gin could pump out 50 pounds of cotton per day. Improvements in the production process allowed for greater volumes to be sold at lower costs. As the price of cotton fell the volume of sales increased further. This increased volume handsomely compensated cotton producers for diminishing prices, and encouraged further improvements in the production process, and consequently even lower prices. In fact, from 1802 to 1860 the general trend in the price of raw cotton was downward.[9] Now there was demand for raw cotton, and with it came a demand for more slaves to pick it.

Profoundly perhaps, but worth noting all the same, slave labor is a form of labor. That the slaveholders saw it as such is evident. An advertisement placed by one R. Loring in the *Pensacola Gazette* declares he has a contract to undertake work on the railroad in Alabama, Georgia and Florida. He is looking for "400 BLACK LABORERS, for which a liberal price will be paid."[10] The *Richmond Enquirer* of Virginia carried an advertisement in 1836 on behalf of one Richard Reins. It declares: "LABORERS WANTED. – The James River, and Kenawha Company, are in immediate want of SEVERAL HUNDRED good laborers. Gentlemen wishing to send negroes from the country, are assured that the very best care shall be taken of them."[11] Philip Roach, placing his advert in the *Alexandria Gazette* of 1837, declares he "wishes to employ by the month or year, ONE HUNDRED ABLE BODIED MEN, AND THIRTY BOYS. Persons having servants, will do well to give him a call."[12] An officer in the employ of the United States, one W.K. Latimer, advertises the need for 60 laborers to work at the naval yard at Pensacola. The advertisement further advises how persons "having Laborers to hire, will apply to the Commanding Officer."[13]

Cairnes thought characteristics particular to species of labor made them amenable to slavery. He thought it was no occurrence of fate that the line dividing North and South also marked an important division between their respective agricultural activities. Cereal crops were produced in the North, while tobacco, rice, sugar, and cotton were produced in the South. In *Cotton is King, and Pro-slavery Arguments* its authors caution slavery's practitioners:

> Slave labor has seldom been made profitable where it has been wholly employed in grazing and grain growing; but it becomes remunerative in proportion as the planters can devote their attention to cotton, sugar, rice, or tobacco. To render Southern slavery profitable

> in the highest degree, therefore, the slaves must be employed upon some one of these articles ... This is a point of the utmost moment, and must be considered more at length.[14]

The nature of the labor employed in cultivating tobacco, rice, sugar, and cotton is similar in each case. So too the nature of the labor employed in cultivating cereal crops is similar in each case. However, there are important differences between these two classes of crop that distinguish them from each other. On occasion distinctions in varieties of crops were enough to preclude them as acceptable to Southern farmers and their slave labor. One planter "cultivated only the coarser and lower-priced sorts of tobacco, because the finer sorts required more painstaking and discretion than it was possible to make" slaves use.[15] The work of cultivating the crops of the North often required the laborers to be dispersed across a large area. There was need too of fewer laborers. Conversely in the South the work of cultivating its crops required the laborers to be many in number, extensively organized and concentrated in a comparatively small area.[16] The Southern politician and advocate of slavery William Harper makes a point like Parker's. Harper contends that, to attain the goal of capital accumulation, and through it to attain advancement, slavery is required. He reasons that when society is at its early stages "people are thinly scattered over an extensive territory, [and] the labor necessary to extensive works cannot be commanded."[17] The people who inhabit these areas exist independently of one another, so while there is an abundance of land, there is "no one [who] will submit to be employed in the service of his neighbor."[18] Consequently the slave is a person whose *raison d'être* is to provide the form of labor compatible with slavery.

Cairnes applies his rationale, comparing the cultivation of different classes of crops using different types of labor, saying:

… tobacco and cotton fulfil that condition which we saw was essential to the economical employment of slaves—the possibility of working large numbers within a limited space; while wheat and Indian corn, in the cultivation of which the labourers are dispersed over a wide surface, fail in this respect. We thus find that cotton, and the class of crops of which cotton may be taken as the type, favour the employment of slaves in the competition with peasant proprietors in two leading ways : first, they need extensive combination and organization of labour —requirements which slavery is eminently calculated to supply, but in respect to which the labour of peasant proprietors is defective; and secondly, they allow of labour being concentrated, and thus minimize the cardinal evil [or defect] of slave-labour — [that is,] the reluctance with which it is yielded [by slaves].[19]

Intriguingly and almost prophetically Cairnes also applies his rationale to sea-faring as one place where slavery might take place: "A mercantile marine composed of slaves is a form of industry which the world has not yet seen".[20] The likelihood of it occurring are poor, he believes, as mutinies "in mid-ocean and desertions the moment the vessel touched at foreign ports would quickly reduce the force to a cipher."[21] This, of course, presumes technological advancement would not one day make it unnecessary for seafaring vessels to arrive at port.

Technology consequently has a role to play. Through its advances new forms of labor emerge and among them, new opportunities to use slavery. Conversely an absence of such advances may serve to shield slavery from developments that would divide its labor into new forms of labor, perhaps rendering slavery redundant. There are, of course, some activities where a division of labor is simply not possible, ones that have remained unchanged since the dawn of time.

What activities are amenable to slavery? History is surely capable of informing. Industries that have hosted slavery in the past will host it again in the future, unless some radical advancement has altered the nature of the labor used in the cultivation of their crops. The explosion of the sugar industry in Brazil in the 16th century, and later in the West Indies in the 17th century, increased the demand for slave labor in the sector.[22] Other industries, such as those of coffee and tobacco, also became known to be predisposed to the use of slave labor and to have benefitted from it enormously.[23] If slavery is used in an activity with which it is not compatible, it will die out and it will not become associated with that activity. Slavery then has its ways of identifying the industries with which it is compatible. Even in his own time Parker was able to conclude how only "coarse staples, sugar, cotton, rice, corn, tobacco, can be successfully raised by the slave in America."[24]

Parker's second point concerns the soil upon which slavery is practiced, which he says, must be extraordinarily fertile.[25] Parker elaborates again, adding how the activity must not be one that, by perpetually carrying it out, exhausts the soil from which it derives. Consider for a moment what a Northerner might expect to see when visiting the South for the first time. What would be the condition of the countryside? Would the Northerner expect to find the countryside bespeckled with the large houses of its planters, prominently situated on vast plantations where a multitude of slaves toiled at picking cotton? Such sights certainly did exist. Perhaps surprisingly, however, they appear not to have been the norm. Olmsted recounts how going on his:

> … way into the so-called cotton States, within which I travelled over, first and last, at least three thousand miles of roads, from which not a cotton plant was to be seen, and the people living by the side of which certainly had not been made rich by cotton or anything

else. And for every mile of road-side upon which I saw any evidence of cotton production, I am sure that I saw a hundred of forest or waste land, with only now and then an acre or two of poor corn half smothered in weeds; for every rich man's house, I am sure that I passed a dozen shabby and half-furnished cottages, and at least 100 cabins – mere hovels, such as none but a poor farmer would house his cattle in the North.[26]

The truth is that much of the land on which slavery had once stood was now devastated. Here again is an instance where slavery is transformed by its own nature. The crudeness of its work meant it was incapable of replenishing the soil on which it was practiced. By 1858 it was estimated 40% of the South's cotton land alone was exhausted.[27]

The reasons behind these issues are complex and some are disputed. Some significance, though, can be attributed to slavery's limitations. The Southern workforce, consisting of a large body of slaves, had to be directed to crops compatible with slavery. That crops like sugar, cotton, rice, corn, and tobacco were compatible with slavery is evident. Why? It is evident because slavery was perpetually used in their cultivation and, had it not been compatible with their cultivation, it could not have been used. No crop rotation was possible. Year after year, the same few crops were planted and harvested. Year after year, the soil was a little less fertile than it had been before and the return from it a little less abundant. One of the consequences of this erosion was that land prices were kept low, as the continuous erosion of the soil destroyed its value.

By the time Olmsted made his journey, slavery was concentrated among some regions. Most of the "cotton crop of the United States … [was] now produced in the Mississippi valley, including the lands contiguous to its great Southern tributary streams, the Red River and others."[28] A famous portrait of Lincoln, by Francis Bicknell Carpenter, entitled *First Reading of the Emancipation Proclamation of President Lincoln*, depicts Lincoln and his cabinet. Almost hidden from sight in its lower right-hand corner, the portrait also depicts a map Lincoln had commissioned, one known as the *Map showing the distribution of the slave population of the southern states of the United States*.[29] What is immediately discernible from this map is how vast tracts of the United States have only a small percentage population of slaves, while others have much higher percentage population. What is also discernible is how those areas with high percentage populations tend to have high percentage populations of slaves in the areas adjacent to them. Conversely the opposite is also true. There is a tendency too for a progression from high percentages to low concentrations *via* a gradual diminution across, rather than an abrupt change between two adjacent counties. The higher percentage populations tend to be in those counties nearest the sea. The exceptions tend to be near to a major inland waterway, particularly the Mississippi River.

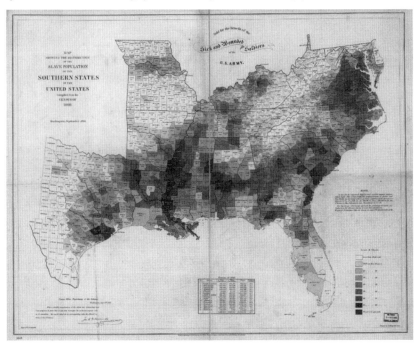

Figure: Map showing the distribution of the slave population of the southern states of the United States.
Compiled from the census of 1860 (Library of Congress 1861).

In the case of the Mississippi River, starting north of Baton Rouge and progressing northwards, the percentage of the population in each county represented by slaves is as follows: West Feliciana (83%), East Feliciana (72%), Wilkinson (83%), Concordia (91%), Adams (72%), Jefferson (81%), Clairborne (79%), Tensas (91%), and so on. At the place along the Mississippi where he toiled as a slave Northup observed there was no need for "those invigorating composts necessary to more barren lands, and on the same field the same crop is grown for many successive years."[30] Indeed the richness of the soil not only allowed existing slave operations to prosper but "the remarkable richness and fertility of the soil … [had the effect of attracting] … a great number of planters."[31] In comparison in Walker County in north Alabama, slaves accounted for just 6% of the population. In adjacent Winston County it was lower at 3%. From the vicinity of these counties one great expanse of low slave population counties opens, sprawling north-eastwards, gradually expanding along its line to its left and to its right as it progresses, before ending in West Virginia almost 500 miles away. Weston contends the "permanency of this fertility … may be deduced from the permanency of the slave population" residing upon it.[32] To a degree then, if the slave population of a particular place is high and it continues to be so for a long time, one may discern the fertility of the soil upon which they toil. That being noted, not all forms of slavery are dependent on the soil.

So potent was the matter of fertility to the issue of slavery that, even when slavery's activities were not linked to the soil, fertility often remained to the fore among its considerations. In some cases, the value of slaves was set not by the profitability of their labor but by the value of the slave as a commodity item in his or her own right.[33] One example of this concerns the breeding of slaves, as was the practice in several states including Kentucky and Virginia. Breeding imposed its own requirements upon fertility. In the testimony of Reverend

C.S. Renshaw, who witnessed two mothers being sold, their infant children taken from them and those children sold for a dollar apiece, he noted how "a young babe decreases the value of a field hand in the lower country, whilst it increases her value in the 'breeding states.'"[34] Whatever the nature of slavery's produce, the issue of fertility could not be permitted to curtail the abundance of its supply.

The issue of fertility meant slavery needed to migrate, and through migration to expand beyond its boundaries, for in depending on the soil for its existence it could only stand still where the fertility of the soil was able to withstand it. Despite even the enormity of the area within the boundaries of the Southern states it was only a matter of time before expansion beyond them was indeed necessary. Historian Genovese, and others, saw it another way, arguing the expansion of slavery was a psychological necessity for the South's slaveholders.[35] If slavery was a benevolent institution, as indeed the slaveholders contended it was, then containing it would itself be morally wrong and it would have the effect of implicitly acknowledging slavery was itself wrong. It became necessary then for the slaveholders to spread their way of life, lending credence to its legitimacy.

Given the prominent space occupied by slavery within the South the expansion of slavery was a political priority. Weston describes the situation:

> The first and essential step in their scheme of ambitious aggrandizement is to extend their favourite institution in one continuous line across the continent to the Pacific Ocean, as far to the north as possible, but, at all events, somewhere, with the expectation that it would prove an impassable barrier to the progress of free labour to the southward. This point being secured, the process of absorption is to be applied to all the regions which intervene between the United

States and Brazil, so that the finest portions of America may become one unbroken and homogenous slave empire. Oceanward, these men contemplate no less adventurous enterprises, than to prop up the tottering fabric of slavery in Cuba, to re-conquer the rebellious blacks of Hayti, and, in due time, to restore the ancient order of things in the British and French West Indies.[36]

Internally as slavery spread to the territories it claimed new land for itself, land that might someday become part of a new State, which might in time be granted admission to the United States. With the acquisition of each state for slavery there came with it the bonus of two seats in the Senate. Already slavery had bestowed the boon of three-fifths of a vote per slave in the House of Representatives. The large influx of foreign migrants arriving at Northern ports in search of a new life would be of assistance to the North in response. In 1850 the free population of the slave states was 6.3 million but, owing to the contribution of votes allocated by the slaves they held, their representation equated to a population of 8.3 million persons, bestowing upon those states 20 representatives more than they would otherwise have been entitled.[37] These 20 representatives were added to the 69 representatives who constituted the free white population of the slave states. Acting together, even if they were not all slave-owners, they became one homogenous body in support of slavery, a veritable Slave Power.[38] At the same time slavery held in its grasp 30 of the 62 seats in the Senate. These two factors, combined with the support of Congressional and Senatorial friends from the North, virtually guaranteed Southern slave interests held the balance of power. There were bigger prizes to be secured. The total Electoral College vote of the time for the presidency was 296 votes, of which the slaveholders commanded 120 votes. It would have been a good candidate indeed who could dispense with 40% of the vote on his first gambit and then proceed on the remainder in the hope of winning. In fact, under such circumstances, the only conceivable way a candidate could be successful when standing in opposition to the slaveholders was if the election was to be determined on the very issue of slavery. Once the presidency was secure for slavery, as it was right up until the dawn of war, the whole of government and democracy itself was secure for slavery:

> Let him enter the wider arena of Federal ambition, and new influences beset him to whatever walk of life he may belong. Is he a statesman? – then to become a cabinet minister, or head of a department, he must sympathise with the governing power. Is he a diplomatist? – foreign embassies are only open to their creatures. Is he a lawyer? – the seats on the bench of the Supreme Court are reserved for those favourites of the Senate whose past history and career are, in a Southern sense, irreproachable.[39]

Many years before, the expansion of the territories took on an added significance for those opposed to slavery. It was realized how, if the progress of slavery were to be curbed, a race must be started to counter each Southern addition of a state with a Northern addition. This kind of competition, a balance of power politics, is one familiar to the sphere of international relations. The race began with the raising of the question of Missouri's admission to the Union. In 1819 the Union comprised 22 States: 11 free states and 11 slave states. The result was a *de facto* balance of power on the issue of slavery. For the North there was some consolation, at least, in knowing the problem of slavery was contained and how it would not spread. Equally, for the South there was consolation that slavery could be maintained, and the Northern way of life would not itself spread, either directly or indirectly, into the South. Time, however, was the catalyst that energized these components, for it was in the same year, in 1819, that Missouri, a slave state, applied for membership of the United States.

Henry Clay, at that time a Congressman for Kentucky, helped settle the question. The "Missouri Compromise" of 1820 granted admission both to Missouri and to the free state of Maine, thus preserving the balance of power. There was another event that year, in 1820, one with far-off consequences: Spain ceded Florida to the United States. Some 15 years passed before further additions were made to the Union. Again, those admitted, the slave territory of Arkansas and that of free Michigan, were granted admission as a pair, keeping the balance of power intact.

The floors of Congress and the Senate proved to be only one forum where the politics of slavery could be played out. Military conflict provided another. In the westward march of the United States "Texas was next; to shut off Texas meant telling southerners no more marching for you."[40] In *A Brief History of the Mexican War* Oliver O. Howard writes how in:

> ... the year 1830 the famous Gen. Sam Houston, at the head of a company of enterprising men and a band of Cherokee Indians, went from the United States into Texas. Their object was to foster revolution, seize the reins of government, emancipate Texas from Mexico, and annex it to the United States. These restless spirits were working in the interests of a Southern policy, hoping so to increase slave territory as to keep a balance of power against the free States, which being formed from the Territories, were increasing in number.[41]

Eventually Houston and his men succeeded in their enterprise and won independence for Texas. In 1836 the Republic of Texas was born. It was 1845, however, before Texas was granted admission to the Union amidst internal and external strife. Internally, Texas' admission tipped the balance of power in favor of the South. Externally, Texas needed to be secured against Mexican claims, raising the prospect of war. The Treaty of 1819, which the United States had signed with Spain, and in which the United States gained the territory of Florida, clearly established the south-western border of the United States with Mexico.[42] Texas was on the Mexican side of the border. The U.S.-Mexican War that followed Texas' entry into the Union commenced in 1846. At about the same time, there was a "Florida Compromise" of sorts, though it is not usually referred to as such, when Iowa and Florida were paired and granted admission.[43] Iowa entered in 1846 with Wisconsin following suit in 1848, restoring the balance of power at 15 states each.

Amidst one war, the seeds of the next are sown. When Congressman David Wilmot, a Democrat, introduced legislation in 1846 he sought to prohibit slavery in any territory that might be purchased or forcibly acquired from Mexico. Known as the "Wilmot Proviso" the legislation sparked "a powerful reaction in the South because southerners correctly identified it as a potentially lethal assault on their political power, on their safety, on their honor."[44] Ultimately the proviso failed, but the stain remained. So incendiary was the proviso, in its attempt to restrict "slavery in the territories, that [the issue it raised] would dominate national politics for the next fifteen years until bullets replaced words."[45] So incendiary was the proviso to the South that it gave rise to the first serious secessionists.

It was with the ending of the U.S.-Mexican War in 1848 that perhaps the most famous, and perhaps the most significant, compromise arose. In 1850 Senator Henry Clay, who had been instrumental in framing the "Missouri Compromise" of 1820, presented a series of five bills. Taken together these bills became known as the "Compromise of 1850." Two elements are particularly important. Under the Compromise, California was permitted to enter the Union as a free state. The fact that California was gold-rich likely did not hurt its cause. The balance was tipped once more, this time for the very last time, in favor of slavery's opponents, at 16 to 15. In time, California dispatched two Senators to the national Senate. One of these was pro-slavery.

To placate the South the Compromise introduced the *Fugitive Slave Law of 1850*.[46] Technically this was an amendment of a much older law, the *Fugitive Slave Act of 1793*. The amendment now permitted the capture of slaves who had escaped from the Southern states to the free states of the North, and their return to their Southern owners.[47] In fact not only did the law allow this, it also imposed a legal obligation upon the citizens and authorities of the Northern states to facilitate every opportunity to do so. In many instances this included facilitating slave hunters from the South who had travelled North in pursuit of fugitive slaves. Northerners, and even those in the North who had been apathetic on the issue of slavery, were horrified.[48] If they had been complicit in the slavery of the South, by virtue of their association with the South *via* the Union, before this moment, they were even more so now. The supposedly private affair of the South's slavery was, as it ever was, foisted upon the people of the North, this time obliging them to be complicit in the very thing they so vehemently abhorred. In February of 1851, a fugitive slave by the name of Shadrach was apprehended by authorities acting in accordance with the law. A small group of locals freed Shadrach from his captors' grasp. They then carried him away to safety, all while a crowd of onlookers stood by and cheered their initiative.[49] It is hard to imagine any more unjust deed the South could have imposed upon the North, or one that could have been so contrary to the interests of the South, than a law that so enflamed the passions of its abolitionists by compelling them to be active participants in slavery.

In 1854, violence broke out in the territory of Kansas when Congress passed the *Kansas-Nebraska Act*, giving the territory's residents a choice. They could choose, in an act of popular sovereignty, to declare their place on the side of slavery or on the side of its abolitionists.

It was a choice Lincoln, then standing for the Presidency, would renounce as being "so perverted" in its attempted use of the term *sacred right of self government* "as to amount to just this: That if any one man choose to enslave another, no third man shall be allowed to object."[50] Lincoln's declaration may itself have amounted to just this, a denunciation of the principle that, if any one state should choose to enslave, no other state should be allowed to object. Implicitly, he also denounced the notion that power is the basis for moral action. In the end, militant factions from both sides flooded into Kansas to confront one another, earning it the name "Bleeding Kansas." That other acts occurred, such as John Brown's raid on Harpers Ferry in 1859 and the ruling of the Supreme Court in the *Dred Scott Decision* on the Missouri Compromise, is duly acknowledged. That there was talk too of dissolving the Union, permitting the re-opening of the transatlantic slave trade, to address the South's changing fortunes is also acknowledged.[51] What is important, however, is how the Compromises, starting in 1820 and continuing as they do for some 30 years, do not mark a path to peace, but a slow march to war. For this is the situation Lincoln illuminated when he described the fruits of those compromises as delivering a nation "half slave and half free."[52]

What is clear is just how very much of what was purportedly an issue for individual States, and for their conception of the good life, was infringing upon the political, economic and social agendas of all of the states of the United States. The slavery of the slave states was infringing too on that part their good life involving their partnership with the free states. Cairnes saw how this was so, and he questioned whether it was possible for non-slaveholding states to be kinsmen of those who advocate for slavery. He had, through the efforts of his book:

> … endeavoured to show that, while the economic necessities of the South require a constant extension of the area of its dominion, and while its moral necessities

require no less urgently a field for its political ambition, it is yet, from the peculiarity of its social structure, incapable of amalgamating with societies of a different type, and has no objects which it can pursue with them in common; and that, consequently, it can only attain its ends at their expense.[53]

If what Weston claimed earlier was the intention is true, and there were others who shared in its expectation, in this one area alone the expansion of slavery would have the effect of setting the United States on the path of perpetual war and conquest, all for the benefit of slavery, and all for the benefit of its slaveholders. That slavery was ostensibly an issue for the states alone did not prevent it from being forced at every turn upon those states that chose not to practice it.

Matters were not helped, when on 4 March 1860 Abraham Lincoln was sworn in as U.S. President. Lincoln was the very first member of the Republican Party, a party he helped establish, to become President of the United States. His party had at its core opposition to slavery. In his inaugural address Lincoln started by saying he did not consider it necessary "to discuss those matters of administration about which there is no special anxiety or excitement" before proceeding immediately to those matters about which both were abundant.[54] "Apprehension seems to exist among the people of the Southern States that by the accession of a Republican Administration their property and their peace and personal security are to be endangered," he conceded.[55] He then sought to reassure the secessionist states of his goodwill towards them by stating: "There has never been any reasonable cause for such apprehension. Indeed, the most ample evidence to the contrary has all the while existed and been open to their inspection. It is found in nearly all the published speeches of him who now addresses you. I do but quote from one of those speeches when I declare that – 'I have no purpose, directly or indirectly, to interfere with the institution of slavery in the States where it exists. I believe I have no lawful right to do so, and I have no inclination to do so.'"[56] If those inclined towards secession derived any consolation from these words they would be soon on-edge again by those that followed, for Lincoln added how "no State upon its own mere motion can lawfully get out of the Union; that 'resolves' and 'ordinances' to that effect are legally void, and that acts of violence within any State or States against the authority of the United States are insurrectionary or revolutionary, according to circumstances."[57] Only the People could unmake what they had made. Only the People could undo the Union. The argument had come full circle.

There was more, however, to upset secessionists. The Republican Party had as a core value its opposition to expansion of slavery in the territories. Lincoln offers no reprieve in his inaugural address saying: "'May' Congress prohibit slavery in the Territories? The Constitution does not expressly say. 'Must' Congress protect slavery in the Territories? The Constitution does not expressly say."[58] While Lincoln's response was not in the negative nonetheless it was a far cry from the zealous assurances once given to Southern slaveholders by political leaders. Nothing short of utter support for the institution of slavery was tolerable. Lincoln and the Republican Party, however, brought with them the assurance slavery would be deprived of one of its vital components. They deprived it of the fertile soil on which it depended. Hemmed-in, it was now doomed morally and viably. For the slave states the choice now was to concede the loss of slavery or to concede the loss of peace.

Parker's third, and final point, asserts how if the source of supply must be abundantly fertile the same must be true of the demand for slavery's produce. Slavery must have "the monopoly of some favorite staple which cannot be produced elsewhere."[59] In The *South Carolina Exposition* of 1828 Calhoun states that exports from the

United States of the time averaged about US$53 million *per annum*, of which the South contributed, through its farming of cotton, rice and tobacco, approximately US$37 million. In contrast the North contributed at the very most US$16 million, less than half what the South produced, while the population of the North was about twice that of the South.[60] All three of these crops relied on the use of slave labor. Sugar, a crop notorious for its use of slave labor, is conspicuous by its absence. Domestic consumption of sugar outstripped supply, leaving no surplus for export and so it does not appear in the figures for exports of this time.[61] By Calhoun's reckoning, this is a staggering sum of money, a staggering proportion of total United States' exports of the time, and all from just three crops. Of these three crops one was designated to be the outright winner. Approximately 205 million pounds in weight of cotton was exported to Great Britain and to Europe in the year of *Calhoun's Exposition*.[62] Cotton, it was said, was king.[63]

Yet 45 years before these figures were provided, in 1783, it appears no cotton was imported into Great Britain or Europe from the United States. A note in one table detailing imports reveals how 71 bags were "seized in England, on the ground that America could not produce so much."[64] Ten years later, in 1793, figures show the United States exported 189,316 pounds. The following year it was 500,000 pounds; the year after 1.6 million pounds; and the year after that, in 1796, it was 6.2 million pounds of cotton. Between 1793 and 1804 Britain's importation and consumption of cotton from all sources grew from 23 million pounds to almost double that figure at 43 million pounds. In contrast United States exports to Great Britain and Europe, which had stood at 189,316 pounds in 1793, grew to almost 222 times that figure at 41.9 million pounds in 1804. In just 11 years total United States cotton exports grew from a point at which they represented a miniscule eight-tenths of just one *per cent* of all the cotton imported and consumed in Great Britain, to a point at which those same exports now equated to 96% of all the cotton imported and consumed in Great Britain. What is clear is the impact of the arrival of Whitney's gin, and the fast-approaching dominance of the South as a global producer of cotton. What ought to be clear too are the profound consequences these figures represented for slaves.

As the years progressed Britain's demand increased, and the South tried to keep up. By 1808 total exports from the United States surpassed total British demand for the first time. In an English weekly magazine, *Household Words* (later edited by Charles Dickens), it is stated how the importation by Great Britain of raw cotton, which in 1808 equated to a total weight of 56 million pounds, rose by 1815 to almost twice that figure.[65] In 1835 the figure was 400 million pounds of raw cotton. By the time one of the installments of Dickens' edited publications went to press in 1852, more than 700 million pounds of raw cotton had been imported that year.[66]

Such was the monopoly of the South in its supply of cotton to England's mills, it was estimated 85% of the cotton imported for processing at those mills came from the Southern states.[67] The remainder of the demand was catered to by supplies from Egypt, the East Indies and from South America. Indeed, such was the monopoly the South had on England's demand a cautionary tale was written of the perils of these commercial arrangements:

> Such is the Cotton trade of England; un-equalled by any industry of any other country in the world. It is not difficult, therefore, to understand how important becomes any question affecting the future supply of this great staple commodity. We are at present dependent upon another nation for the ... [material] of our national prosperity, and that nation depends upon the labour of a race of slaves. Let any great social or physical convulsion visit that country, and England would feel the shock

from Land's End to John O'Groat's. The lives of nearly two millions of our countrymen are dependent upon the cotton crops of America; their destiny may be said, without any sort of hyperbole, to hang upon a thread. Should any dire calamity befal the land of cotton, a thousand of our merchant ships would rot idly in dock; ten thousand mills must stay their busy looms; two thousand thousand [(two million)] mouths would starve for lack of work to feed them.[68]

If the division between North and South marked a division in the type of labor used in each and a division in the crops each grew, then so too the division between the South and Great Britain marked a division of its own. Only the crudest part of the operation, the cultivation of cotton and the separation of lint from seeds, was performed in the South where slavery was used. Even then this latter part of the operation was for the most part performed by machine. It was in England's cotton mills, under a manufacturing regime, that the raw material was transformed into something of superior quality, which in its completed form was estimated by 1832 to represent "about two-thirds of all the woven fabrics exported from the empire."[69] Yet the divide that existed between England and the South in this regard was traversed by the economics of their dependency upon each other and upon the fact that the material they handled was largely the same, since most English cotton fabric originated from Southern plantations.

The symbiotic nature of relationship between the commodities of slavery and the produce of industry is revealed when one appreciates how the relationship worked in the opposite direction too. "To render Southern slavery profitable in the highest degree" its slaves had to be engaged with a commodity suited to its ways, and those had to be "sustained by a supply of food and draught animals from ... agriculturists; and before the planter's supplies are complete, to these must be added cotton gins, implements of husbandry, furniture, and tools, from ... mechanics."[70] The limits of slavery as a form of labor precluded it from producing the supplies and tools it required. These it acquired through the assistance of the North. Even in its own time it was understood how slavery "is not an isolated system, but is so mingled with the business of the world, that it derives facilities from the most innocent transactions."[71]

In *Cotton is King, and Pro-slavery Arguments*, its authors declare of the interaction of slavery and business to:

> ... the superficial observer, all the agencies, based upon the sale and manufacture of cotton, seem to be legitimately engaged in promoting human happiness ... But turn a moment to the source whence the raw cotton, the basis of these operations, is obtained, and observe the aspect of things in that direction. When the statistics on the subject are examined, it appears that nine-tenths of the cotton consumed in the Christian world is the product of the slave labor of the United States. ... It is this monopoly that has given to slavery its commercial value; and, while this monopoly is retained, the institution will continue to extend itself wherever it can find room to spread.[72]

"Look at your bills for groceries," another urges, "and what do they contain? Coffee, sugar, molasses, rice—from Brazil, Cuba, Louisiana, Carolina; while only a mere fraction of them are from free labor countries."[73] To comprehend these things, the text's pro-slavery advocates add, is merely to comprehend the nature of the world as it is and to expect otherwise is unstatesmanlike:

> He who looks for any other result, must expect that nations, which, for centuries, have waged war to

> extend their commerce, will now abandon that means
> of aggrandizement, and bankrupt themselves to force
> the abolition of American slavery![74]

Lest there be any ambiguity, they add: "This, now, is what becomes of our cotton; this is the way in which it so largely constitutes the basis of commerce and trade; and this is the nature of the relations existing between the slavery of the United States and the economical interests of the world."[75] It is why Weston despairs at "how immense a sacrifice of human life has been made, to enable the civilized world to be supplied at cheap prices" with commodities such as "sugar, rum, and coffee."[76]

This hand-in-hand relationship between free and slave labor was at the foundation of Ruffin's advocacy for slavery of one class over another. Knowing how slavery was a viable outcome, and being resigned to its inevitability, Ruffin realized how he and his own class might be subject to it. Ruffin then does not see slavery as exclusively a race issue, though there is certainly a strong "master class" element to his politics. He does not see slavery as something apart from labor, but rather part of it. His views are as complex as they are radical. Other forms of slavery, such as political slavery, are possible too, he believes. He thinks, for example, "England has subjected Ireland to both political and class slavery of the severest and most crushing oppression."[77] Indeed he thinks that, if the term slavery were properly applied, it would be recognized how:

> ... the most destitute people of nearly all the world – and
> especially of the more civilized, wealthy, refined and
> highly improved communities – are, in different modes
> of subjection and of suffering, held under a much more
> stringent and cruel bondage, and in conditions of far
> greater privation, painful and inevitable coercion, and
> of suffering, than our negro slaves; and, therefore,

should as much be deemed subjects of slavery in an extended and proper sense.[78]

"Enormous," he says, are "the numbers of the miserable wretches made slaves by the home industrial system and policy of England."[79] Yet that very same England, the one that practices its own variety of slavery, he contends, is quick to offer words that stand "in contrast with the true facts of English action."[80] To avoid the prospect of slavery being practiced upon the South for the interests of others, the South must practice it on others for its own interests.

England, always so diligent in protecting her interests, did make efforts to prevent so precious a commodity becoming monopolized by a foreign entity, one over which it had no control. It looked to its colonies in the hope they might provide the answer. Ultimately, however, these efforts failed and when they did "the golden apple, fully ripened, dropped into the lap of ... [the South's] cotton planters."[81] Having secured power at home through a political balance of power, the Slave Power had now secured economic prosperity for itself and for its posterity through cotton. This too was noted of these developments:

> ... the history of the cotton-plant shows how powerful a control an obscure plant may exercise, not only over the social character of a people, but over their general material prosperity, their external political power, and their relations with the world at large. The cotton shrub, which seventy years ago was grown only in gardens as a curiosity, yields now to the United States an amount of exportable produce which, in the year ending June 1850, amounted to seventy-two millions of dollars, of which from thirty to forty millions were clear profit to the country. With its increased growth has sprung up that mercantile navy, which now waves

its stripes and stars over every sea, and that foreign influence which has placed the internal peace, we may say the subsistence of millions, in every manufacturing country in Europe, within the power of an oligarchy of planters.[82]

Nonetheless a threat did come and, when it came, it came from within, as the "Tariff of 1828". That the measure arose out of some political mischief-making which subsequently went awry is largely irrelevant. With the ending of the Napoleonic wars in Europe, and with the gradual restoration of peace, American goods were no longer in demand as once they had been. The peace that brought remedy to Europe brought stagnation to America, and she was beginning to suffer. Her suffering reflected an emerging need for new markets for her produce and manufactures. In a speech Henry Clay put it so: "This market may exist at home or abroad, or both, but it must exist somewhere, if society prospers; and, wherever it does exist, it should be competent to the absorption of the entire surplus production. It is most desirable that there should be both a home and a foreign market. But with respect to their relative superiority, I can not entertain a doubt. The home market is first in order, and paramount in importance."[83] At a time when this home market was greatly needed, goods made in other countries were flowing into the United States. Once in place the tariff allowed government to counter the influx of these foreign goods and to encourage their replacement with goods made at home. Problematically the policy was one made for Northern manufacturers, and not for their Southern compatriots.

To the South it was akin to a three-pronged assault. The first of these prongs was deliberately aimed at British goods. The charges added to these goods at their point of import meant they must be sold at higher prices, but this meant Britain, a good customer of the South, would have fewer sales in the North and consequently less capital to spend in the South. Consequently, the volume of cotton being sold must decline. The second prong, while not necessarily deliberate, was perceived to be real all the same. The South was dependent on manufacturers to supply goods it could not, by virtue of the limitation of slavery, make for itself. The cost of these goods now necessarily rose. It could purchase directly British goods on which the tariff was applied. Alternatively, it could buy goods from the North, some of which were imported from Britain and consequently more expensive than hitherto, and some of which were from the North but were more expensive than it had been accustomed to paying. The profitability of sales must now also be less. The answer, it would appear, would be to increase the price the South sought for its goods, but the goods made in the South were mere commodities, readily swapped for a cheaper variety if it suited the buyer. Southern cotton producers could not increase prices to compensate for the additional burden of cost because doing so would undermine their monopolistic position. They must then absorb the burden. The third and final prong threatened to deliver the *coup de grâce*, for even by doing nothing and absorbing the burden there was the prospect their trade in cotton could nonetheless be wiped out. By imposing a tariff on U.S. imports, there was the prospect of the British imposing one of their own, raising the price of U.S. cotton imports into Britain, and destroying the market for it. There was also the possibility Britain would simply purchase cotton from some other quarter, with the same effect.[84]

Calhoun was concerned once the foreign market was destroyed for Southern produce, there was no prospect of that produce being consumed by the home market in the North.[85] How could the North consume it? The North's own part of the economy was much smaller than the contribution made to exports by the South. Its populace, though twice that of the South, generated only a fifth of its revenues *per capita*. The North simply did not have the revenues to be the exclusive buyer of Southern goods. The market for those goods would be ruined and, once ruined, the South would have to become the rivals of, and not the consumers of, the goods of the manufacturing States, but he holds out no hope of this being a realistic prospect saying how "without capital, experience, or skill, and a population untried in such pursuits ....[t]he result is not doubtful."[86] The North with its "superior capital and skill" would defeat them in the open field of such a battle.[87] Hitherto the South's slavery was like a blessing bestowed upon it. The business model was simple. From cotton in its crudest form, a staple was produced in the South in vast quantities, before being shipped to foreign shores where it was in unsurpassable demand, and where at those shores those who demanded it could not produce it for themselves. Year-after-year Southern cotton producers sent more cotton. Never was it sufficient to quench the insatiable demand for it. Year-after-year Southern cotton producers had need of more slaves. Never was the supply sufficient to stay the voracious appetite for their labor. Demand perpetuated demand: slavery perpetuated slavery. It was well known that this was so. One advocate of slavery even went so far as to claim the existence of a calculation linking cotton production to the population of slaves, equating the production of one bale of cotton to one slave. Hence it was said that when "the slave population was two millions, the average produce of cotton was two millions of bales," though this claim appears dubious.[88] Nonetheless it recognizes the very real link between cotton production and the demand for slaves.

The tariff threatened to end it all. The South, it was said, had "been drugged, by the slow poison of the miserable empiricism of the prohibitory system, the fatal effects of which ... could not so long have [been] resisted, but for the stupendously valuable staples with which God has blessed ... [it], and the agricultural skill and enterprise of ...

[its] people."[89] Throughout its period of dominance the cotton market had been beset by all sorts of crises, including the immersion of its predominant customer, Britain, in war. This, however, did not affect business. The tariff on the other hand did. From the combination of these, one of slavery's advocates concurs with the sentiments of the *London Economist* that "legislative restrictions on traffic, permanently affecting the habits of the people submissive to them, and of all their customers, have a much more pernicious effect on production and trade than national outpourings in war of indignation and anger— which, if terrible in their effects, are of short duration."[90] Considering the circumstance Southern slaveholders now found themselves in, it is small wonder they labeled the measure the "Tariff of Abominations."

The first of Parker's points illustrates how slavery was never something distinct from labor. Slavery was never something unto itself; it was always part of labor. Certain tasks were amenable to it; others clearly were not. As further testament to slavery's relationship with particular activities, developments in those industries were able sometimes to wipe it out and at other times to create new opportunities for its use, or for the extension of its use. The second of Parker's points illustrates the importance of supply. The soil where it was practiced needed to be abundantly fertile if it hoped to withstand relentless extraction. If the soil proved to be anything less than abundantly fertile then slavery consumed it to the last, before moving on. Slavery moved on in one of two ways: it either sought out new fields for its activities by migrating to them, or it remained where it was and found alternative activities that presented it with fields of a different sort. Knowing how slavery is dependent on fertile soil one can measure the fertility of the soil for slavery by the length of time it can remain at a particular place. All of it served to ensure there was an abundant supply. Parker's third point pertains to the issue of demand. For slavery to exist, though limited in its application, it needed a monopoly on some insatiable demand. Parker's points reveal something else too. They reveal how the Civil

War was, to a degree, about the issue of supply, while the fight over the "Tariff of Abominations" was, to a degree, about the issue of demand. These elements, supply and demand, form the constituent parts of a market, one whose tendrils extended from America to Britain, and beyond.

Chapter 4:

The Profitability of Slavery

That there was a market is sure. That it was rational is not. Wouldn't it have been more in the interests of the South to have used free labor rather than slave labor? Wouldn't it have been both more profitable and more productive, considering the advantages exhibited by free labor? If the use of slavery was not rational, why then was it used? It raises the possibility slavery was used by the slaveholders in defiance of rational behavior because of a commitment, perhaps a sociological one, to means over ends. On the other hand, it may have been the case slavery was indeed rationally used in the South. At the outset one would think slavery should be more profitable than free labor. The business case appears simple. Rather than paying his laborers a wage the slaveholder keeps all the profits generated by them. Frugality in the slave's subsistence is also rewarded: by providing only the bare necessities of life the cost of maintaining a slave should also be lower than the equivalent of maintaining a free laborer. If indeed slavery was rationally used in the South, it raises questions about the viability of approaches that might have been used to end it.

Despite the apparent simplicity of the case for the economics of slavery the answer may not be so simple as it at first appears.[1] Slavery in America was diverse. It was practiced as an economic system across the South, and it was practiced by individuals as part of both their business and domestic activities. It could consequently be divided into both macroeconomic and microeconomic elements. Even when its macroeconomic elements were excluded its diversity was not. Slavery was practiced on plantations that were close to routes to market, and on plantations that were distant from them. It was practiced on plantations that cultivated cotton, sugar, rice and tobacco, on plantations that were small in size, of moderate size and on some of immense size. Some slaves were coopers, some carpenters, some blacksmiths, some worked in mines, some in logging operations, others toiled at the laying of railroad tracks, others still were servants in taverns and places of rest, and so on. Slavery was employed in private houses, where slaves worked as cooks, housekeepers, nurses and servants. Some of these activities were associated with the making of profit; others were not. Thus, micro-economically slavery was sometimes motivated by the making of profit and at other times by the reducing of costs. Some slaves benefited their masters through the commodities they cultivated. Others benefitted them through the domestic labor they performed. Others again benefitted them by being the commodity cultivated for the purpose of being sold.

On whose account is the question of slavery's profitability asked? Is it on account of the slave in the field or the one at the house? It seems reasonable that the field hands, who accounted for 90% of the slaves in the South, and whose labor was employed to raise crops for profit, should be its focus. Certainly, it cannot be asked on account of the slaves whom it benefitted not at all. With whom should one make the comparison? Manual labor was beneath a free man of the South: it was slave's work. On what basis then could the comparison be made, when the work was done by the slaves and eschewed by the Southerners? One could look to the North, but there one finds the crops were different and the processes involved in cultivating them consequently different too. There were some exceptions, but could one base the conclusions on the exceptions? A multitude of other factors might be brought into the equation. The question that at first seemed so straightforward now appears complex when all these things are considered.

At the level of macroeconomics slavery produced mixed results. There is much more to the successful operation of an economy than the enrichment of a few, no matter the extent of their enrichment. This, though, was either not understood or not heeded in the South. The "interests of all owners of all soil in the Slave States," even if not engaged in the production of crops using slaves, and also all of the capital of the South, even if not engaged in slavery, were nonetheless "forced to be co-partners in an association in which … [it did] not share the profits."[2] Some have contended slavery was not profitable as a large-scale economic system, that its macroeconomics made it untenable, and that in the long-term it would have brought about its own demise. The truth, Olmsted advises, "has been overlooked that the accumulation of wealth and the power of a nation are contingent not merely upon the primary value of the surplus of productions of which it has to dispose, but very largely upon the way in which income from its surplus is distributed and reinvested."[3] Cairnes backs him up saying, "those who are acquainted with the elementary principles which govern the distribution of wealth, know that the profits of capitalists may be increased by the same process by which the gross revenue of a country is diminished, and that therefore the community as a whole may be impoverished through the very same means by which a portion of its number is enriched."[4]

Cairnes and Olmsted were content to conclude that this was in fact what was happening with the system of slavery at the South. Together they indicted the system. It enriched the few at the expense of everybody else. It was like a parasite. It thrived on the destruction of everything around it, nourishing itself, but contributed nothing to the system sustaining it. Olmsted asks:

> ... where will the returning traveller see the accumulated cotton profits of 20 years in Mississippi? Ask the cotton-planter for them, and he will point in reply, not to dwellings, libraries, churches, school-houses, meals, railroads, or anything of the kind; he will point to his negroes – to almost nothing else. Negroes such as stood for five hundred dollars once, now represent a thousand dollars.[5]

Cairnes says, "the economic advantages possessed by slavery, which were the inducement to its original establishment and which cause it still to be upheld, are perfectly compatible with its being an obstacle to the industrial development of the country, and at variance with the best interests, material as well as moral, of its inhabitants."[6] He adds "the interests of slave-masters ... are no more identical with the interests of the general population in slave counties in the matter of wealth, than in that of morals or politics."[7] Slavery didn't just separate South from North. In the South it devoured any prospect of there being a communal life, a society, or a country, all for the benefit of a few slaveholders. Not all agree with this assessment, however.[8]

More importantly perhaps, at the level of microeconomics the question is equally complex. One approach to the question might be to delve into the *minutiae* of what went on at different plantations to gather the habits of the planters and the data available about the operation of their businesses. Certainly, one can see certain patterns in the daily lives of some slaves. For example much of the routine of life on the plantation for those who worked in the fields seems to consist of: being awoken by the sound of a horn, often before sunlight; preparing and consuming breakfast, preparing some food and water to take to the field to be consumed during a short break at mid-day; the procession from the huts to the fields; the repetitive nature of the work and the long hours spent doing it; in the case of cotton, the counting of the yield for the day during the picking season, and the prospect of punishment if it was not to satisfaction; the procession back to the huts, sometimes in darkness; and the preparation and consumption of the evening meal.[9] Long days were just one feature of slavery of the time.

Slavery brought with it more than the assurance of long days: it brought the assurance of a multitude of them. For everything there is a season. The harvesting of any crop can occupy only a portion of the year, but in the South there was never reprieve. In the cultivation of sugar the planting of the crop commenced in January, immediately after the conclusion of the previous one which ended with the sugar manufacturing process. The land was first ploughed to loosen the soil. When this was done it was ploughed again to create drills into which the sugar cane could be planted.[10] Having prepared the land, the work now turned to the stacks of cuttings kept from the previous year. When these carefully prepared stacks were opened the cane, despite being stored for some months, came out green, sweet and moist. Some work was needed to prepare it further and a portion of the top part of the stalk was cut off to be used in planting. Once this was done the cuttings were gathered and loaded into carts to bring them to the fields. There was much yet to be done. Olmsted observed groups of slaves engaged in this repetitive and unskilled task. One slave brought with him as many cane cuttings as he could carry to the two colleagues of his group in the field. There he deposited the cane before returning to get more. A second slave took the cane and planted it before moving on. A third slave covered with soil what the one preceding him had planted.[11] All of the planting was concluded by March and the process began of repeatedly tilling the soil proximate to the young cane by ploughing. By early July the cane was five or six feet high and, through repeated tilling, it now sat atop beds of soil, seven feet wide. Between these beds there were deep furrows to drain excess water. These needed to be cleaned out at this point to ensure their efficiency in the event of downpours. When the work was done the crop could be left to tend to itself for the next three months, but the toil of its slaves did not cease. Preparations were then made for the season in which the hardest work of all occurred, the grinding season. During this time timber was cut, gathered, carted and stored, for use later in the boiling of the cane juice. There was much work to be done at this time too to repair and to improve the sugar-house where the process would be carried out.[12] During this time too portions of the best part of the crop were selected to provide cuttings for the following season. These selected portions were cut at the root, and stacked in such a way as to protect them from frost.[13] By October the grinding season, which saw out the remainder of the year, had arrived. Olmsted identified this season as the time that required "the utmost possible activity and the utmost labour."[14] It was during this time that every person at the plantation, sometimes even the planter and those he employed to oversee the work of his slaves, worked for as many as 18 hours each day to secure the profits of the crop. When it was done, the process started all over again.

Northup offers a similar account, albeit a shorter one, of his work at Bayou Boeuf when he records how from the sounding of the horn an hour before daylight "the fears and labors of another day begin; and until its close there is no such thing as rest."[15] In his account of the year he says, "[p]loughing, planting, picking cotton, gathering the corn, and pulling and burning stalks, occupies the whole of the four seasons."[16] The other tasks he performed, such as gathering wood, pressing cotton and tending to the hogs, he dismisses as being "but incidental labors."[17]

That the planters were astute is certain. That they were fools to pursue slavery when other forms of labor would have been in their interest is unconvincing. Nowhere is their astuteness more evident than in their allocation of work. Northup saw how it was done and he reveals how when "a new hand, one unaccustomed to the business [of picking cotton], is sent for the first time into the field, he is whipped up smartly, and made for that day to pick as fast as he can possibly. At night it is weighed, so that his capability in cotton picking is known. He must bring in the same weight each night following. If it falls short, it is considered evidence that he has been laggard, and a greater or less number of lashes is the penalty."[18] Each laborer thus set his or her own quota, for the planters had learned how some laborers were more adept at tasks than others. Northup's colleague Patsey was so proficient at picking cotton she could readily pick 500 pounds of cotton a day. In comparison, Northup, working as best he could, only ever picked about 200 pounds daily. Northup would never find himself being punished for not producing as much as Patsey. If, however, he found on a given day he had produced considerably more than he had on any day previous, then he might well be punished for holding back and his quota would be increased to reflect his true capabilities. It went without saying how, if he failed to meet his own quota he would certainly be punished. So astute were the slaveholders, so thrifty in the management of their affairs, and in the management of those of their slaves, that they understood these things. They understood how differences between their slaves made it difficult to compare the productivity of one with that of another. Despite this challenge, they overcame it. By allocating quotas they were able to exact every iota of advantage. Olmsted saw this kind of quota system in operation during his journey through the South, and he provides a description of its thoroughness:

> As on most large plantations, whether of rice or cotton, in Eastern Georgia and South Carolina, nearly all ordinary and regular work is performed by tasks: that is to say, each hand has his labour for the day marked out before him, and can take his own time to do it in. For instance, in making drains in light, clean meadow land, each man or woman of the full hands is required to dig one thousand cubic feet; in swamp-land that is being prepared for rice culture, where there are not many

storms, the task for a ditcher is five hundred feet: while in a very strong cypress swamp, only two hundred feet is required; in hoeing rice, a certain number of rows, equal to one-half or two-thirds of an acre, according to the condition of the land; in sowing rice (strewing in drills), two acres; in reaping rice (if it stands well), three-quarters of an acre; or, sometimes a gang will be required to reap, tie in sheaves, and carry to the stack-yard the produce of a certain area, commonly equal to one fourth the number of acres that there are hands working together. Hoeing cotton, corn, or potatoes; one half to one acre. Threshing; five to six hundred sheaves. In ploughing rice-land (light, clean, mellow soil) with a yoke of oxen, one acre a day, including the ground lost in and near the drains – the oxen being changed at noon. A cooper, also, for instance, is required to make barrels at the rate of eighteen a week. Drawing staves, 500 a day. Hoop poles, 120. Squaring timber, 100 ft. Laying worm-fence, 50 panels per hand.[19]

Olmsted also noted how some of these tasks were not excessively hard to conclude and how sometimes the more adept slaves were able to attain their quota by about 2pm. That being the case, Olmsted concedes to having heard at least one man boast how he was able to extract twice what was customary from his slaves. Olmsted says: "Thus we get a glimpse again of the black side. If he is allowed power to do this, what may not a man do?"[20] He observed of Virginia "it is the custom of tobacco manufacturers to hire slaves and free negroes at a certain rate of wages per year. A task of 45 lbs. per day is given them to work up, and all that they choose to do more than this they are paid for."[21]

So is it in knowing what each day returned, that one finds the advantage of slave labor over free labor? Or is it in the combination of the assuredness of daily returns, the multitude of these days, and the long hours? When viewed in this way slavery appears to be so coldly calculating, and perhaps this was the case. Not one cent was spent without knowing and, even more, being assured of what it would return. It was in this direction Ruffin looked when he came down on the side of slavery over free labor. That slave labor was slower and more inefficient than labor undertaken freely, he was willing to concede.[22] However he maintained how even when there was much work to be done, when wages were high, and when free laborers could be contracted to do the work at high rates, those laborers worked only part of the time available to them. When the rate of work of free and slave were compared, it was the free laborer who won out, but this was only part of the equation. Ruffin estimated the free laborer only worked about a third of the time available to him because this is all the free laborer required to cover his subsistence. The slave laborer worked all the days available. Over a three-day period when the free laborer produced just one day's output, the slave, who despite being slower was more continuous, produced twice that output, and at the very most at the same expense to the employer irrespective of the choice pursued.[23] Problematically for Ruffin, even if this were the case, did it say more about the social effects of slavery on the South's free laborers, than it did about the efficiency of slave labor, given how so little was produced in the South by free labor? A Mr. Helper put it thus:

> In one way or another we are more or less subservient to the North every day of our lives. In infancy we are swaddled in Northern muslin; in childhood we are humored with Northern gewgaws; in youth we are instructed out of Northern books; ... in the decline of life we remedy our eye-sight with Northern spectacles, and support our infirmities with Northern canes; in old age we are drugged with Northern physic; and, finally, when we die, our inanimate bodies, shrouded in

> Northern cambric, are stretched upon the bier, borne
> to the grave in a Northern carriage, entombed with a
> Northern spade, and memorized with a Northern slab!
> [24]

Cairnes says of the slaveholders and of their Southern compatriots how, without "cultivating one of the arts or refinements of civilization, they can possess themselves of all its material comforts. Without employing an artizan, a manufacturer, a skilled labourer of any sort, they can secure the products of the highest manufacturing and mechanical skill."[25] There was a whole class of people in the South for whom there was no work, and no prospect of it. The slave Singleton noted how "[m]ost of the work of the South in those days was done by slaves."[26] Cairnes concludes "the free labour of the South possesses none of that superiority to slave labour, which is characteristic of free labour when reared in free communities."[27] This may well have been the case, but then again, should the two ever have been compared?

Slavery's productivity was only part of the tale, as it permitted the slaveholders utility in another direction too. It offered the slaveholders control over the expense of the lives lived by their slaves. There is much commonality among the many accounts of food given the slaves residing on plantations. Most slaves appear to have received, at a minimum, a peck of corn per week. This measure was based on volume, not on weight, and equated to a quarter of a bushel. It was not much. Indeed, a great many of the slaves were in all probability half-starved. Much of the preparation of the food occurred at night when the corn was milled. Northup recounts how "at a late hour, they reach the quarters, sleepy and overcome with the long day's toil. Then a fire must be kindled in the cabin, the corn ground in the small hand-mill, and supper, and dinner for the next day in the field, prepared."[28] Jacobs records how when she "arrived on the plantation we heard the sound of the hand-mill. The slaves were grinding their corn."[29] Several slaves at that plantation received meat. She records:

> On that night the slaves received their weekly allowance of food. Three pounds of meat, a peck of corn, and perhaps a dozen herring were allowed to each man. Women received a pound and a half of meat, a peck of corn, and the same number of herring. Children over twelve years old had half the allowance of the women. The meat was cut and weighed by the foreman of the field hands, and piled on planks before the meat house. Then the second foreman went behind the building, and when the first foreman called out, "Who takes this piece of meat?" he answered by calling somebody's name. This method was resorted to as a means of preventing partiality in distributing the meat.[30]

The generosity of the planter in bestowing so bountiful a blessing upon the poor slave need not overwhelm, however, as Jacobs also records how among:

> ... those in waiting for their allowance was a very old slave, who had faithfully served the Flint family through three generations. When he hobbled up to get his bit of meat, the mistress said he was too old to have any allowance; that when ... [slaves] were too old to work, they ought to be fed on grass. Poor old man! He suffered much before he found rest in the grave.[31]

A Mr. Shepherd, a slaveholder who resided 30 miles north of Charleston, on the Monk's Corner road, owned five families of slaves and the food that he ate, meal and meat, was the same given to his slaves, but he estimated this was true of but one in 100 planters.[32] Olmsted informs how in Virginia the "general allowance of food was thought to be a peck and a half of meal, and 3 pounds of bacon a week."[33] On one plantation in South Carolina he observed the planter had "as lately given a less amount of meat than is now usual on plantations, having observed that the general health of the Negroes is not as good as formerly, when no meat at all was customarily given them."[34] Further south, in Louisiana, Olmsted encountered a slave who told him how it was habit among the French planters not to give out meat to their slaves, even though the law required it. The tale recounted by the slave reveals how all that was law was not practice: "Oh, but some on 'em don't mind Law … Law never here; don't know anything about him. *Very often*, dey only gives 'em dry corn – I knows dat."[35] The same slave was able to point to the plantation where he resided as a place where the slaves were better off. They were better fed and better clothed than most.

Good fortune, or lack of it, played a part too in the nourishment of slaves. Some in the grain-growing parts of the South may have fared better than those who labored in non-graining parts.[36] In Northup's case the nearness of a swamp provided an opportunity to find some additional food and he describes hunting for opossums. However, he recalls just how difficult this was to avail of, as "after a long and hard day's work, the weary slave feels little like going to the swamp for his supper, and half the time prefers throwing himself on the cabin floor without it."[37]

There was nothing sumptuous about the cabins where the slaves lived. They were basic, at best, and the slaves were packed into them. Often there was no window, no wooden floor, no stove, and no chimney. During the warm season the smoke from the fire needed to be kept up at night to keep the gnats and mosquitoes at bay. During the cold season the cabins offered little warmth. When it rained, or when there was a storm, they offered little shelter. It was upon the floor, and not in a bed, that most slept. Few, if any, had a blanket to cover them. The cost of clothing a slave was put at $16 *per annum*.[38] Some put it at just half that figure.[39] This is not to say that the experience of the slave on the matter of clothing was the same everywhere. Olmsted notes at one South Carolina plantation the clothes worn by the slaves were "uncouth and cumbrous, dirty and ragged."[40] Some slaves wore only the coarsest garments, and wholly inadequate footwear. Indeed, a great many slaves may have been practically naked. Others may have fared better, being able through some degree of industry to make a little money, which they could then use to purchase some much-needed clothing. With food strictly controlled, with shelter and even clothing insufficient to meet their most basic needs, slaves had good cause to be ill, but illness offered no reprieve from slavery.

Some scrutiny has been given to the cost of medical care provided to slaves to compare it to that provided to free laborers.[41] Unsurprisingly, not all slaves received medical care. Reverend Moulton recalls that another "dark side of slavery is the neglect of the aged and the sick."[42] Some, when they fell ill, were simply left to die. Others would be tended to, not by a physician, but by the slaveholder or by one of the slaves. So thrifty were some of the slaveholders the physician was paid only if the slave recovered.[43]

Slavery was exempt from some costs entirely. Certainly, there were no educational costs. Educating slaves was socially taboo and prohibited. Yet slavery brought costs particular to its practice too. One such cost was that of oversight. One person estimated the cost of overseers at about $22.50 per slave and he considered it likely that an overseer could tend to just 20 slaves.[44] Others give accounts of overseers tending to more than double this number, thus lowering the cost of their employment.[45] Even when costs were seemingly inevitable, the ever-thrifty planters sometimes managed to weasel out of them. The compensation of the overseer may have been not in the form of an assured payment but as a portion of the crop, an arrangement that put the interests of the slaves and those of their overseer immediately at odds.[46]

In *An Address on the Progress of Manufactures and Internal Improvement, in the United States,* Jones looks at the prices associated with hiring labor from adult male and female slaves, as well as slaves who were children. He looks too at the cost of feeding and clothing them for the period of their hire. He approximates the taxes. Based on his calculation, he asserts the prices paid to free laborers will "average about three times" that of slaves, while at the same time the slaves "in steadiness, will far surpass the great mass of the whites."[47]

Could so calculating and thrifty a group of people as the slaveholders be found wanting on the issue of their profits? It seems most unlikely. On this basis alone one might decide slavery was indeed more profitable. Why? It was profitable because the slaveholders practiced it, and had it proved not to be the most profitable option they would surely have ceased practicing it. The *Natchez Ariel* asked this question in relation to hemp factories of Kentucky in 1827: "Why are slaves employed?"[48] The answer the *Natchez Ariel* gives is: "Simply because experience has proved that they are more docile, more constant, and cheaper than freemen."[49] That combination of compliance, constancy and cheapness is key. Weston asserts:

> It is vain to deny that slave labor, in its immediate application, where it is used, costs less than free labor. If it was not so, it certainly would not be used. It is not sufficient to say that the slave performs less labor that the freeman, that he performs his work badly, that he breaks his tools, that his position makes him a shirk and thief, and that no stimulus is so efficient as wages. All this being true, and this being known to be true, slave labor is nevertheless employed, and not because the employers are under any delusion as to the positive or comparative value of a day's work of a slave, but because they know that taking cost and value together, it answers their purpose better than anything else within their reach.[50]

Some claim investing in slaves alone produced a return of 10% on market rates.[51] It is claimed too that an approximation of the trends in profitability of growing cotton can be obtained by comparing the overall trend of its prices with deviations from the trend. What they show is that the 1850s were a time when the profits of the cotton planters experienced incredible growth, and it was a time too when that growth outshone the fabled wealth of the 1830s.[52] Consequently any claim the slaveholders were an unsophisticated pre-capitalist class that made the pursuit of profit secondary to the pursuit of power and its way of life is thrown into doubt.[53]

Olmsted gives an account of one Louisiana sugar plantation owned by a person identified only as Mr. R., who experienced the bountiful profits of slavery for himself. The plantation contained 900 acres of tillage land, all enclosed in a single field bounded by a cypress post and rail fence.[54] Drainage was provided by two five-foot-deep drains running parallel to one another, set 20 feet apart, through the center of the field. Mr. R. had purchased the plantation just three years prior to Olmsted's visit. Most planters, Olmsted was informed, were required to take on a heavy burden of debt, typically comprising 75% of the total capital requirement, to make the purchase. "Buying a plantation," Mr. R. advised Olmsted:

> ... whether a sugar or cotton plantation, in this country, is essentially a gambling operation. The capital invested in a sugar plantation of the size of mine ought not to be less than $150,000. The purchaser pays down what he can, and usually gives security for the payment of the balance in six annual instalments, with interest (10 *per cent. per annum*) from the date of purchase.[55]

If fate should deliver a bad crop the planter will have to refinance portions of his debt at higher rates of interest, sometimes at terms not less than 25% *per annum*.[56] Mr. R. proclaimed how he had been especially fortunate returning three good crops in succession. In the previous 12 months he had produced sugar and molasses. The molasses alone covered all his expenses for the year and the sugar had yielded him a profit of 25% on his whole investment.[57] If the current year proved as good as the last then Mr. R. will own the plantation, free from all debt, in just four years.[58] There is no suggestion Mr. R. was anything but a shrewd operator.

Olmsted records how the 1,474 sugar plantations in Louisiana in 1849 produced a total of 236,547 casks of sugar. Among them there was little homogeneity, with a few producers benefitting to the greatest extent. Half of the casks were estimated to have been produced on fewer than 200 plantations. The profits that flowed to these few plantations, Olmsted thought, were staggering.[59]

That there were immense disadvantages to using slave labor was certainly the case. Cairnes gives three great disadvantages: it is wanting in versatility; it is unskillful; and it is given reluctantly. Of the first and second, that the labor of slaves lacks versatility and that it is unskilled, one might ask whether these are necessarily disadvantages. They were not disadvantages *per se* if the task did not require, or did not permit, the work to be done skillfully and if its nature was so straightforward and so repetitive as not to be curtailed by the limitations of slavery. In this way the first and second disadvantages could have described the quality of the labor furnished by the slave, or it might instead have described the nature of the labor, irrespective of who did it. Some slaves did undertake skilled work and some of these excelled at it, despite the severe restrictions imposed on them. Similarly, there is no reason to suppose slaves, as human beings, with due regard for the restrictions imposed upon their education, would be any less intelligent than their free counterparts. At one plantation where some of its slaves worked as blacksmiths, carpenters and mechanics the planter proudly extolled the "excellence of their workmanship, and said that they exercised as much ingenuity and skill as the ordinary mechanics that he was used to."[60]

It seems then that the first two disadvantages articulated by Cairnes should be interpreted as referring to the nature of the labor. In stating the third disadvantage, that the work is given reluctantly, it was a criterion that could only have been made with reference to the person of the slave. The slave, as Ruffin explains, receives as his reward "the same support, in food, clothing, and other allowances, whether he works much or little" and the slave's task is to balance his reward with the risk of sparing "himself as much as possible, and to do as little work as he can, without drawing upon himself punishment."[61] This certainly was true, but then again look to the prudence of the planters in measuring the productivity of their laborers through a system of quotas. It was specifically designed and employed to counter just this disadvantage.

Others claimed the reluctant nature of slavery manifested in other ways too. Specifically, they pointed to the poor tools given to slaves as proof of how slaves would break their tools regularly. They looked to the poor quality of the animals in the South as evidence of poor animal husbandry by the slaves who tended to these animals and to the poor fertility of the soil as proof of the inability of slaves to apply manure to it with the care it required. However, it is questionable whether some of these are proof of slave labor's inadequacies, or whether instead they are in fact part of slavery's design. It was observed for instance how as "late as 1850 the average value of occupied land in the South Atlantic states was only $5.34 per acre, and in the Southwestern states, $6.26 per acre. Good farming land was always so cheap and plentiful that its owners scarcely regarded it as a permanent investment, and they felt they could afford to be wasteful of it."[62] Olmsted encountered the same attitude: "when I ask, if a little painstaking here and there would not save much fertility, that he should reply, that inasmuch as land enough, equally good, can be bought for six dollars an acre, the whole fertile matter can be better lost than a week's labour."[63] Ruffin too notes how land may be valued in two ways, with one value based on the productivity and profitability of the land, and the other based on its value as an item of trade or speculation.[64] It is the first of these, and not the second, he claims is the most beneficial, and least injurious, to the farmer. Under the slave regime it suited slaveholders not to find land expensive, just as under the regime of the North it suited employers not to find labor expensive.[65] The incentive then may not have been towards caution in relation to every item under slavery's control, but towards an extravagance of a very different kind, towards a wastefulness of labor and a wastefulness of soil.[66] The focus may not have been upon doing tasks well, but upon bringing them to the nearest point of completion where might be judged to be done. Slavery rewarded not quality, but quantity.

Nowhere were the differences between slavery and free labor more evident than in the fact it was possible under slavery's economic system for the laborer to be sold as a commodity. Nowhere was labor so extravagantly spent, and at the same time nowhere was it so extravagantly priced, as under slavery. Here too one sees the difference between their respective economics: under free labor the outlay usually occurs gradually as the laborer labors, whereas under slavery the outlay for labor occurs all at once, in advance of any labor. To seek to understand one approach in the context of the other may be not to understand it at all. To make the comparison, or even to pose the question, in terms of the individual labor of the slave *versus* that of the free laborer may then be flawed. The two appear to be so incompatible as to be different things, and their labor to be but one element of a broader system. To make a real comparison the question might be posed instead whether, for similar capital employed, slavery returned more profit than free labor?

Ruffin gives an answer in just these terms. He notes how when slavery is used, in those activities best suited to it, in agriculture it requires large space and for the best results the operation should be extensive requiring many laborers. He concedes how using slavery leads to wasteful practices. In contrast agriculture using free laborers will use smaller areas and fewer workers. The proportion of capital to labor will be different in each. One would have expected free labor systems to have a lot of capital and only some labor, whereas slave labor systems have little capital and much labor. To make a meaningful comparison the large slave plantation needs to be compared with the operation of a small free laboring farm. Critically Ruffin believes that, "in proportion to their respective amounts of capital and labor, the small northern farmer would make and save double as much profit and accumulation as would a large southern slaveholder," but critically, he nuances his conclusion.[67] He adds how:

> … of all the before experienced northern farmers who have bought land and settled in Virginia, and who, either with or without slaves, attempted to exercise their boasted northern skill in farming on a large scale, I have never heard of one who did not fail, or, at best, fall much below the results of the ordinary management of his more careless and wasteful neighbors.[68]

According to Ruffin then, free labor is more profitable than slave labor, but he does not presume the two can be brought into competition in the first place, for Ruffin contends that in the South where the crops were of a particular type, free labor could not be employed, as it was not suited to those crops. According to Ruffin it is only when economic conditions are so turbulent, when the fabric of society is torn asunder, when all are reduced to the condition of slavery of an altogether different kind, one of starvation and suffering, the economic case for using slave labor over free labor disappears.[69] Ruffin asserts:

> [Under] such conditions, slaves (if they could not be sold and removed to some other country, where needed) would be readily emancipated by masters to whom they had become burdensome. Soon, under

> the operating influence of self-interest alone ... slavery
> would come to an end.[70]

The question of slavery's profitability cannot then be understood without first understanding the very meaning of free and slave labor. There are several possible interpretations of these terms. Free labor could be interpreted as labor freely given, or it could refer to labor incompatible with slavery. Equally slave labor could be interpreted as labor exacted through coercion, or alternatively as labor compatible with slavery. In both instances, the first of these two interpretations focuses on the laborer and the second on the nature of the labor. Consider again the example of the pins given by Adam Smith in *An Inquiry into the Nature and Causes of the Wealth of Nations*. He stresses how a tradesperson unacquainted with the trade of pin-making, and without any of its machinery, could scarcely manage to make one pin over the course of a day, let alone as many as 20 pins in a day. When the labor was modernized, machinery introduced and the operation broken into tasks and spread among 10 laborers 48,000 pins were made each day, or 4,800 pins per tradesperson per day. The labor became less representative of the process of making any given pin. However, suppose pin-making defied modernization, and that consequently all the labor of making just one pin was fulfilled by one person, then the playing field is leveled. Whether the laborers are free or enslaved matters little, at least from the point of view of their productivity, which will be largely the same. The slave, however, works longer hours and more days and costs less to maintain, so even if disadvantaged by a slower rate of work, the slave is advantaged by the constancy of it. Over several days, the slave makes many more pins and costs less. Making large numbers of pins under these circumstances requires many more laborers than if the operation had not been defiant of modernization. The questions then of profitability, and of the meaning of free labor *versus* slave labor, are not independent of the labor.

Free labor is labor incompatible with slavery. It is labor that possesses none of the characteristics making it amenable to slavery. Slave labor is labor compatible with slavery. Free labor and slave labor are distinct economic systems. It almost goes without saying how a laborer who works in either under conditions of coercion is a slave, or a slave laborer. A laborer who works of their own choosing in either system can be said to be one whose labor is freely given, or a free laborer. These distinctions are used hereafter. A slave laborer might be employed in activities amenable to free labor, but very few indeed would be suited to it and, owing to the nature of their engagement, it would not be productive. For these reasons slave laborers are not a competitive source of labor for free labor activities. A free laborer, one working freely, might choose to engage in work amenable to slavery, though owing to the nature of the work, when the choice is put to the market most choose not or to do so only occasionally. For this purpose, the population available to carry out the work amenable to slave labor might be said to be sparse, in accordance with Parker's first point. This is likely the reason too why Ruffin and his contemporaries saw no prospect of the South's laborers being a competitive source of labor for the cultivation of the South's crops. Whether people want to perform these activities or not, economically the cultivation of these crops may have been highly remunerative, especially when cultivated by a great number. Slavery overcomes the hurdle of consent by depriving the slave, through violence, of his or her own will. Overall this is what Ruffin maintains is the case when he states the "slave system ... gives much more command and control of labor in a new country of sparse population, and makes it continuous in effort, and therefore, even if slower and less effective for short times of actual employment, it is far more efficient and profitable on the whole than would be" labor given freely.[71] It is the nature of the crop, or the activity, that determines the nature of the labor required for its cultivation, and that determines too the system of economics that rewards its cultivation.

The question of whether slave labor is more profitable than free labor is a flawed one. The two cannot be brought into competition: they are two different things. The question could be changed to whether the work of free laborers is more profitable than that of slave laborers. The answer is itself dependent on the context of the labor. Slaves cannot compete with the work of free laborers working in a free labor system, because of the advantages of the latter over the former. However, if the nature of the labor required to produce the work is crude, and if it can still find a market, despite being produced by laborers whose work lacks versatility and whose work is given reluctantly, then it is a suitable candidate for slavery. In this arena, one of labor amenable to slavery, free laborers cannot compete with slave labor, because the nature of the crop deprives them of advantages they would normally possess in a free labor system. Additionally of the things produced by slaves, a great many of them are harvested from some natural resource, rather than being something created anew. The produce of slavery is a commodity. Price is critical. If a prospective buyer finds the item is priced too high, a different seller can often be found selling it cheaper.

The rewards of slavery come when much work is done, or when the rewards come sporadically, over a long period of time, or in any combination of the two. Moreover, where free labor looks northwards to its advantages, to its capacity for creativity, for its profit, slavery looks southwards to those of its own. Through slavery's capacity for thrift, whether in the maintenance of the slave or in providing the paraphernalia of his or her work, its profit is yielded. There is then an economic benefit, as well as a psychological one, to depriving slaves of even the most basic necessities of life. On the whole then, where the activity is profit-seeking and where it is amenable to using slave labor, a fact that can be ascertained by finding where it had been used before, then it will be more profitable to use slave labor. For this reason, likely, the slaveholders did not invest in, or place any economical or moral value on, the supposed advantages of free labor systems because under slavery those advantages could never accrue to them, and they may actually have been disadvantageous. There is evidence to suggest this was a lesson they learned only with experience.

In *An Address on the Progress of Manufactures and Internal Improvement, in the United States*, Jones gives the example of the relationship between the raw material the cotton mills used and the fabric they produced. The production of each yard of cloth required a quarter pound of raw cotton. In 1815 a yard of cloth could be sold for 25 cents. The cost of raw material for that yard was 5 cents, leaving 20 cents to cover the profit and the labor costs, "and yet very few … made money, because of want of machinery, or of management and skill."[72] Three years later a yard of cloth was selling for 21 cents. The cost of the raw materials was now 8 cents, leaving 13 cents to the manufacturer to cover the profit and the labor costs, and with this increase of raw material costs most manufacturers were ruined. However, in 1827 a yard of cloth could be sold for only 9.5 cents. The cost of raw material for that yard was now just 2.5 cents. Now there were only 7 cents left over to cover profit and labor costs, and yet "the business of making such goods, though made cheaper than they are made in England, is a good one!"[73]

At first glance the example appears not to make sense. In the first instance the profit made on the sale of a single yard of cloth is the most. In the second the selling price has reduced, but so too has profit. Yet in the previous two instances neither saw the manufacturers do well. In the third example the price charged is lower than ever, the cost of raw material is similarly low, the profit per yard sold has never been as low and yet business is booming. Jones does not specifically say why this is the case. He does expect his audience will know, and many of them certainly would have understood why at lower profit per yard the business of producing fabric was better than it had been before. The reason is cotton, as a commodity, exhibited a tendency to sell disproportionately more as the price fell. As the volumes of sales increased, and did so dramatically, despite the low profit made on any one sale, those volumes pushed overall profitability skywards, and with it the prospect of reinvestment and further reductions in production costs. Between 1822 and 1827 the production of cotton cloth by Northern manufacturers tripled, but during the same period its selling price declined 35%.[74] Economists refer to this phenomenon as *elasticity of demand*. In this instance it applied to both the sale of raw cotton and the sale of manufactured cotton goods. The marginal increase in the volumes of sales, over the reduced profit made on any one sale, compensated for the loss in the profitability of unit sales. In this way, counterintuitively, lowering price did not compromise profits. On the contrary, a lower price was an absolute necessity to their overall maximization. So too was an abundance of cotton to sell.

If indeed slave laborers may be used more profitably than free laborers, and there is much to suggest that they can be when conditions are right, there are far-reaching and ominous consequences. First, any suggestion that slavery was used in the South for purely sociological reasons, perhaps even for purely irrational reasons, such as to gain for example social status by conspicuously consuming slave labor, is immediately repudiated. One can find repudiation of this suggestion in the writings of some of slavery's advocates. In the concluding chapter of *Cotton is King, and Pro-slavery Arguments* one such advocate, David Christy, denounces sociological reasons as the source of slavery. In fact, he expressly repudiates all fealty to slavery. It is not slavery he serves. It is only a means to an end. He declares: "King Cotton cares not whether he employs slaves or freemen. It is the cotton, not the slaves, upon which his throne is based."[75] On the basis of the evidence it does indeed seem slavery was the more profitable option when it was properly applied. On this same basis it was not irrational. On the contrary, it was coldly rational in pursuing its self-interest through market rationale.

Second, the disestablishment of the institution of slavery cannot bring about an end to slavery. Here too Christy has something to say on the matter when he declares how King Cotton "has no evidence that … men can grow his cotton, except in the capacity of slaves."[76] Though wars may come and go, no matter their cost in terms of loss of life and human suffering, the intrinsic economics of crops remain intact, and consequently too the politics of their cultivation. From this perspective slavery in the South was merely the legal implementation of an already long-established economic practice and, while the U.S. Civil War could bring about its end as civil and societal institution, the war could not compromise its economic underpinnings. Armed with this knowledge, one could foresee how acts of slavery would continue in the aftermath of the Civil War no matter what the war's outcome. If this were to occur, and the institution were to be wiped away, such acts could nonetheless be properly understood as a continuation of the practice rather than as a departure from it.

Third, the engagement of free laborers in competition with slave laborers will not eliminate slavery. Free labor and slavery are two distinct systems, and they advance on two different fronts. Free trade is certainly to the advantage of free laborers in free labor systems, and through the improvements it produces there is the prospect of destroying labor amenable to slavery. However, not all these improvements produce freedom. Some create opportunities for labor where there were none before. And some of these opportunities are for slave labor. Certainly, where the improvements of free labor cannot destroy slave labor, free trade may be counterproductive, and it may even promote slavery. This realization is often hidden from view. In its absence the tactics employed to restrain slavery are tantalizingly viable, but no good will ever come of them. On this point Christy says:

> King Cotton is a profound statesman, and knows what measures will best sustain his throne. He is an acute mental philosopher, acquainted with the secret springs of human action, and accurately perceives who can best promote his aims. ... It is his policy, therefore, to defeat all schemes of emancipation. To do this, he stirs up such agitations as lure his enemies into measures that will do him no injury ..., and sustains the supremacy of King Cotton in the world.[77]

Fourth, though slavery and free labor may overall be distinguished from one another, this is not to conclude they exist entirely independently of one another. It is true the fruits of slavery often flowed directly to the person who controlled it, but it is true too these fruits sometimes flowed to other beneficiaries, in the form of cheap goods, through intermediaries in the form of free labor manufacturers. The relationship between the South's cotton producers and Britain's cotton cloth manufacturers is a case in point. The South's slaves produced the commodities so desired by Britain's manufacturers. Those manufacturers imported and processed these commodities before selling them to their own customers. Manufacturer and producer were amply rewarded. In this way slavery was not just a precursor to industrial advancement; it was a potential supplier of some of industry's staples. The relationship worked in the other direction too, as Britain's manufacturers provided the South with the abundance of affordable supplies so vital to her slave operations. Thus, while the manufacturing sector may have viewed slavery as being primitive, slavery was capable of being a good customer of the sector all the same.

A great many in the South understood these points. In fact, they were resigned to the necessity of them. They saw the world as comprising two parts: one free and one slave. Within the South they created both parts. What they created, however, was not confined to the South for though the North was free, it too had a relationship with slavery. The South could clearly see the hands of those who stood in opposition to slavery were not quite as clean as the North's abolitionists might have understood. Just in case, Christy adds:

> In speaking of the economical connections of slavery, with the other material interests of the world, we have called it a tripartite alliance. It is more than this ..., the abolitionists do not stand in direct contact with slavery; they imagine ... But they, no less than their allies, aid in promoting the interests of slavery. Their sympathies are with England on the slavery question, and they very naturally incline to agree with her on other points. She advocates Free Trade, as essential to her manufactures and commerce; and they do the same, not waiting to inquire into its bearings upon American slavery. ... The free trade and protective systems, in their bearings upon slavery, are so well understood, that no man of general reading, especially an editor, or member of Congress, who professes anti-slavery sentiments, at the same time advocating free trade, will ever convince men of intelligence, pretend what he may, that he is not ... woefully perverted in his judgment ... England, we were about to say, is in alliance with the cotton planter, to whose prosperity free trade is indispensable. Abolitionism is in alliance with England. All three of these parties, then, agree in their support of the free trade policy ... slavery and free trade nationalized![78]

There are other consequences to the conclusion that slave laborers may be used more profitably than free laborers. Fifth, there must be some skepticism about the role of markets as vehicles whose purpose

119

exclusively maximizes autonomy. Markets may serve to maximize the autonomy of consumers, but at the same time they may deplete the autonomy of those whose role it is to supply. So much of what occurred to the South's slaves, the reason behind their enslavement and the course of the lives they endured, was dictated by purely market interests. In fact, such was the degree to which this was true that the two were inextricably linked. Even when a market is found to be free of slavery one cannot conclude it is unconnected to another market entirely dependent upon slavery. In this way markets have the capacity to make the true nature of transactions opaque. This is not to say that markets are not capable of spreading freedom, or that a great amount of the freedom in the world has not been attained through them, but rather that in some instances they can have the opposite effect to the severest possible degree. It very much depends on the nature of the market, and the market very much depends on the nature of the crop it cultivates. Christy acknowledges this too, and he acknowledges the role of the consumer, when he declares of King Cotton how he "receives no check from the cries of the oppressed, [the pace of his progress is not slowed by the cries of his victims,] while the citizens of the world are dragging forward his chariot, and shouting aloud his praise."[79] Lastly, economic rationale can be relied upon to model slavery's behavior.

Chapter 5:

Shaping the Slave's Fate

The initial requirement for slaves was fed by abducting black Africans from their homes and transporting them in ships *en masse* to America's slave markets. After the introduction of the prohibition of 1808 most of America's slaves originated not from abroad, but from within its own borders. The narrative of the victim abducted from home and transported in grueling conditions over harsh seas to a foreign land gradually became less representative of the tale of slaves. Slavery was now an almost entirely domestic enterprise, one that preyed not on black Africans, but on the black Americans who were their descendants. Generations of slaves were born into slavery. They often stayed where they were born for many years before being sold, and some remained where they were born for the entirety of their lives. When Chief Justice Taney delivered the opinion of the Supreme Court in the *Dred Scott Decision* he declared the slave a thing "bought and sold, and treated as an ordinary article of merchandise and traffic, whenever a profit could be made by it."[1] Taney used a word suggestive of movement, but movement was no longer part of the narrative. Two vitally important distinctions can be made. Slavery and smuggling are not the same thing. Where borders are concerned, smuggling is always an illegal act requiring the illicit passage of people or goods across them. Slavery, however, does not always require movement, hence it does not necessarily always require smuggling, and even where people were moved it was not always illegal to do so. Additionally, the word *traffic*, as used by Taney, *does not mean movement but trade*, in this case a trade in human beings, a trade that requires a market, and a market, as has been seen, requires both supply and demand.

The slave market presents a formidable image, one unlike any other market one could witness. Can slave markets be reconciled then with other markets? By the laws of the time there were those who were free and there were others who were not. Only a slave could legally be sold at a slave market. An interesting point can be made concerning the fate of Solomon Northup, a free man of the North, who was kidnapped, brought to a slave market, and sold into slavery for 12 years. What makes Northup's story exceptional was not so much that he endured this experience, but how he was able to escape it and, by recounting it, to leave a permanent record. In his book Northup does not presume he was the only free black person to experience such trials, saying: "I doubt not hundreds have been as unfortunate as myself; that hundreds of free citizens have been kidnapped and sold into slavery, and are at this moment wearing out their lives on plantations in Texas and Louisiana."[2] Once the arrangements had been made for Northup's release his master, Epps, put it to him that he was in fact a free man. Northup acknowledged this was the case. "[W]hy did you not tell me that when I bought you?" a confounded Epps enquires.[3] Northup replies, "Master Epps, you did not take the trouble to ask me; besides, I told one of my owners – the man that kidnapped me – that I was free, and was whipped almost to death for it."[4] His reply illustrates how it didn't suit those selling him to have it known, and once paid for by Epps it wasn't convenient for him to know either.

Northup recalls how only some months prior Epps had told a contracted laborer, Bass, of an offer to purchase Northup, which had been declined:

> I walked up to them, as if he had never thought before
> to take any special notice of me. "Yes," replied Epps,

taking hold of my arm and feeling it, "there isn't a bad joint in him. There ain't a boy on the bayou worth more than he is – perfectly sound, and no bad tricks. D--n him, he isn't like other n*****s; doesn't look like 'em – don't act like 'em. I was offered seventeen hundred dollars for him last week." "And didn't take it?" Bass inquired, with an air of surprise. "Take it – no; devilish clear of it. Why, he's a reg'lar genius; can make a plough beam, wagon tongue – anything, as well as you can. Marshall wanted to put up one of his n*****s agin him and raffle for them, but I told him I would see the devil have him first."[5]

Everything about Northup was to the satisfaction of Epps. He was strong, hardworking, skilled, and compliant. To Epps, Northup was worth every cent he had paid for him. Now Epps was at the loss of his property, and this is exactly how Northup describes the scene, how Epps' "whole manner and language exhibited a feeling of anger … and of fretfulness at the idea of losing so much property."[6] There was more too, when Epps confessed "if he had only had an hour's notice … he would have run … [Northup] into the swamp, or some other place out of the way, where all the sheriffs on earth couldn't have found" him.[7] It was not in the interest of the slave trader to inform Epps that Northup was a free man who, unlikely as it was, could be set free by the law if Northup's plight came to its attention. Neither was it in Epps' interests to set Northup free once he had paid for him, nor to sell him on, given the characteristics Northup possessed that Epps so valued. It was certainly not in Epps' interests to have Northup taken from him, or even to hand him over to be freed when that was the proper thing to do. After all, it would hardly have been good business.

Of course, there were opportunities to right injustices such as this. Weston is critical of those who espouse the belief mankind is "governed wholly by interests," adding how such thinking is "received only by those shallow intellects which cannot comprehend the complicated organization of the human, and which find a relief in the simplicity of a theory which represents it as moved only, as a balance is, by the preponderance of material and homogeneous weights."[8] This is certainly true. Human beings do have the capacity to act justly, even when it is not in their interest to do so, and doing justice regularly necessitates the putting aside of interests. Nonetheless Weston cautions too how, in judging slavery, one must realize "that many things in it justly repulsive cease to be so, because familiar and accustomed; that, in this as in other matters, self-interest warps and clouds the judgement; and that the temper and habits formed by slaveholding are peculiarly unfavourable to sound reasoning upon it."[9] It seems reasonable that once men have reduced others to the level of fulfilling their own interests, the nature of those interests should dominate in governing the fate of those so reduced. Is not this after all what Taney observed when he declared the slave to be nothing but a commodity to be traded as suited the interests of the trader? Beecher Stowe recognized as much saying how "suppose that something should bring down the price of cotton once and forever, and make the whole slave property a drug in the market, don't you think we should soon have another version of the Scripture doctrine? What a flood of light would pour into the church, all at once, and how immediately it would be discovered that everything in the Bible and reason went the other way!"[10] It is also why, with utter despair, one of her characters asks, "how can I bear to have this open acknowledgment that we care for no tie, no duty, no relation, however sacred, compared with money?"[11] It is also why Beecher Stowe addresses the traits associated with markets.

One of these traits is competition. The *Niles' Weekly Register* of Baltimore advises dealing "in slaves has become a large business; establishments are made in several places in Maryland and Virginia, at which they are sold like cattle; these places of deposit are strongly built, and well supplied with thumb-screws and gags, and ornamented with cow-skins and other whips oftentimes bloody."[12] It was a business Weston denounced as "the disgrace of our age and country."[13]

Engaging in the business of slavery by no means assured success. Planters could be wiped out financially by any number of variables. Poor market conditions sometimes meant not enough produce could be sold to cover costs. Fluctuations in the price paid meant that at times there was nothing to be made from sales. Bad weather conditions sometimes destroyed entire crops. Such conditions could also leave roads and rivers impassable, making it impossible to get crops to market at an opportune time. The infestation of the crop by pests could render it worthless. Disease sometimes afflicted the crop and other times those who toiled in its cultivation. Accidents befell men and beast, maiming and killing, depriving the planter of their use. These are but a few instances of bad luck that could make the venture futile in any given year. A series of failures brought the prospect of having to refinance debts at higher and higher rates of interest, with the ever-increasing likelihood of ruination. The journalist Olmsted noted success "in sugar, as well as cotton planting, is dependent on so many circumstances, that it is as much trusting to luck as betting on a throw of dice."[14] All the same, many planters did grow wealthy. Year after year they were rewarded by bumper crops. With the money they received they were able to acquire more land, sometimes from neighbors who had not done so well, to build new storage and processing facilities, and to pay off their creditors. Importantly, they were also able to buy more slaves. In all arenas of business there are both successes and failures. Some fare better than others in both regards. Luck, though not the only determinant, also had a role to play in dictating the place ultimately occupied within the market by the planters. It had a role too in determining the space occupied by the slaves and in shaping their fate.

Good fortune might occasionally grant a kind master. There was a chance, but the odds were against it, and those odds declined each time they were tested at the marketplace. Beecher Stowe writes:

> We hear often of the distress of the negro servants, on the loss of a kind master; and with good reason, for no creature on God's earth is left more utterly unprotected and desolate than the slave in these circumstances. … The number of men who know how to use wholly irresponsible power humanely and generously is small. Everybody knows this, and the slave knows it best of all; so that he feels that there are ten chances of his finding an abusive and tyrannical, to one of his finding a considerate and kind one. Therefore is it that the wail over a kind master is loud and long, as well it may be.[15]

William Henry Singleton experienced this for himself when his mistress died. True to Beecher Stowe's characterization he recalls:

> On the day of the funeral all of us slaves on the plantation, between seventy-five and a hundred, men, women and children, followed her body to the cemetery, about five miles away, where she was buried.

> It was a very sad occasion, for all the women were crying and most of the men too, as well as the children. We knew that she was the best friend we had and that now our lot would be harder. Shortly after that my master married again, but our new mistress did not have the kind heart our old mistress had had.[16]

Knowing that this to be so, one of Beecher Stowe's fictional characters, realizing how though he is comparatively good to those he holds as slaves, but that to hold them at all is to test fate and to condemn them at some future time, decides to release them all, announcing "in the case of my [falling into] debt or dying, – things that might happen, – you cannot now be taken up and sold."[17] Parker too knew how so much of what went on in slavery was governed by the proportion of men who had the capacity to act cruelly in support of their interests *versus* those who had the restraint to allow themselves to act justly. He writes: "Man is certainly not cruel by nature; even in the barbarous state. In our present civilization man is far from brutal. There are many kind and considerate slave-holders whose aim is to make their slaves as comfortable and happy as it is possible; men who feel and know that Slavery is wrong, and would gladly be rid of it; who are not consistent with the idea of Slavery."[18] Like Beecher Stowe, who perhaps drew inspiration from him, he believed such kind people were in the minority, accounting for only about 10% of all slaveholders.

At other times poor fortune in one quarter could deliver one from harsh consequences in another. Beecher Stowe's character George, the one who had masqueraded as a Spanish gentleman, was married to another of her characters, Eliza. Beecher Stowe notes how it is often the case women of mixed ancestry, mulattos or quadroons, possess an "air of refinement," a "softness of voice and manner," and "beauty of the most dazzling kind."[19] Eliza, though of mixed ancestry, was "not a fancy sketch."[20] It may have been just as well, for it allowed Eliza, Beecher Stowe writes, to reach "maturity without those temptations which make beauty so fatal an inheritance to a slave."[21]

Irrefutably, skill was another factor exerting a bearing on one's place in the market. In the 1700s South Carolina managed to cultivate rice and the prospective commercial opportunities soon became apparent. All through the 18th century South Carolina's economy was dominated by its cultivation. At first South Carolina's planters struggled with the crop. With persistence, and with the experience gleaned from failure after failure, they eventually succeeded. The planters realized they were not the only ones experienced in farming rice, as many of the inhabitants of Africa's west coast were skilled in growing rice too. With demand in South Carolina, with a supply in Africa, and with abundant money to be made, the result was a foregone conclusion. It was at Charleston, at the time called Charlestown, South Carolina's capital and center of commerce, where demand and supply might be united. Slave traders soon learned South Carolina's planters were "willing to pay higher prices for slaves from the 'Rice Coast,' the 'Windward Coast,' the 'Gambia,' and 'Sierra-Leon' and slave traders in Africa soon learned that South Carolina was an especially profitable market for slaves from those areas. Consequently when slave traders arrived in Charlestown with slaves from the rice-growing region, they were careful to advertise their origin on auction posters or in newspaper announcements, sometimes noting that the slaves were 'accustomed to the planting of rice.'"[22]

Through Northup's very real experience at Bayou Boeuf he was able to witness the influence of skills innate to the individual. Northup himself was so valued by Epps because of characteristics particular to Northup. Epps had identified Northup's intelligence, his tendency to do what he was told, his work ethic, his exceptional ability to do skilled work and his physical strength as being of value.[23] Perceptively Northup saw how the world of slavery about him was fashioned by market conditions, factors over which he and his counterparts had little control. Some slaves were more amenable to the labor of their employment than others. One of his counterparts, Patsey, was able to pick cotton with both hands and for this reason she "was known as the most remarkable cotton picker on Bayou Boeuf."[24] This skill made Patsey especially valuable, distinguishing her from all the other cotton pickers, and would have contributed to the price attained for her had she been sold.

In Arkansas about 1860, the average price of a slave was $900. Many of those sold for this price were sold as mere laborers. However, some had other skills: in carpentry or in blacksmithing. The demand for skilled slaves such as these was enormous. As a result, some sold for as much as US$2,800.[25] Through their skills some slaves were able to shape the market to their advantage. Beecher Stowe's most despotic character was Simon Legree and the slaves under his control suffered terribly. Exceptionally, one of his slaves, a woman by the name of Cassy, "had always kept over Legree the kind of influence that a strong, impassioned woman can ever keep over the most brutal man."[26] Cassy had interpersonal skills that became critical to her existence. She was able to shape her experience of slavery by recourse to these skills. However, just because Cassy's particular skills endowed her with a different experience of slavery, one comparatively easier than her counterparts, it didn't mean she was any less a slave. Her experience merely denoted her place in the market.

This is an important insight for it shows how the market was not uniform throughout. The market was not homogenous and there were niches to be found within it. One person who appreciated this was a Benjamin Davis of Hamburg, South Carolina, who in September of 1838 took out an advert in Charleston's newspapers, excitedly advising the readership of:

> 120 Negroes for Sale – The subscriber has just arrived from Petersburg, Virginia, with one hundred and twenty likely young negroes of both sexes and every description, which he offers for sale on the most reasonable terms.

> The lot now on hand consists of plough boys, several likely and well-qualified house servants of both sexes, several women with children, small girls suitable for

nurses, and several small boys without their mothers. Planters and traders are earnestly requested to give the subscriber a call previously to making purchases elsewhere, as he is enabled and will sell as cheap, or cheaper, than can be sold by any other person in the trade.[27]

Price clearly was a factor on which Benjamin Davis was not going to be outdone, but his advertisement offered much more in terms of value than affordable slaves. In advertising these slaves as newly arrived and as having arrived from Virginia, a slave-breeding state, it may be inferred these slaves were effectively "fresh produce" of that State, and not yet worn out by daily toil. Their youthfulness serves to reinforce this conclusion. There was value for Davis too in their diversity. Some were male, among whom many possessed the physical strength required for ploughing. Others were female, some of whom appear to have been accompanied by their children. It is likely all of these ended up working in their master's fields. Yet among the males and females were some who had skills and characteristics that immediately distinguished them from most others in the group, suiting them to work at their master's house. Each analysis of the group brought its own proportions. It was these seemingly trivial insights that sometimes hid the truth about slavery from those in the North.

One opportunity for furthering the cause of slaves presented itself when Northerners occasionally visited households where slaves were employed. Surely, these Northerners thought, they would have the opportunity to see for themselves the condition of the South's slaves and to interrogate the slaves about their lives. The slaves who resided at their master's house were commonly referred to as "house slaves." These house slaves were in the minority, with those who worked in the fields, the field slaves, being in the majority. House slaves were often better fed and if they were not given enough food they could nonetheless avail of sources of it around the house. They were certainly clothed considerably better than the field slaves. Olmsted notes how "house-servants were neatly dressed, but the field-hands wore very coarse and ragged garments."[28] At one house he further observed how several "of the house-servants, as is usual, are mulattoes, and good-looking."[29]

In recounting her own experience Jacobs, who escaped from slavery, records of her first owner: "My mistress was so kind to me that I was always glad to do her bidding, and proud to labor for her as much as my young years would permit."[30] When she was just 12 years old Jacobs' mistress died and she ended up in the hands of another. She continued to be a house slave, but fortune was less kind to her on this occasion:

> Yet I would have chosen this, rather than my lot as a slave, though white people considered it an easy one; and it was so compared with the fate of others. I was never cruelly overworked; I was never lacerated with the whip from head to foot; I was never so beaten and bruised that I could not turn from one side to the other; I never had my heel-strings cut to prevent my running away; I was never chained to a log and forced to drag it about, while I toiled in the fields from morning till night; I was never branded with hot iron, or torn by bloodhounds. On the contrary, I had always been kindly treated, and tenderly cared for, until I came into the hands of Dr. Flint. I had never wished for freedom till then. But though my life in slavery was comparatively devoid of hardships, God pity the woman who is compelled to lead such a life![31]

Now one must be clear, as Jacobs was herself clear, how being a slave, whether employed in the field or in the house, always entailed suffering. That being noted, house slaves were not the embodiment of slavery's ills, but more akin to its exceptions. They were certainly its elite. There was consequently a sort of class system within slavery. Jacobs acknowledges this when she refers to "companies of slaves from the plantations, generally of the lower class."[32] Yet it was these exceptions, the house slaves, visitors from the North would meet when they came to the South. It was these exceptions who would be wheeled out by the slaveholders as proof positive for those visitors of how allegations of cruelty in slavery were without the slightest foundation. If the general demeanor of a particular house slave was not in keeping with the illusion the slaveholder wished to create then the slave was conveniently kept out of sight. It was the experience of these elite few, a small few who resided at slavery's apex, that informed the opinion of visitors on the plight of the whole. What then did the Northern visitor:

> ... know of the half-starved wretches toiling from dawn till dark on the plantations? of mothers shrieking for their children, torn from their arms by slave traders? of young girls dragged down into moral filth? of pools of blood around the whipping post? of hounds trained to tear human flesh? of men screwed into cotton gins to die? The slaveholder showed him none of these things, and the slaves dared not tell of them if he had asked them.[33]

Reverend Horace Moulton, who resided in the South for a time, knew slavery was not homogenous. Of his account of slavery, in which he seeks to encompass the spectrum of slavery's daily realities, Moulton says it:

> ... will apply to *field hands* who compose much the largest portion of the black population, (probably nine-tenths,) and not to those who are kept for kitchen maids, nurses, waiters, &c., about the houses ... where persons from the north obtain most of their knowledge of the evils of slavery.[34]

Slavery, and the market for slaves, lacks homogeneity in other ways too. Not all forms of slavery are rooted in economics. Even so, market rationale still holds true, as slavery exists to supply an individual, or a group of them, with a particular demand. Jacobs proposed a strategy for those who wished to learn the truth of the South's slavery. She writes, "If you want to be fully convinced of the abominations of slavery, go on a southern plantation, and call yourself a negro trader. Then there will be no concealment; and you will see and hear things that will seem to you impossible among human beings with immortal souls."[35] This was but one instance where the fate of the slave depended on a flawed premise, the premise being how the condition of a few house slaves was reflective of the entire body of slaves in the South. It was not. These were slavery's "successes", if slavery could be credited with such a thing, which it readily paraded. Once the flawed logic was accepted, gathering the results of the experiment was straightforward enough. The conclusions, however, did not reflect the reality, but only the flaws inherent to the starting point. Such was the deception of slavery. Such was the misfortune of the South's slaves.

That slavery was legal in the South is certain, but when market interests conflicted with legal constraints those interests did not always yield to them. In the South a black person had a commercial value he or she did not have as a free person in the North, whereas in the North a black person had an intrinsic value he or she did not have at the South. When slaves escaped and fled to the North they lost all commercial value, gaining for themselves an altogether different one. The process could work in reverse too. Any free black person seized in the North could be brought to the South at little cost to their abductor and sold at their full commercial value. The fate of Solomon Northup was a case in point. That Northup believed a great many other free blacks were seized from the North and sold as property was certain. Judge George M. Stroud of the Criminal Court of Philadelphia noted how despite "the city of Philadelphia['s remoteness] from those slaveholding states …, and where also the market is tempting, it has been ascertained, that more than thirty free colored persons, mostly children, have been kidnapped here, and carried away, within the last two years."[36] This, however, was only the tip of the iceberg.

In 1808 the law prohibiting the transatlantic slave trade came into effect, but slaves were as valuable as ever, perhaps even more so. The commercial realities remained intact irrespective of their status in law. A story is recounted of a slave ship, whose service was probably engaged by slaveholders, sailing to within a short distance of Savannah, having been blown off course by unfavorable winds.[37] Contrary to law this ship had some 500 slaves aboard, so the crew could not make for port. Instead, they opted to make for a safe place where they could drop anchor and offload their cargo under the guise of replenishing their stores. Fate, though, was not on their side and a Revenue vessel travelling along the shore discovered their presence and the nature of their business. The slave ship was seized. Thereafter both vessels made for port at Savannah where the cargo of slaves was unloaded, and the ship's crew confined to jail. In due course a show trial was conducted, though the crew suffered no ill effects as a result, unlike the slaves they had carried away from Africa. Within a few weeks a third of the slaves had died from disease. After a time, 20 or 30 of the remainder were hired out. The rest were divided among some of the planters of the region. None were returned home. It was the market, and not the law, that triumphed.

In 1819 Congress heard of 13,000 Africans thought to be smuggled into the United States annually to be sold as slaves in the South.[38] Of this time Reverend Horace Moulton wrote, "[w]ere you to visit all the plantations in South Carolina, Georgia, Alabama and Mississippi, I think you would be convinced that the horrors of the traffic in human flesh have not yet ceased. I was surprised to find so many that could not speak English among the slaves, until the mystery was explained."[39] The Reverend thought it was an easy enough accomplishment to distribute newly arrived slaves across the South once they had been safely landed at Florida.

Some estimates put the figure for slaves illegally imported into the United States at about 1,000 *per annum* during the years between the introduction of the prohibition and the outbreak of war.[40] Estimates of the time put the figure at between 13,000 and 15,000 annually.[41] At the very least an approximate total of 51,000 slaves were imported this way during these years. By the time the transatlantic trade was ended 9.5 million Africans had been forcibly shipped from their homes to the New World. Most of those enslaved ended up, not in the United States, but in Brazil. Despite the enormity of slavery in the South it accounted for only 6% of the entire slave body moved from Africa.[42]

Governor Hammond of South Carolina, an advocate of slavery, was fatalistic about the inevitability of the slave trade. In correspondence Hammond writes of a Mr. Grosvenor, a representative of Britain's parliament, The House of Commons. Grosvenor said he had 20 objections concerning the abolition of the slave trade. The first of his objections was how it was impossible to abolish the trade. The remaining objections, in light of the first one, Grosvenor asserted, he need not give.[43] "Can you say to yourself, or to the world, that this first objection of Mr. Grosvenor has been" overwhelmingly refuted, Hammond asks?[44] "Does it not really seem that Mr. Grosvenor was a Prophet? That though nearly all the 'impossibilities' of 1787 have vanished, and become as familiar facts as our household customs [, those of domestic slavery,] under the magic influence of Steam, Cotton and universal peace, yet this wonderful prophecy still stands, defying time and the energy and genius of mankind," he adds.[45] He points to the vast losses of life and the great sums of money fruitlessly spent by the British trying to overturn slavery, all to no avail. With the economic realities of slavery in mind, Reverend Moulton declared as a "dead letter" any law that genuinely expected to end the slave trade simply by making it "piracy to traffic."[46] The *New Orleans Courier* of 1839 summed up the situation thus: "Human laws have, in all countries and ages, been violated whenever the inducements to do so afforded hopes of great profit."[47] Such was the extent of these concerns that in their own time the question was posed: "If it be concluded that the domestic slave trade is both cruel and opposed to sound policy, it would still remain to be considered whether the interests and passions, which can be rallied to its support, present insuperable obstacles to any attempt to put an end to it."[48]

It was the prospect of profit that gave the slave cause to tremble, for the slave knew profit was at the heart of her torment. Even before the outbreak of the Civil War the sheer immensity of the loss of human life resulting from the cultivation of the tropics' sugar crop alone was known. The crop had "destroyed more life than all the European wars of the twenty years which followed the French Revolution."[49] It was where profits were greatest, one found human life was cheapest, Weston contended. A Dr. Demming of Richland county in Ohio, reported how while on a tour of the South aboard the steamboat Fame, he had the opportunity to talk to a Mr. Dickinson and a group of slaveholders. Mr. Dickinson advised how during part of the season of cultivating sugar it was necessary to have twice the labor required at other times. However, thrifty to the last, some slaveholders in Louisiana had worked out how, if the slaves were made to work, quite literally, day and night, all the work could be done during these busy times with the same number of slaves as was available during other times. When this was done costs were reduced and the rewards of slavery were increased. There were, however, risks associated with this enterprising plan. Sometimes slaves died but, so long as the costs incurred through the deaths of slaves were less than the savings returned from overworking them, it was good business. Some further developed the economics of the scheme. By looking at the relationship between death and cost reduction, in terms of risk and reward they had ascertained "they could afford to sacrifice," or risk, a full team of slaves once every seven years, and still reap the rewards.[50] Mr. Dickinson and the slaveholders in his company make it clear this business acumen was applied in the cultivation of sugar at the time.

Ruffin points to a banking crisis recent to his time. The very substantial business of cultivating tobacco in Virginia was carried out using slaves. When problems beset the banking system business came to a halt and the slaves were left with nothing to do. Ruffin's complaint is not so much that the tobacco manufacturers experienced hardship, as it is that the slaves came through the crisis relatively unscathed. Their owners were left with the burden of feeding and clothing them, even though no work, and consequently no profit, was to be obtained. The slaves were, he says, "perfectly idle, and returning no compensation whatever to their employers."[51] In 1845, during his very first year on Epps' plantation, Northup experienced the effects of profitability's absence and re-emergence. Across the region, during that first year, caterpillars infested and subsequently destroyed most of the cotton crop. This was a disaster for the slaveholders, but not so for the slaves. Northup recalls there was little for the slaves to do and although they had once worked unceasingly, they were now idle for about half of the time. It was only later when word reached the planters of Bayou Boeuf of high wages to be earned, and the equally high demand for slaves, on the sugar plantations of St. Mary's parish that the reprieve ended. Northup explains:

> This parish is situated on the coast of the Gulf of Mexico, about one hundred and forty miles from Avoyelles. The Rio Teche, a considerable stream, flows through St. Mary's to the gulf. It was determined by the planters, on the receipt of this intelligence, to make up a drove of slaves to be sent down to Tuckapaw in St. Mary's, for the purpose of hiring them out in the cane fields. Accordingly, in the month of September, there were one hundred and forty-seven collected at Holmesville, Abram, Bob and myself among the number. Of these about one-half were women.[52]

Weston asks where in the United States slaves found conditions severest. It was not in the northern slave states, the slave-breeding states, but in Louisiana and Texas. In those states where slavery was the most profitable, it was also the most severe. Indeed, slaves who lived in the breeding states knew the reputation of Louisiana and Texas for cruelty and, when they irked their masters, they were sometimes threatened with the prospect of being sold to these places. Weston asks, "Is it not notorious, that the States upon the Gulf of Mexico, in which forced labour is most productive to those who own it, are made use of by the northern Slave States, not merely as markets in which to dispose of slaves as a matter of profit, but as a Botany Bay furnished to their hands, to which their slaves are sent by way of punishment?"[53] As the profits of the business rose the damage inflicted upon the slaveholders through the death of any one slave diminished. What is more, as profits rose, it became tempting to pursue profit unto its most extreme point, to impose more burdens upon the slaves, until their lives were literally and financially spent. They were, after all, mere commodities, readily replaced.

That is not say, however, slaveholders were unconcerned with costs, but rather how some costs were more bearable than others. Only in the United States and in Haiti, would slaves be made permanently free through violence. Even when laws were passed in other jurisdictions granting emancipation, freedom came only gradually, if it came at all. It was the children of slaves who were emancipated, and not their parents. These children continued to be born into slavery and it was only at their 18th, 21st or perhaps even 28th birthday that freedom was granted. The intention of this gradual emancipation was to make it as cost neutral as possible, not to the slave, but to his or her owner. In those instances where emancipation was granted quickly it was estimated the rates of return attained through the labor of slaves were so high as to compensate for 40% of the cost of the slave during the short time of his or her retention. Other measures, such as the compensation of owners from government funds, went a long way to make up the shortfall. Even when freedom came to slaves, it was always at their expense, and never at that of the profitability of their masters.[54]

So contrary were the interests of the *business of slavery* to the *welfare of slaves* that one would come at expense to the other. Weston points out how the only thing a slave could truly hope for was the demise of his or her master's business.[55] Only then, when the factors of cost and profit were obliterated, only when slavery's market rationale was invalidated, when the conjoined elements of supply and demand could be separated, could there be hope. There wasn't much basis for such an aspiration of course. Unless accompanied by some widespread economic catastrophe, of the kind described by Ruffin, the more likely outcome would have been the sale of the slave to another master. Nonetheless it is an insight that raises doubts over the capacity of markets to be, of themselves, guarantors of freedom. Weston concurs, expressing his appreciation for the space occupied in civilized society by property rights while at the same time, making the point how nowhere were such rights exercised more wholeheartedly than in the slave society of the South.[56]

Once free, the slaves would have time to ponder which of these factors, the supply or the demand, had been the principal agent of his or her enslavement. One person who may have been able to intuit the answer, through his own experience, was none other than George Washington. Having inherited Mount Vernon from his late brother in 1754, Washington increasingly acquired more slaves. In *The Domestic Architecture of Slavery at George Washington's Mount Vernon*, Dennis J. Pogue notes how Washington eventually stopped buying slaves and how his decision was the consequence of many considerations. Nonetheless, Pogue makes it clear, economics were foremost among those considerations. Against a backdrop of a tobacco market that was declining internationally and his failure to produce a crop capable of commanding a premium price, Washington found himself increasingly in debt.[57] Quite simply there was no demand for the crops Washington was able to supply. By 1766 Washington changed the direction of Mount Vernon's business and gradually improved finances. This was achieved by diversifying his estate's commercial activities. Some of these activities were more favorable to utilizing the power of animals than human labor. Washington now found himself with more slaves than he needed. The commercial options were clear. He could sell the slaves at auction or hire them out. Pogue conveys how Washington, now in his final year, was averse to the commercial choices before him. In a letter, Washington sets out his opposition to the trade in human beings. He roots his opposition in morality, even as he acknowledges the commercial reality of the position before him. As to the option of hiring out his slaves, Washington considers it to be almost on a par with auctioning. To pursue the option, he comprehends, he would have to break up families and to send their members hither and thither. He ponders what he can do, as in doing nothing he foresees his financial ruin.[58] Fortunately, his persistence at changing the fortunes of Mount Vernon was rewarded. Fortunately too for Washington's slaves, and for their families, his principles did not allow them to be subjected to the trials of the market.

Another similar example, though anecdotal, is found in the experience of those slave traders who specifically targeted slaves from areas of Africa experienced in the cultivation of rice. On occasion these traders could not obtain slaves from targeted regions and consequently the slaves they had for trading did not have skills making them of value to prospective customers. Much later, having traversed the Atlantic Ocean with their cargo of slaves and having arrived at Charleston, the traders learned of their mistake. The mismatch between the supply of their cargo and the demand of rice planters meant that if sales were made, they were always at a price lower than anticipated. Even so, sales could not be taken for granted. Sometimes it was futile for them even to try, and the traders learned the expensive lesson of being in the possession of a supply of goods for which there is no demand. They were left to gather their slaves back into their ship, to sail away, and to try their luck at another port.[59]

Not all ports were open to slavery, however. That slavery must expand to survive has already been established. Yet some of slavery's advocates proposed it would be in the interests of those who stood in opposition to slavery to permit it to expand. They claimed once it had spread to new places it would die out entirely in those places where it had originated. The results were a mixed bag, for with the expansion of slavery new markets were found and, always dynamic, slavery was transformed at its origins, not eliminated. This was the basis for the establishment of the Breeding States, which became outlets for slaves, rather than employers of their labor. Weston denounces the proposal saying the "idea that anything has been gained ... is a delusion and a snare; a cheat in those who propagate it, and a pitfall for the unwary."[60] From 1790 until 1860 some 835,000 slaves were exported from these States.[61] He points to the progress of Delaware in ridding itself of slaves. He observes how, in the time since the Revolution, it alone had made "substantial progress" and how it had done so by prohibiting the sale or removal from the state of slaves. He says the "prohibition is the sole explanation of her progress."[62] He notes how, had the good citizens of Delaware been given the option to sell slaves "they would have raised them."[63]

Three things were learned. First slavery was adaptable: it could adapt to suit the times, and to avail of new opportunities. Through this adaptability it always retained within itself the power of its own perpetuation. Second, slavery was not diminished by letting the demand for it spread. The opposite was true, as by allowing slavery to spread it created new opportunities for itself. It found new footholds while at the same time solidifying old ones. Third, slavery only acted to fulfil its own interests and those of its beneficiaries. Even when it made moral appeals, as it appealed to abolitionists that it was in their interests to permit it to spread, these appeals were informed by no interests other than its own selfish ones, and these interests were achieved by wretchedly exploiting human brokenness.

Ruffin had a different perspective. Instead of being a source of brokenness, slavery was a remedy for it. All around he perceived there was human misery, yet everywhere there was demand, and in this demand the capacity to remedy misery. For the world's tribal peoples, the quality of their lives was a matter beyond their control. It was a matter determined by the fertility of the land they inhabited, and the abundance of the waters around them. Even in those countries where life was more developed, in the industrial economies, he perceived, one observed people crushed by their inability to command their labor to fulfill the demands of life. Ruffin saw slavery as an opportunity to rehabilitate individuals so that, via the coercion of the slaveholder, these individuals conformed with the market of their own supply and demand, while at the same time conferring benefits on society. Ruffin argued how, if even among the most primitive of societies some could have taken it upon themselves to become slaveholders, they would soon have learned the fruits of its labor. "Hence," he says, "among any savage people, the introduction and establishment of domestic slavery is necessarily an improvement of the condition and wealth and well-being of the community in general, and also of the comfort of the enslaved class."[64] However, Ruffin recognized how the supply of brokenness was not enough in itself to create the slavery he advocated as therapeutic. In order for slavery to exist a society must not be completely devoid of "regular industry ... [or] of the artificial wants which induce a demand for, or the desire to possess the accumulated products of labor."[65] Critically, he emphasizes how "[w]ithout the existence of such a demand for the services of slaves as will induce and compensate the providing for the regular and sufficient support, domestic slavery cannot be begun."[66]

It is on this question, of which is the more important, the supply or the demand, that something remarkable happens: fervent abolitionism becomes unified with passionate advocacy. Given the primacy of demand, and the subservience of supply to it, Beecher Stowe asks, "But who, sir, makes the trader? Who is most to blame? The enlightened, cultivated, intelligent man, who supports the system of which the trader is the inevitable result, or the poor trader himself?"[67] One of her characters furnishes the answer, laying the accusation, "it is you considerate, humane men, that are responsible for all the brutality and outrage wrought by these wretches; because, if it were not for your sanction and influence, the whole system could not keep foothold for an hour. ... the whole thing would go down like a millstone. It is your respectability and humanity that licenses and protects [t]his brutality."[68] When it comes to the question of which is the greater, Ruffin and Beecher Stowe are agreed it is the demand, and thereby the role of the customer, that is deserving of primacy.

In *Time on the Cross* Fogel and Engerman make a point about slavery in the New World predating the rise of cotton there. Of the 9.5 million slaves shipped across the Atlantic, 80% were imported prior to 1810.[69] The rise of cotton only commenced in the middle of the 1790s and the crop may be considered to have been still at its early stages by 1810, so cotton cannot account for the demand for slaves during this time. Tobacco too provides no explanation. During the 18th century, when the slave trade was booming, the supply of tobacco into Europe only increased at a rate of approximately 350 tons *per annum*.[70] No, it was neither the customers of cotton nor those of tobacco who paid the ferryman Charon to carry these souls over the Styx to this earthly Hades. Fogel and Engerman pronounce it was Europe's love of sweet delicacies, rather than its fascination with cotton cloth or its tobacco addiction, that dictated the scale of the Atlantic slave trade of this time.[71] It was European consumers of sugar who consumed 7.6 million lives.

In his pre-Civil War writing slavery's advocate David Christy poured scorn upon attempts to stop the trade. Even when the planters of the South had only a small part of the market for cotton, the rewards were substantial enough to stop them from emancipating their slaves. By the time of his writing, the South's planters had secured a monopoly on the supply of cotton. The popularity of cotton, and the choices made by its consumers, raised unassailable obstacles in the path to freedom of the cotton industry's slaves.[72] Christy points to the conduct of the churches of his time. A great many of them denounced slavery, but in denouncing it they did so from the viewpoint of its immorality, without comprehending what else they might have done. Christy points to the flaw in their approach by noting how, though they were to be found in opposition to slavery, it never occurred to them to address the phenomenon where it could truly be hurt. If slavery was to be dealt a blow, it must be directed at its customers. Political parties opposed to slavery similarly failed to capitalize on this economic reality. Christy writes:

> This was a radical error. ... As long as all used their products, so long the Slaveholders found the ... [religious anti-slavery] doctrine working them no harm; as long as no provision was made for supplying the demand for tropical products, by free labor, so long there was no risk in extending the field of their operations. Thus, the very things necessary to the overthrow of American Slavery, were left undone, while those essential to its prosperity, were continued in the most active fashion; so that, now ... we may say, emphatically, COTTON IS KING, and his enemies are vanquished ...[73]

Weston points to contemporary extracts from Southern newspapers detailing the recent price of slaves sold at auction: "Jack, aged four years, $376;" "Two small girls sold, one for $880 and the other for $350;" "two boys, the eldest five years old, brought $487; the other, two and a half years old, brought $325."[74] He asks:

> Is it wonderful that the "brood mares" with such prices for their young, should be well fed and well groomed? Is it wonderful that the desire should be most ardent to extend institutions, under which "*Jack, aged four years,*" will sell on the auction block for three hundred and seventy-six good, hard dollars; while three hundred

and twenty-five dollars is thought cheap enough for a boy "two and a half years old?" And, finally, taking human nature as it is, who is most blameworthy: he who raises "*small girls*" for sale under the temptation of these prices, or he who creates, or connives at creating, the markets upon which such prices depend?[75]

All then, abolitionists and advocates alike, are agreed. When pondering the greater role in creating the market for slavery, the supply of slaves or the demand of customers, it is the customer who is the most blameworthy. One of Beecher Stowe's characters, a brutish slave trader, sums it up: "'So long as your grand folks wants to buy men and women, I'm as good as they is … tan't any meaner sellin' on 'em, that 't is buyin'!'"[76]

Section 2

Chapter 6:

The Ambassador

Today slavery has been remade. In testament to its dynamism, it has several new names. Sometimes, for example, it is known as *trafficking in persons (TIP)*. At other times it is referred to as *trafficking in human beings (THB)*. It is most popularly referred to as *human trafficking*, or simply as *trafficking*. Conscious of the array of names given to the phenomenon, and of the confusion this likely causes, some prefer instead to refer to contemporary occurrences simply as *modern-day slavery*, a name distinguishing it from the practices of the past, *chattel slavery*, where slaves were legally held as personal property. Though chattel slavery has been consigned to history, the practice of slavery has not.

The accomplishment of the *United Nations Convention against Transnational Organized Crime and its Protocols* is of critical importance. It provides the only internationally agreed definition of the phenomenon, and it permits cases in different jurisdictions to be properly and uniformly labeled as acts of human trafficking. The convention is supplemented, as its name suggests, by protocols. These are the *Protocol to Prevent, Suppress and Punish Trafficking in Persons, Especially Women and Children* and the *Protocol against the Smuggling of Migrants by Land, Sea and Air*. As the convention was agreed at the Sicilian city of Palermo, it is more often, and loosely, referred to as the *Palermo Protocol*.[1]

The protocol comprises three parts: the act, the means and the purpose, providing a framework that addresses: what, how, and why.[2] When these three component parts are taken together the resulting definition describes human trafficking as:

> the recruitment, transportation, transfer, harbouring or receipt of persons, by means of the threat or use of force or other forms of coercion, of abduction, of fraud, of deception, of the abuse of power or of a position of vulnerability or of the giving or receiving of payments or benefits to achieve the consent of a person having control over another person, for the purpose of exploitation. Exploitation shall include, at a minimum, the exploitation of the prostitution of others or other forms of sexual exploitation, forced labour or services, slavery or practices similar to slavery, servitude or the removal of organs.[3]

A separate definition is given to describe human trafficking where children are involved. A child is any person who has not reached the age of 18.[4] This definition excludes any reference to the means of trafficking as they become irrelevant in instances where children are its focus. The definition is thus the "recruitment, transportation, transfer, harbouring or receipt of a child for the purpose of exploitation shall be considered 'trafficking in persons' even if this does not involve any of the means set forth."[5] The approach adopted by the *Palermo Protocol* is often referred to as a 3P approach, which addresses the issues of protection, prevention and prosecution.

A new front, whose tendrils extend to every corner of the globe, has been opened in the war on modern slavery. Part of this new front is to be found at the very heart of America's seat of government, on a line that runs east to west across the White House's North Lawn, which then passes the West Wing and the Eisenhower Executive Office Building, before it proceeds up Washington D.C.'s G Street NW for two blocks to the *Office to Monitor and Combat Trafficking in Persons*. This office is part of the U.S. State Department. It is from this office that the United States' Ambassador-at-Large, and a dedicated team of experts, guide the Administration's response to the global slave trade. In 2009, Ambassador Luis CdeBaca, a former civil rights prosecutor, took up the reins of that response.

In an interview with the Ambassador, during the twilight of the Obama Administration, he was asked whether the increase in the estimated number of global victims, growing from approximately 12.5 million to 27 million, is evidence of the problem worsening, or whether it reflects improvements in the techniques used to estimate the numbers, or is a combination of both.[6] The Ambassador points to the challenges. This increase is only one of several such increases that have occurred over the years. Certainly, there have been improvements in the application of methodologies for estimating the number of slaves, and some of the increase can be attributed to these improvements. Definition, as ever, also proves to be an important starting point. Earlier definitions focused upon trafficking as a cross-border phenomenon. Trafficking, of course, is not necessarily related to the movement of persons, or to their movement across borders. Certainly too, one can smuggle slaves but not all that is smuggled, even when human, is a slave. Migrants wishing to gain entry to a country may choose to be illegally smuggled into it, but enslavement is never a choice, and consequently smuggling and human trafficking are two different phenomena. Modern slavery, as defined by the *Palermo Protocol*, is a practice then that occurs not only across borders, but within them. The term *internal trafficking* is used to denote forms that occur within a jurisdiction. Even when used by traffickers, "movement," the Ambassador says, "is simply a time in the process."

The agreement of the *Palermo Protocol* meant that for the first time there was a holistic view of the process. The definition acknowledges that trafficking can certainly entail movement, but nonetheless it does not confine trafficking to movement, or even make movement necessary for trafficking to occur. As the definition came closer to reflecting the reality, the prospective population from which victims might emerge was enlarged and consequently so too the estimated number of victims. Something else happened. The Ambassador explains how the new definition served to re-orient the focus of slavery, which shifted from movement, and consequently from a jurisdictional matter, to victimization, and consequently to those who are living as slaves. One could not help but be struck by the intensity of the importance of this new focus to the Ambassador, to his staff, and to their mission. On the Ambassador's office table rested a treasured item, a book containing a collection of drawings, a token of appreciation bestowed by one who had known what it meant to be a slave, to one who had dedicated his life to freeing slaves. In every sense one finds that slavery remains today an issue close to the heart of America's politics.

The continuing refinement of these estimates raises the question of whether in time they might grow again. The Ambassador is circumspect. He recounts the experiences of one U.S. city police chief who said that neither the city's police nor residents thought human trafficking was a problem, but then again the city did not have a task force, and the city was not quite sure what was meant by human trafficking. It was only after the city established a task force, when it learned what constituted human trafficking, and having arrested 31 traffickers for violation commensurate with its new-found understanding, that it came to realize it did indeed have a problem. The problem, of course, was always there. Yet, only when measures were taken to address the phenomenon was it found. The lessons of the anecdote of this police chief's experience go far beyond his city's boundaries. It is a parable that resonates globally as readily as it does locally. As states and cities around the world make progress in training their personnel to identify instances of human trafficking, and as they establish task forces to combat it, the Ambassador is confident the "number of identified traffickers and identified victims will definitely go up." However, he distinguishes between the estimates and the actual number enslaved, adding that one cannot, of itself, "read that to mean trafficking is getting worse." He points to a lack of research in assessing under-reporting. This research is a step that has yet to be taken in assessing the relationship between estimates and actual victims, and it must be taken if the true extent of the problem is ever to become known.

In 2000, the same year as the landmark agreement on the *Palermo Protocol*, the United States government passed groundbreaking measures of its own. *The Victims of Trafficking and Violence Protection Act* is comprised of three legislative acts. The first is the *Trafficking Victims Protection Act of 2000* (TVPA), which establishes the Interagency Task Force to Monitor and Combat Trafficking, to be chaired by the Secretary of State. Other members include the Administrator of the United States Agency for International Development, the Attorney General, the Secretary of Labor, the Secretary of Health and Human Services, the Director of Central Intelligence, and other officials as the President may deem necessary.[7] The TVPA amends the *Foreign Assistance Act of 1961* to allow the President to provide assistance to foreign nations as part of their fight against human trafficking, while at the same time it establishes the policy of not providing "nonhumanitarian, nontrade-related foreign assistance to any government that— (1) does not comply with minimum standards for the elimination of trafficking; and (2) is not making significant efforts to bring itself into compliance with such standards."[8] Additionally the Act specifies the minimum standards by which governments across the world should be assessed. The 3P approach of the *Palermo Protocol* is evident too in the TVPA. Section 106 of the Act is entitled "Prevention of Trafficking," while Section 107 is entitled "Protection and Assistance for Victims of Trafficking," and Section 108 compels government to prosecute traffickers.

In another amendment to the *Foreign Assistance Act of 1961* the TVPA requires the annual publication of a report, the *Trafficking in Persons Report,* scrutinizing "the nature and extent of ... trafficking in persons ... in each foreign country. ... With respect to each country that is a country of origin, transit, or destination for victims of ... trafficking in persons, an assessment of the efforts by the government of that country to combat such trafficking."[9] Today there are four tiers: Tier 1, Tier 2, Tier 2 Watch List, and Tier 3. A Tier 1 country is one that is designated to be fully compliant with the minimum standards. A Tier 2 country is not fully compliant, but it is nonetheless making significant efforts towards full compliance. The Tier 2 Watch List adopts the conditions of Tier 2 but adds the criteria: the country is one in which there are a lot of victims or one where the number of victims is increasing significantly, and there is little evidence of government effort over the past year to combat trafficking or the determination that efforts are being made is based on the assertion of government. A Tier 3 country is one which does not meet all the criteria, and one which is making no substantial effort to rectify the deficit in its efforts.[10] Each year, usually around late June, governments across the world await the publication of the State Department's report detailing its global perspective on slavery, and the tier ranking they have attained for the current year.

Countries are allocated a tier ranking based on their compliance with the minimum standards. Those standards have themselves changed over the years and there are 12 of them. The first, for instance, asks whether "the government of the country vigorously investigates and prosecutes acts of severe forms of trafficking in persons, and convicts and sentences persons responsible for such acts, that take place wholly or partly within the territory of the country, including, as appropriate, requiring incarceration of individuals convicted of such acts."[11]

In June 2014 the State Department issued its *Trafficking in Persons Report* of that year. In it Pope Francis is quoted as saying to President Obama: "I exhort the international community to adopt an even more … effective strategy against human trafficking, so that in every part of the world, men and women may no longer be used as a means to an end."[12] Scarcely one month later, in testimony given to the Senate Committee on Foreign Relations (Subcommittee on East Asian and Pacific Affairs), Ambassador CdeBaca described as "a means to an end, not an end unto themselves" the United States' tiered approach.[13] Was the testimony of the Ambassador, and the prominent inclusion in the *Trafficking in Persons Report* of Pope Francis' exhortation, a sign the tiered approach was being re-evaluated? The Ambassador answers that he sees the tiered approach as "something that works." The assessment of the Office to Monitor and Combat Trafficking in Persons has global importance, and the prospect of being downgraded is an incentive to states to pass anti-trafficking legislation. The tiers themselves, the Ambassador shares, are designed to look at each country's application of the minimum standards, and each year as the publication of the *Trafficking in Persons Report* looms there is an opportunity to do just that. Ambassador CdeBaca describes the criteria of the standards as "very common-sense things … [for] anyone who is looking at a trafficking problem and how a government is relating to it."

In effect the annual evaluation equates to "a diagnostic, and the tier rankings have to flow from a fair application of the diagnostic, the facts in law under those standards." To assess the impartiality of the process one can look at instances of countries, not on a good standing with the United States, being upgraded when they took measures to counter trafficking, and this is a common enough occurrence, he advises. One can look too at instances of countries with whom the United States has close relationships and who nonetheless found their rankings downgraded because they fell short in a particular year. The Ambassador expresses his confidence in the therapeutic effect of this process, and he has seen "countries who have been on Tier 2 Watch List, and even Tier 3, make very strong progress over the years." He acknowledges some governments, in making improvements, are motivated solely by public perception. Others, he notes, claim they are not. Nonetheless it is the effect the allocation of rankings produces, that Ambassador CdeBaca and his staff pursue. To ensure clarity about where the problems lie, and what can be done to ameliorate them, considerable effort is made in the *Trafficking in Persons Report* in the form of both narrative and recommendations. What matters to the Ambassador then is not the tiers *per se*, but "how the tiers are used, how the tiers are reacted to". The tiers then are not static things, but dynamic, and through their dynamism a country can move up or down.

On countries that attain Tier 1 ranking the Ambassador is emphatic the designation reflects the overall attainment of minimum standards, nothing else. Even then that's not the end of the story. "Now that's one of the things that I think everybody always needs to remember is the minimum standards are minimum standards," he says. He likens the attainment of Tier 1 ranking to the school grading system. An "A Grade" is attained by achieving 90% or above, so even by achieving the grade one has not necessarily attained a perfect score. "A Tier 1 doesn't mean that you are getting an 'A.' A Tier 1 literally is like getting a 'C,'" he says. "Because, I don't think that we can say that there is a country out there that's got this solved," he adds. Tier 1 status is not the end of a long journey, but the beginning of it.

Some of the most innovative responses to the issue of human trafficking come from jurisdictions that are not Tier 1 countries at all. This is reminiscent of a point from another quarter. In an article entitled *Human Traffickers Evade Conviction* Nikolaj Nielsen describes national laws across the EU as a "mixed bag ... [which] can produce surprising results."[14] He notes how Bulgaria, despite the many problems the country faces with organized crime and corruption, has one of the highest rates of convictions for human trafficking "because prosecutors only need to prove aggravating circumstances such as 'forced use' and 'deception' to put traffickers behind bars."[15] The Ambassador notes the good work of the Royal Thai Police in prioritizing the issue within their jurisdiction, as a case in point. Another is Myanmar's Central Body for Suppression of Trafficking in Persons (CBTIP), a dedicated small group striving to tackle human trafficking. Nigeria's National Agency for the Prohibition of Trafficking in Persons (NAPTIP) is commended by the Ambassador for its innovative cross-disciplinary approach, combining the work of police, social workers and prosecutors, to casework.

Innovation alone, however, is not the answer to a country's problems, he observes. Despite the achievements of many groups around the world some find their country remains on the lower rungs of the tier ranking system, because of deficits in fulfilling the minimum standards. A whole host of factors, some of them extraneous, can come into play. For example, corruption may undermine the efficacy of government policy, meaning that what exists as policy is very different to the realities on the ground. Specifically, in Myanmar's case, Ambassador CdeBaca refers to the state-sponsored forced labor enshrined in law under its 1907 *Villages and Towns Act,* which has an inescapable bearing upon its tier allocation.[16] On the other hand some countries have made big improvements in their approach to human trafficking, but when one scrutinizes the record of these countries in other quarters one finds it is far from ideal.

One other noteworthy initiative to highlight the plight of slaves across the world is the *Global Slavery Index*. The index is guided by the University of Nottingham's Professor of Contemporary Slavery Kevin Bales. According to its estimates, which have increased over the years, globally there are millions today eking out an existence as slaves.[17] The index echoes the words of Ambassador CdeBaca when it states in its annual report how it is "important to note that we are not asserting that there has been an increase in modern slavery around the world over the last year. We believe that the majority of this increase is due to the improved accuracy and precision of our measures, and that we are uncovering modern slavery where it was not found before."[18] The *Global Slavery Index* provides a number of insights. First, it estimates the prevalence of slavery, providing an actual estimated number of slaves, in each of the world's countries. Second, it measures government response to the problem. Third, it measures the vulnerability of persons in each of the world's countries to the phenomenon of slavery. It too ranks countries, but it does so on each of these three insights.

The Ambassador's Office to Monitor and Combat Trafficking in Persons has innovations of its own. In reaching out to activists from different sides of the debate on slavery, and in questioning how demand for the produce of slaves might be reduced, an online survey was devised. The State Department funded the creation of the Slavery Footprint, an online resource that, according to its website, "allows consumers to visualize how their consumption habits are connected to modern day slavery."[19] In other words the survey allows participants to see how many slaves are required to provide them with their everyday staples. It is probably of great surprise to most who take the survey to learn that, on average, the answer is 37 slaves.[20]

Illustrating how, once again, definitions have a very tangible bearing on the fate of victims the Ambassador gives an account of how judicial systems have sometimes misunderstood the tier ranking system entirely. When confronted by the case of a victim of trafficking who is seeking to remain in the country of their exploitation, because returning to their country of origin would only serve to expose the victim to traffickers again, judges have turned to the tier ranking system. Finding how the country of origin was Tier 1 they interpreted this ranking, presuming the definition was linked to the trafficking situation in that country, as posing a low risk of trafficking, which of course is not what the tier ranking means. Victims who could, and should, have been protected were siphoned off from the population identified as being vulnerable to re-exploitation. Instead, they were returned to their countries of origin and to the very real prospect of being enslaved once more. The bitter irony is that these victims are sometimes dispatched from countries that are themselves Tier 1 countries, where protecting victims of slavery is a priority in attaining that status, yet whose actions are sometimes at odds with such protection. When victims are let down, whether they are in a Tier 1 country or a Tier 3 country matters little. Here is part of the meaning of the Ambassador's statement that importance of the tiers is not in the score they allocate, but in the effect they aspire to produce.

With so many millions enslaved, one might expect to hear of impending court cases, successful prosecutions and sentencing hearings. Yet, this has not always been the case. In recent years the *Trafficking in Persons Report* has included details of global trends in cases from prosecution to conviction. The statistics provided in the report are indicators, rather than precise figures. In 2006, there were approximately 5,808 prosecutions, leading to 3,160 convictions. That same year some 21 new or amended pieces of legislation were introduced to tackle human trafficking. In 2013, there were about 9,460 prosecutions, leading to 5,776 convictions. A total of 44,758 victims were identified and some 58 new or amended pieces of legislation introduced.[21] The

2020 numbers for prosecutions and convictions are comparable to those of 2013, though many more victims are now being identified. Prosecutions then tend not to be the norm, and it is well-understood that, when they occur, convictions are often very difficult to secure.

Being comprised of three parts (acts, means, and purpose) the *Palermo Protocol* definition presents a formidable challenge to prosecutors seeking to secure convictions in countries whose law incorporates it. At a very minimum a prosecutor must successfully make their case for each of the three parts. To fail in one is to fail in them all. The question was put to the Ambassador, a former civil rights prosecutor, whether a mistake is made by countries when the *Palermo Protocol* definition is adopted *verbatim* into national law, rather than as a series of discrete offences that might better serve the purpose. "I think it is a mistake for countries to have laws that slavishly repeat the language of the *Palermo Protocol*. I think that what we have seen is that countries that did that, in the early years right after 2000, had a lost decade in which they really failed to fight human trafficking," he says. The Ambassador notes Britain's political discussions on *The Modern Slavery Bill*, whereas for him the development that was "groundbreaking and determinative was the passage of the 2009 *Coroner's Act*, which focused more on slavery and less on trafficking. What we have seen through the years since 2009, in the UK, is that you're getting ... more arrests, prosecutions, many more victims helped."[22] On the reason behind these positive developments the Ambassador is clear it is the arrival of new law, in place of "post-Palermo law that just wasn't very useful." In the U.S. the Ambassador sees how virtually no cases are brought under *U.S. 1590 Code – Trafficking with respect to Peonage, Slavery, Involuntary Servitude, or Forced Labor* because it places too much emphasis on the acts of slavery, rather than focusing upon the fact a person was enslaved. "All you really need is a law that says if you're enslaving somebody you're guilty under a trafficking chapter of the criminal code, and then you're Palermo compliant," he says. All of this underpins something else. Acts of human trafficking are difficult to prosecute, and consequently the numbers prosecuted globally reflect the difficulty of convicting offenders, and not the absence of offences. Speaking from his experience as someone who partook in the U.S. side of the negotiations on the *Palermo Protocol* he adds how "none of us felt that we were negotiating the text of a criminal statute. For the purposes of the political statement of the protocol we were trying to capture something that described the entire phenomenon."

Capturing that phenomenon is important, as the *Trafficking in Persons Report* of 2014 reminds. It says that "[l]anguage matters. ... The conflation of terms, as well as the failure to use the correct definition to describe human trafficking, can confuse and mislead audiences. Human trafficking is a complex crime that many communities are still trying to understand, and using outdated terms or incorrect definitions only weakens understanding of the issue."[23] This is not the first time attention has been drawn to the use of language, to its importance, to the myths that result from its misuse, to the repercussions for efforts to combat it or indeed to the very real consequences for victims that arise from these myths. Damningly the 2012 report states: "[m]yths and misperceptions about trafficking in persons and its complexities continue to hinder governments' ability to identify victims, provide them the services they need, and bring their traffickers to justice."[24] It identifies "[n]arrow definitions and continued stereotypes of trafficking as a problem."[25] It notes victims of human trafficking are sometimes wrongly identified as illegal migrants or, even worse, as criminals. The pathway to human trafficking can commence by engagement in illegal activities, as in the case of foreign migrants working without work permits, but this does not excuse the abuse inflicted or the crime perpetrated. Persons who were engaged in illegal activities but who subsequently fell victim to traffickers, could and should be rightly identified as victims of slavery. The "challenges are made worse by the unfortunate tendency to conflate human trafficking and human smuggling," the report adds.[26] The unfortunate politics of these happenings mean victims, who should have been protected, are instead punished for being victims.

The 2012 *Trafficking in Persons Report* emphasizes human trafficking has become synonymous with particular manifestations but that this is itself flawed as slavery encapsulates a wide variety of activities. Specifically, the report emphasizes too how statistics must be handled with caution because human trafficking is an illicit activity. Some statistics, for example those relating to prosecutions or those relating to the number of victims located, are representative of only part of the picture, not the entirety of it. All of this serves to illustrate just how important is understanding to efforts to combat the phenomenon, and how important is definition in efforts to encapsulate the population upon which the status of victimhood should be bestowed.

The Ambassador shares too how, at times, definitional issues have historically been politically useful to governments, often at the expense of victims. From about the 1890s there was an international effort by countries to deal with slavery. In the wake of Japan's ascendency in the Pacific after the Russo-Japanese War the country had enough power to block a convention from defining trafficking as anything other than a cross-border phenomenon. Slavery within the jurisdiction, or internal trafficking, remained a private matter untouched by international agreement. Japan did this to protect its practice of *geisha*. The notion that trafficking of the time should be confined to the cross-border trade in human beings was "not because that was the problem, it's because that's what governments were willing to do." This definition of human trafficking stayed around for a long time after its emergence in the early 1900s. Of course, the definition did not reflect the reality of slavery. Whether slavery was cross-border, or otherwise, mattered little: it was still slavery. By conditioning the definition to stipulate that it must be cross-border the government of Japan was able to divide the slave population, effectively excluding domestic slavery from being recognized as such. It also served to impose limitations on the conversation about slavery, by limiting it to external forms of slavery. Of course, the definition did not reflect reality. It was just a ploy used to satisfy the interests of a political agenda.

Thus, the development of the *Palermo Protocol* was a major progression. It established a global standard and broke down some of the historic barriers that were willing only to recognize slavery as a cross-border practice. Human trafficking law was transformed from something that existed on paper to a response to the problem. Additionally, the problem was no longer one that belonged to part of government but to all of it. One can see the progression from the concepts of slavery and trafficking as being distinct, to being unitary. Again, the Ambassador emphasizes how little it matters to victims what slavery is called, or the distinctions one makes between the forms it takes. What matters to the victim is their enslavement, and the pathway to ending it. Unexpectedly the concepts become clearer and more useful, as the distinctions made between them become a little fuzzy. Ambassador CdeBaca has a historical parallel for this insight. The Civil Law, he explains, originated as a set of standards established by the Roman Empire to be applicable across the domain. The role of the lawyer was not to interpret it, but to follow it. The Common Law, on the other hand, which emerged from an England isolated from the Roman Empire, is more intuitive and permits violations of various forms to nonetheless be recognized as manifestations of the same entity. When it comes to slavery, it for this Common Law perspective that the Ambassador appeals.

Chapter 7:

The Modern Slave Trade

Human misery is the rock upon which slavery is built. War, poverty, disease, famine, natural cataclysm, political upheaval, social persecution, and a great many other causes contribute to the misery endured by millions across the world daily. Exhausted, impoverished, and despondent, victims of these crises sometimes try to flee by casting their lot in with the rest of the world's migrants, refugees, and asylum seekers.[1] Opportunistic human smugglers see these crises in a different light to the sympathetic. They see these crises as opportunities to exploit, and as opportunities for personal gain by extorting what they can from people desperate to flee. Paradoxically while the smuggling of people does not constitute human trafficking, the vulnerability that required them to be smuggled in the first place certainly makes them amenable to it. For this reason, there is a close relationship between the tale of migrants, refugees and asylum seekers and the tale of those who fall prey to human traffickers. Each year hundreds of thousands make a crossing of the Mediterranean Sea from their homes in the Middle East and Africa. Many never make it to shore, with individual disasters accounting for the lives of hundreds and even thousands. Some years ago, within just five months of joining the international humanitarian effort to assist, the Irish naval service recorded the rescue of more than 8,200 people. For some alas, even if rescue comes, another tragedy awaits ashore. That being so, even the seas are no longer immune to slavery.

The technological advances of the 20th and 21st centuries have transformed the world's fishing industry. Radio communication allows boat captains to contact supporting vessels, to be resupplied and refueled. The same technology allows those captains to be updated on approaching weather conditions. Satellite navigation systems allow captains to know their precise location. Diesel engines allow greater flexibility in traversing oceans. Refrigeration allows crews to be fed and for their catches of fish to be preserved. It was the Irish economist John Elliot Cairnes who considered, prior to the U.S. Civil War, how slavery could be used in maritime pursuits, were it not for the fact that traffickers would face the prospect of their slaves escaping once they arrived at port. Free of the restrictions Cairnes once identified, today's boats can stay far out to sea for long periods of time, sometimes even for years, and work without cessation. They are free in other ways too. Through the advancements of technology, they are free to practice slavery.

In reporting for *The Guardian* newspaper Kate Hodal and Chris Kelly record the tale of Myint Thein, who for "the past two years, ... has been forced to work 20-hour days as a slave on the high seas, enduring regular beatings from his Thai captain and eating little more than a plate of rice each day. But now that he's been granted a rare chance to come back to port, he's planning something special to mark the occasion: his escape."[2] As testimony to slavery's economy, the fish these boats harvest are not even necessarily valued varieties. Instead, they are often described as "trash fish," with some of them being immature and others even inedible. Still these fish have a commercial value as they can be sold to factories that grind them down to make fishmeal. Producers sell it in turn to other producers who feed it to their farmed prawns. They in turn sell these prawns to some of the world's premier supermarkets. The demand is huge, with Thailand reportedly exporting 500,000 metric tonnes (over 550,000 U.S. tons) of prawns annually. Problematically for the industry, the enormous demand for prawns is not matched by a corresponding supply of workers. Thailand's Ministry of Labor is reported to have estimated the number of additional workers required by the industry at 50,000.[3] One captain told reporters that as fishing in Thailand is hard work, force is needed to get some of the workers on to the boat.[4] Some of the enslaved have witnessed murders. One recounted witnessing 20 of his fellows killed before him while at sea, with one of them tied, limb by limb, to four different boats and systematically pulled apart. No doubt this barbarous act fulfilled its intention on those who witnessed it. A representative of one of the locally situated companies producing prawns from Thailand's fishmeal is reported to have acknowledged the problem of slavery in the supply chain, but to have defended his company on the basis that the market obscures the true nature of the transactions, stating "we just don't have visibility."[5] Such is the extent of the problem that reporters Hodal and Kelly declare the modern-day Thai fishing industry to be "built on slavery."[6] A report by London's *Environmental Justice Foundation* notes "[s]uccessive Governments have appeared more concerned about working in concert with industry to reassure international purchasers of Thai seafood and maximise catch volumes, at any expense."[7] The coast of Thailand is just one place where the sea has been transformed, where new slave plantations have emerged, a new frontier where tightly knit teams of slave laborers can toil without end.

Remarkably, a document issued by the U.S. Department of State entitled *The Intersection Between Environmental Degradation and Human Trafficking* immediately rekindles one of Parker's points how the soil upon which slavery is carried out must be remarkably fertile, and if it is not fertile slavery will contribute to its degradation. The document notes vessels engaging in these practices have repeatedly "used banned fishing gear, fished in prohibited areas, failed to report or misreported catches, operated with fake licenses, and docked in unauthorized ports – all illegal fishing practices that contributes to resource depletion and species endangerment."[8] Parker's other two points are present in the tale of Myint Thein and his compatriots. First, the population available for the work is sparse, either because there are not enough people available to do the work, and more likely because there are not enough people consenting to do the work at the terms being offered. Second, the slavery is made possible by its monopoly on a favorite staple that cannot be acquired elsewhere, at least not as cheaply. In this instance the staple is consumed by prawns. By a circuitous route, one finally arrives at the source of the demand, the companies purchasing prawns from Thailand, and the customers of those companies who consume their prawns.

Figure: A boy aboard a jermal sieves small fish. A jermal is a rickety wooden fishing platform, one usually perched precariously on stilts. They are found in the shallow waters of north Sumatra where there are 1,000 such platforms hosting a total of 5,000 children. The working days are often exhaustingly long, the conditions dangerous, the rewards few, and workforce exploited. © U.R. Romano

Wars are often the catalyst for great transformation and innovation. In late 1941 a young Russian tank commander was injured while fighting to protect his homeland from Nazi invaders. During his time in hospital, he observed how frequently injured compatriots complained about the poor quality of the weapons issued to them. Inspired by these complaints he undertook to design a better weapon. Mikhail Kalashnikov's rifle arrived too late to have a bearing on the Second World War, but the immensity of its impact thereafter is beyond parallel. Developed in 1947, it is of course the AK-47 or Kalashnikov rifle. Within two years it was being used by Soviet troops. It fires in two modes: semi-automatic and automatic. In the former each suppression of the trigger fires a single shot. In the latter the rifle continues to fire, while the trigger is suppressed, at a rate of 600 rounds per minutes until all its ammunition is expended. Its characteristic long banana-shaped magazine contains 30 rounds of 7.62 × 39mm ammunition, which fire from the rifle's muzzle at a velocity of 710 meters per second and are effective to 300 meters.[9] The combination of its reliability, the ease with which it may be used, and its low cost, has made it a popular weapon. It is so popular in fact some estimate the number of Kalashnikov rifles in the world at about 100 million weapons, and they are thought to kill some 250,000 persons each year. Today, among the dozens of variants of the original, some cost as little as US$10.

Prior to his death at the age of 94 Kalashnikov, who first went into a church at the age of 91 and was later baptized into the Russian Orthodox Church, expressed his remorse in a lengthy letter to his church's patriarch. He regretted how the weapon he had designed to defend against one of the worst tyrannies the world has yet seen, is today found in the hands of a new tyranny.[10] There was cause enough for the aged Kalashnikov to be sorrowful. Among the assorted features of his rifle is one that adds to the weapon's popularity: when loaded it weighs just 4.9 kilograms.[11] In fact it is so light even a child might carry it and this development, combined with the weapon's other characteristics, has given rise to the child soldier.

The *Trafficking in Persons Report* of 2014 lists Burma, the Central African Republic (CAR), the Democratic Republic of the Congo, Rwanda, Somalia, South Sudan, Syria and Yemen as countries where government-backed armed groups using child soldiers are to be found.[12] The report also notes how the definition of a child soldier covers, in addition to children bearing arms, children serving as cooks, porters, messengers, medics, guards, or even sex-slaves, in these groups.[13] Some children fulfill other roles such as, for example, acting as spies. Approximately 40% of child soldiers are thought to be girls.[14] Nobody knows for sure how many children are exploited in this way, but estimates put the number at 250,000.[15] In the Central African Republic alone some 10,000 children are reportedly engaged as soldiers.[16] Early in 2015 UNICEF welcomed the largest-ever demobilization of children in a conflict zone up to that time, when some 3,000 South Sudanese children were expected to be demobilized. An initial group totaling 280 children was released by the South Sudan Democratic Army (SSDA) Cobra Faction, with the youngest of these just 11 years old. In the 12 months prior to the announcement of the demobilization it was estimated 12,000 children, mostly boys, had been recruited by armed groups in South Sudan.[17] The terrorist group, Islamic State of Iraq and Syria (ISIS), has also been noted for its use of child soldiers, with some appearing in its recruitment videos, and with several videos featuring a child executing prisoners.

One group has come to global prominence through the notoriety it has gained for itself. The *Lord's Resistance Army* (LRA) morphed out of a supposedly divinely inspired movement against the Ugandan government. At the time of its transformation, it had a new leader. His name is Joseph Kony. For nearly 30 years he and his group have brought terror to Uganda and to its neighbors. The LRA is responsible for the deaths of 100,000 people, and for the abduction of 60,000 children.[18] Violence has played a key role in the forcible recruitment of children into its ranks. Some are threatened and left with no choice but to participate. Others are forced to commit horrific acts of violence, including murder and mutilation, against even their own family members, and against their own communities, permanently alienating them from both, and to a large degree too from their own selves. Children may also find themselves ordered to kill other group members, who are themselves children, when those members have sought to escape or have refused to follow orders. The LRA was eventually driven out of Uganda, though its rebel forces remain scattered across the Democratic Republic of Congo (DRC), Central African Republic (CAR) and southern Sudan. Joseph Kony is wanted by the International Criminal Court but has yet to be apprehended.

Not all the world's child soldiers find themselves fighting for terrorists. In northern Nigeria, some children are to be found fighting for a pro-government self-defense militia called the Civilian Joint Task Force (CJTF) in the fight against the Nigerian terrorist group Boko Haram. In *The Child Soldiers Fighting Boko Haram*, Philip Obaji Jr. shares how high ranking CJTF members concede that children comprise nearly 25% of the forces fighting the terrorist group. Given the size of size of these forces this equates to approximately 2,500 child soldiers. Obaji Jr. further shares the sentiments of a senior member of the CJTF who attempts to justify the use of child soldiers on a numerical basis. Boko Haram fighters have numerical superiority and in response child soldiers have been used to bulk up CJTF forces, this senior member declares.[19] It is widely accepted children should not be participants in military conflicts and states now have legal obligations to ensure children are protected. To this end the United Nations has adopted the *Optional Protocol to the Convention on the Rights of the Child on the Involvement of Children in Armed Conflict*.

Technological advancement in an industry also brings with it the prospect that opportunities for modern slavery might be destroyed through the destruction of labor. Camel racing is a popular activity in the Persian Gulf states. Over the past 20 years camel races have grown in popularity and have done particularly well in the United Arab Emirates, where there are approximately 14,000 racing camels today. The country has 15 racetracks, of which 12 were built during the 1990s to meet the growing interest. The distances of the races vary with some being just 4 kilometers long, while others are an exhausting 10 kilometers long. Races themselves are purported to be chaotic and dangerous, with as many as 70 or more camels partaking in a single race. In the recent past, though perhaps to a lesser extent now, very young boys were used as camel jockeys. These children were, according to information provided by the city of Dubai, aged between 6 and 7, and weighing around 20 kilograms so as not to impede the progress of the camel.[20]

In 2010, journalist Paul Peachey, writing for Britain's *Independent* newspaper, reported "[y]oungsters had been killed or hurt, suffering head and spinal injuries and damaged genitals."[21] Tellingly, journalist Ron Gluckman wrote of being told by one Western worker how "[y]ou won't see any Arab children out there."[22] The city of Dubai acknowledges that the use of children as jockeys, an essentially dangerous activity for any person let alone a child, eventually led to their being supplied to the industry by human traffickers.[23] The scale of the exploitation is nothing short of staggering. In just this one corner of the globe, in just this one industry, it "was estimated that 15,000 children had been taken from the district [of Rahimyar Khan alone, in southern Punjab, Pakistan] to the UAE and Gulf States as camel jockeys."[24] This is only part of the tale though, as other children have been trafficked from other parts of Pakistan, Bangladesh, Mauritania and Sudan.[25]

Some relief from the problem of human trafficking in the sector was achieved by the development in Japan of small light-weight robot jockeys. These robot jockeys are described in *Wired* magazine in 2005 as comprising a computer running the Linux operating system combined with GPS hardware and further hardware to monitor the camel's heart.[26] Another development was the imposition of a ban on the use of very young children. The ban allowed older children, of 15 years of age or older, to continue racing. There is evidence to show that the ban is not always adhered to, primarily because the best jockeys are those who are lightest.[27] In a demonstration of its commitment to the plight of the children exploited as camel jockeys *Wired* magazine revisited the issue in 2015. It found earlier robots were problematic on a variety of technical fronts. Nowadays they have been replaced by more sophisticated and better performing ones.[28] The problem has not been completely eradicated, but it has been remarkably transformed.

Modern slavery is to be found too today where the slavery of old was to be found before. The world's sweet tooth continues to furnish a demand for sugar, and, in places, this is still catered to by slaves. Benin, for example, has experienced the victimization of its children from its northern regions with many recruited by traffickers for work on farms in neighboring countries. Some of these children end up working in the cultivation of cocoa, the ingredient from which chocolate is derived.[29] The industry is worth US$90 billion a year but this does not make it impervious to slavery. Uzbekistan is another example of finding slavery where it was to be found before. The country was rebuked in the *Trafficking in Persons Report* for the exploitation that occurs during the harvesting of its cotton crop.[30] Angola was noted to have exploitative practices in the cultivation of its rice crop.[31]

Where modern slavery is found, the work done by slaves is typical of that carried out in its older forms: it is typically crude in nature;

it is repetitive; and it requires long hours. One commonplace manifestation of human trafficking in various places around the world is the use of victims for the purpose of begging. Aside from the cost to the individual exploited there is virtually no cost to the exploiter. A person can be made to sit in a suitable location with a begging bowl without need of anything else. Indeed, the more desperate their condition the more closely it fulfills the goal of their exploiter. A well-dressed and healthy-looking beggar does not get much sympathy or, more importantly for the trafficker, much money. The *Trafficking in Persons Report* gives the tale of Shanti, a 10-year-old girl, from Ajmer, Rajasthan, who was trafficked, along with seven other children, to New Dehli when she was just seven years old. The State Department's account says she was:

> ... forced to beg from eight in the morning until 11 in the evening, to tear her clothes and to avoid bathing for months. She was given only one meal a day so that she would look thin and malnourished and elicit more money from the passers-by. She and 12 other children showing signs of physical abuse were rescued in a raid. The children had been beaten and were given a kind of tobacco named 'gul' to numb their senses while experiencing harsh conditions.[32]

The report also expressed its concern over "an increasing problem of Albanian children, often of the Roma ethnicity, being subjected to forced begging and other forms of compelled labor in Greece, Kosovo, and within Albania."[33] The practice has led many jurisdictions to look at begging, especially that carried out by children, with a very different perspective. One need not be a child, though, to be forced to beg. La Strada International, for example, reports that its Polish office has encountered "a number of cases of Moldavian women forced into begging in Poland."[34] In another case police arrested four people in the Italian city of Bergamo for using force on an elderly man to get him to beg and for punishing the man if he didn't meet his daily quota.[35]

Even the most trivial of things can contribute to slavery. Mica is a mineral whose name is unfamiliar to most, though tens of thousands of children in India toil in the unrelenting work of mining it from the earth. The world's largest deposits of mica are found in the Indian state of Jharkhand. Reporters Ben Doherty and Sarah Whyte record the plight of 12-year-old Mohammed Salim Ansari, a child laborer, who mines about 10 kilograms of mica each day, which pays him just US$0.40 daily for his efforts. The features of the tale they tell in their report are predictable. They record, for instance, that the mineral is "in demand from all corners of the globe."[36] The work is described as "hard and dangerous."[37] Furthermore the children "risk snake and scorpion bites, and the hollowed-out caves they mine in often collapse. They suffer cuts and skin infections, as well as respiratory illnesses, such as bronchitis, silicosis and asthma."[38] The industry, they say, is "dependent on a huge unskilled workforce, forced into working for lower and lower prices."[39] Business is good, all the same, despite low prices, perhaps even because of them. Their report contrasts the small with the large, the tale of the individual with that of the international trade that supports it. India officially exports 15,000 metric tonnes (over 16,500 U.S. tons) of mica in crude form each year, Doherty and Whyte note. However, in the year 2011 to 2012 India exported nearly nine times this figure, more than 130,000 metric tonnes (over 143,000 U.S. tons), with most of it going to China, they claim. There are many applications for mica, but in testament to the fact that slavery often exists right before one's face, one is particularly ironic. Mica is a common ingredient in cosmetics as it gives them their luster, being used to produce the sparkles that appear in some of them. The price paid for these luxuries is a far cry from the price paid to Salim, and many like him, for their daily bread. Those who purchase these products know little more about their origin, than those who mine them know about their destination. Doherty and Whyte find how "[t]hose who work at the mine are unaware of where their product ultimately ends up, and those who buy the mica are willfully blind to where it comes from."[40] The reporters disclose how two decades ago the government sought to shut down mines across the state of Jharkhand as part of an initiative to better regulate the mining of mica. They disclose too how these efforts "have driven child labor further, literally and metaphorically, underground."[41]

Slavery today is big business. It has become customary to point out how the market in human trafficking is estimated to yield US$32 billion annually, though this figure is now quite old, making this market the third largest criminal industry today, behind the illegal trades in weapons and narcotics. More recently it has been asserted human trafficking yields profits many more times this figure annually.[42] The *Global Slavery Index* of 2014 identifies India, China, Pakistan, Uzbekistan and Russia as countries where 61% of today's slaves reside.[43] The United Nations' *Global Report on Trafficking in Persons 2014* discloses victims of human trafficking have originated from 152 countries and have been found in 124 countries across the world. The burden of human trafficking falls hardest upon women, and thereafter upon children. Between them they account for 82% of all victims detected, of whom 49% are women, and 33% are children, of whom 21% are girls. Regionally, among victims detected, sexual exploitation accounts for most of those victimized in the Americas, Europe, Central Asia, Africa, and the Middle East. Only in East Asia, South Asia, and in the Pacific is the picture different, where forced labor accounts for 64% of victimization. While most of those convicted for trafficking offenses are men, women also play a role, accounting for 28% of convicts. Most of those convicted (64%) are nationals of the country in which their conviction has been secured.[44] The United Nations report also notes how, though most countries now legislate against human trafficking, the few who do not, or the few who legislate only partially, leaving some victims not covered or some forms of exploitation not covered by law, nonetheless account for 2 billion persons globally.[45] Though the figures give some appreciation for the scale of the suffering inflicted by traffickers, the depth of the suffering endured by the afflicted is beyond measurement.

The 2014 *Trafficking in Persons Report* describes the United States as a Tier 1 country, adding that it "is a source, transit, and destination country for men, women, and children – both U.S. citizens and foreign nationals – subjected to sex trafficking and forced labor, including domestic servitude. Trafficking can occur in both legal and illicit industries or [in] markets."[46] According to the Department of Homeland Security's *Blue Campaign* at least 100,000, and as many as 300,000, children in the United States are at risk of being trafficked for commercial sexual exploitation in the United States. Polaris (formerly Polaris Project), a nonprofit, non-governmental organization based in Washington D.C., provides a map of communiques received during 2014 relating to human trafficking.[47] It immediately evokes Lincoln's map showing the distribution of slaves in the South.[48] Both show hotspots, particularly along coastal areas and in areas where the major cities exist. One must be cautious, however, in reaching conclusions. Lincoln's map was based on figures obtained from the *Census* of 1860. Polaris' map is based on data from several sources, obtained by various means. While Lincoln's map purported to show the entire landscape of the situation on the ground, the Polaris map shows only what was reported to it. Perhaps the factor that is most striking between the two, however, is how slavery is no longer a phenomenon confined to the South.

Polaris' map is a reminder too how slavery is not a homogenous entity. For instance, not all modern-slavery's forms are motivated by money. The plight of sex slaves, for example, is a case in point. Forced marriage is another. The United Nations' *Supplementary Convention on the Abolition of Slavery, the Slave Trade, and Institutions and Practices Similar to Slavery* specifically addresses this form of abuse. It commits parties to its *Convention* to end practices where an inducement, of any kind, is accepted by a third party and where, in accepting the inducement, a woman is forced to marry against her will. It prohibits practices enabling marriage to be used as a property right, which in turn enable a husband to transfer his wife to another person. It prohibits other practices too, such as the treatment of widows as though they were merely part of their late husband's inheritance.[49] Often those who are forced to marry are mere children. The United Nations' Office of the High Commissioner for Human Rights provides the tale of Helen, a 15-year-old Sudanese girl married to a 50-year-old man. The office reports how girls of Helen's age "and younger are five times more likely to die in childbirth than" women in their twenties.[50] The scale of the problem is immense, with the U.N. reporting how, in the developing world, a staggering one in seven girls is a child bride before her 15th birthday.[51] The problem, it says, is global, though it is more frequent in Asia and Africa. It recounts how, aside from death through childbirth, these child brides are exposed to domestic violence, to HIV / AIDS, and to a life of poverty.

In some instances, the origins of the problems are man-made. In an article entitled *Bare branches, redundant males*, the *Economist* magazine observes how years of sex-selective abortions have favored males over females. Haryana, one of India's richest states, has the country's most distorted gender ratios with 114 males of all age groups for every 100 females. Sex-selective abortions are common in India. They are popular in China too, where the country's recently ended one-child policy, and the cultural tendency to favor males over females, have produced problems of their own, with 116 male births for every 100 female births during 2010 to 2015. In India, the figure was 111 male births to 100 female births for the country overall during the same period. Citing figures from the United Nations, the *Economist* declares some 109 million girls and women to be missing when the populations of India and China are combined. They are missing, it says, because had sex-selection not been permitted in India and China, the natural ratio, which also favors males, of 105 male births to 100 female births would be the case. Other factors, such as decisions not to have children, or to have fewer of them and reduced rates of fertility, contribute to the imbalance. In India alone, even if the ratio of male to female births "were to return to normal and stay there, by 2050 the country would still have 30% more single men hoping to marry than single women."[52] From the male perspective there will be fewer choices, and perhaps even none, in finding a wife. The female perspective is different as at the peak of this imbalance, in China during 2050 to 2054, for every 100 women seeking a husband there may be as many as 186 men seeking a wife. In India, the peak is projected to occur 10 years later when there may be as many as 191 men for every 100 women. *The Economist* notes how, aside from the profound social problems these trends present, "abduction of women for sale as brides is becoming more common."[53]

One would think the macabre practice of human sacrifice had been consigned to history. It is not an occurrence one would associate with slavery and, like witchcraft, it likely is not a topic one would expect to find mentioned in the *Trafficking in Persons Report*. Yet, as recently as 2013 India's western state of Maharashtra introduced legislation against human sacrifice.[54] Among the articles of the *Maharashtra Prevention and Eradication of Human Sacrifice and other Inhuman, Evil and Aghori Practices and Black Magic Act* are some that prohibit the promotion and the practice of human sacrifice. Information on the extent of the problem in India is hard to find. Even when prospective cases are found there is sometimes an alternative explanation. All the same there have been some compelling cases. In 2003 it was claimed 25 people had been murdered as part of human sacrificial rites over a six-month period in India's northern state of Uttar Pradesh.[55] That same year a married Indian couple resorted to sacrificing 6-year-old Monu Kumar, a child they had kidnapped from their neighborhood, when they could not have a child of their own.[56] In 2010 Indian police arrested three men following the discovery of a decapitated body of a man in the Birbhum district of West Bengal, about 200 kilometers from the state capital Kolkata. The body had been dismembered and its parts found near a part of the temple dedicated to Kali, the Hindu goddess of power. The head was found smeared with red pigment and surrounded by flowers and sticks of incense.[57] In 2012 two men were arrested in central India for allegedly murdering a 7-year-old girl before they cut out her liver as part of a ritual to deliver a better harvest. Both reportedly confessed to the crime.[58] In 2013 *The Times of India* reported a court in the state of Chhattisgarh had sentenced a witchdoctor to death for beheading an 11-year-old boy as part of a sacrificial rite intended to improve the witchdoctor's good fortune.[59]

In the Americas the cult of Santa Muerte, which translates as *Holy Death* or *Saint Death*, is linked to human sacrifice. The central character of this cult is female, sometimes referred to as *La Dama Poderosa*, which translates as *The Powerful Lady*. Her worshippers portray her as a skeletal figure wearing long robes. In some depictions she is carrying a scythe; in others she carries a scythe in one hand and a globe in the other. Her depiction is not unlike the Western representation of the *Grim Reaper*, whose origins may be found in the Greek mythology as Charon the ferryman who carried the dead souls to the underworld. It is appropriate that she should have so close a relationship with the underworld, as the violence fueled by Mexican drug cartels is linked to her ascendency. She has other associations too and is worshipped as a patron of outcasts. Some of her followers are hardened criminals closely associated with the drugs cartels, and some of them are willing to make sacrifices to gain the favor, and the protection, of Santa Muerte.

In an article entitled *Santa Muerte: Inspired and Ritualistic Killings* serialized in the FBI Law Enforcement Bulletin, Dr. Robert J. Bunker says how though the number of such killings has been few, especially when compared against the backdrop of violence inflicted by the cartels and gangs on Mexican society, it has been sufficient to draw attention to the practice and to be a cause for concern.[60] Some of the victims have been adults, including members of one cartel sacrificed by another. Others have had no association with criminality. Children and even infants have been among the victims murdered in the name of Santa Muerte.[61] Items, including small shrines, found at the crime scenes of these murders indicate they are linked to the cult. "Law enforcement professionals who encounter Santa Muerte artifacts and related narcotics cult paraphernalia at crime scenes should not dismiss them hastily," Dr. Bunker warns.[62] Not all these sacrifices have occurred south of the border with the United States. Dr. Bunker believes the earliest such killings to be identified in the United States relate to the events of 2005 and 2006 in south Texas during which time a member of a Mexican drugs cartel engaged in several homicides. This cartel member subsequently boasted to another acquaintance, in a telephone call intercepted by agents of the U.S. Drug Enforcement Agency (DEA), that having killed his victims he gathered their blood in a vessel and toasted Santa Muerte.[63]

Even when slavery is economically motivated, some of it is cost-reducing rather than profit-making.[64] The household has become a place, as it was before, where slavery may be conducted. Today its occurrences there are usually referred to as *domestic servitude*. Surprisingly, the foreign diplomats of several countries have been identified as potential perpetrators of this form of exploitation. In November of 2014, an Irish labor tribunal awarded €80,000 ($88,000) each to three staff members of the United Arab Emirates ambassador in Ireland. The three worked as many as 15 hours per day, seven days a week, and were effectively each paid less than €2 ($2.20) per hour.[65] Only a few months earlier, in March, the South African *chargé d'affaires* in Ireland was posted to another country after a former employee claimed to have worked 17-hour days, and to have been paid only €1.66 ($1.82) per hour.[66] As a consequence, there have been calls in several jurisdictions for a review of diplomatic immunity to ensure it affords no protection where slavery is concerned. Such is the extent of the association between some diplomatic corps and practices of domestic servitude that the United States has addressed the matter as part of its collection of legislative measures against slavery.[67]

Many of the world's slaves today are in a situation of *debt bondage*, a situation also known as *bonded labor*. A loan, sometimes of a seemingly trivial amount for those in the Western world, may have been obtained, and the laborer has agreed to work until it has been paid in full. The problem with the arrangement is that, for some, the owner of the loan may never count the debt as repaid no matter how much work is done and, for others, the debt is handed down from generation to generation, as an inheritance that enslaves one generation after the next. Some, however, are paid a wage and, through their work, they may eventually escape.

Scorn should be poured nonetheless on the notion of *slave wages*. Enslavement cannot be understood by the wages the slave is paid, or not paid. One's status as a slave is not diminished by improvements in wages, any more than it is increased by a deterioration in wages. Money may provide the motivation for slavery, but it is the use of violence in the form of force, deception or coercion that makes one a slave, and maintains one's enslavement. In 2014 the *Trafficking in Persons Report* asserted:

> The forced labor of an estimated 20 to 65 million citizens constitutes India's largest trafficking problem; men, women, and children in debt bondage – sometimes inherited from previous generations – are forced to work in industries such as brick kilns, rice mills, agriculture, and embroidery factories. A common characteristic of bonded labor is the use of physical and sexual violence as coercive means. ... Trafficking victims in India at times are injured or killed by their traffickers; for example, a labor contractor in the State of Odisha chopped off the hands of two bonded labor victims in 2013.[68]

Irrespective of the contractual details of these arrangements they are entirely illegal. The *Palermo Protocol* requires debt bondage to be criminalized.[69] Millions of people, particularly in South Asia, are enslaved using this form of slavery. In fact, bonded labor is the world's most common form of slavery. Its prevalence attests to just how simply one can be enslaved.

In an article entitled *Why India's Brick Kiln Workers 'Live like Slaves'*, the BBC's Humphrey Hawksley reports the scene before him as like something out of ancient times. Lines of women and men stride up and down steps in single file. Doubtless the nature of this work has not changed much over eons. The work is difficult, Hawksley is told by one of those at the scene.[70] There is plenty to be done, and there must be ample demand, with 1,500 bricks being made each day. Already one can see how bricks and the process of their production present many of the characteristics one associates with slavery. In *Labour in Brick Kilns: A Case Study in Chennai* Guérin *et al.* say how the production of bricks in these operations is based on three characteristics. First, they say the work involves virtually no capital investment. This is consistent with what Hawksley observes as it seems as though there is no investment of any kind, but then again that would be consistent with an economics of slavery that invests almost nothing while extracting everything. Hawksley notes the absence of any safety equipment at the scene. He also notes how there are significant commonplace workplace issues including the withholding of wages and stories of worker sickness.[71] In fact, in their study of brick kilns in the city of Chennai in the Indian state of Tamil Nadu, Guérin et al. see how, even when a little investment is supplied, it is often the workers who supply it. Tools, for example, usually consisting of molds, are provided by the workers. Even the carts to move the bricks are supplied by the workers, who finance them through loans. Having avoided some of the costs of the operation of the business, the real costs to the owners come by way of labor, which Guérin et al. say accounts for between 45% and 60% of the total annual cost of the operation.[72] Second and third, they say the work is "continuous and cyclic" and that, once commenced, it "does not tolerate any halt."[73] Conditions are hard and the working day is anywhere from 12 to 16 hours.[74] Any cessation during the period of operation represents a heavy loss to workers. Only during the rainy season, from about August to December, are operations concluded, but always in the confidence they will resume, in the same way, when it too comes to an end. Undoubtedly the facts Guérin et al. obtain from their exploration of brick kilns at this corner of India are equally true of other operations across the country and beyond.

According to information from India's Central Pollution Control Board an estimated 140,000 brick kilns produce anything from 240 to 260 billion bricks annually. It is a staggering figure, one which has been growing by 5 to 10 per cent annually, and one which equates to the production of 200 bricks per annum for every man, woman and child in India. To accomplish this feat hungry kilns consume, every year, 500 million cubic meters of clay and fuel equivalent to 35 to 40 million tonnes (39 to 44 million U.S. tons) of coal. At the same time the kilns spew out 66 million tonnes (73 million U.S. tons) of carbon dioxide gas.[75] Sulphur oxide gases are also produced. The impact on the environment is of grave concern and it is not helped by the fact that many of the kilns burn material inefficiently or by the nature of the material they select to burn as fuel. Nivit Kumar Yadav is a Senior Programme Manager with the Delhi-based advocacy group Centre for Science and Environment (CSE). In an interview with Mr. Yadav he lists the assortment of fuels burned: coal, biomass, heavy fuel oil, agricultural waste, timber and even tyres.[76] "These pollutants coming out are creating a huge environmental problem. The pollutants are not only responsible for degrading air quality but also have an ill effect on the people working in the kiln", he explains.

The process of making bricks involves mixing clay with water, shaping the wetted clay into bricks using molds, drying the bricks using either sunlight or some artificial means, and firing the bricks in the kiln. 99% of the bricks produced in India are made in this way.[77] Clearly the operation is manually intensive. With so many bricks to make and with so much of the process being dependent on manual labor it can hardly be surprising that 9 million people are thought to be employed by the sector.[78] Mr. Yadav points to yet another characteristic of the operation of brick kilns which will appear familiar. "Most of the kilns are operating on leased land and they don't own the land on which they operate (except in few cases). Clay is a major raw material for these kilns and once availability of clay from nearby surrounding is finished the kiln entrepreneurs shift to some other location", he observes.

In contrast to their employees who work long hours, the owners of these kilns are seldom, if ever, present. Instead, the kilns are run by managers employed by the owners. The managers engage the services of brokers to give advance payments to workers who may be locals or as is often the case migrants from other parts of India. Compounding the vulnerability of these internal migrants, is the fact that they commonly belong to groups widely discriminated against in the country. The advance payments, and the debt bondage that comes with them, serve two purposes: they act to lure new employees and they act to impose control over existing ones.[79] The importance of this system of payment, and all that comes with it, is so well understood by the brick kiln owners they claim "without advance, we cannot work."[80] The system proves even more effective at engaging the services of these internal migrant workers who, comparatively poorer than local workers and even more desperate for a source of income, will labor for 20% to 30% less than their local counterparts.[81] Poverty serves other roles too in the plight of these migrants. It serves to keep them from departing. In contrast, local laborers will not work under the system of advance payment. Consequently, their work is not bonded labor.

Figure: A 9 year-old bonded child laborer molding bricks at a kiln in Orissa, India. The bricks in the background represent one day's work. © U.R. Romano

Poverty plays other roles too. Unlike the ever-absent owners of these kilns, the full attention of every laborer must be put to the task at hand. Without time for childcare, or the means to source it elsewhere, laborers are compelled to bring their children to work with them. UNICEF India reports how girls and boys are used to knead the mix by standing in the combination of clay, straw, ash, coal dust, and water. Children are used too in the transportation of molds to the baking centers and in the drying of bricks under the sun. The owners of the kilns disavow any responsibility, claiming there is little they can do if the parents of these children choose to engage their children in the kiln's work.[82] It is all against the law, the BBC's Hawksley is told by a labor activist working for a human rights group. India has instituted a series of laws over many years to prohibit this kind of abuse. Some of those laws encompass issues of labor and of slave labor. Others prohibit the exploitation of children. It happens nonetheless.[83] Not all that is law is practice.

Guérin *et al.* observe how in Chennai a subsistence allowance is paid to the bonded laborers weekly, but only during the period of operation, and how even this is dependent on the quotas attained in production.[84] Their figures collected from 2003 to 2004 show, for example, the payment of 40 Rupees ($0.64) to molders for every 1,000 bricks molded. The remuneration given to laborers, based on a survey of some 246 surveyed, averaged at 108 Rupees ($1.74) per 1,000 bricks molded. Some were paid as much as 130 Rupees ($2.09), while others were paid as little as 79 Rupees ($1.27) for the same output. Honesty is itself a problem, for many of the laborers are illiterate and thus poorly equipped to keep count of the actual work they have performed. Even for Guérin *et al.* calculating the state of a given laborer's account proved to be a challenge, and their assessment was dependent on the financial accounts provided to them by the kiln's manager.

There is more, for the kiln owners impose deductions, either in the form of 50 bricks per 1,000 produced, or as a weekly deduction of 500 bricks, upon the bonded migrant workers claiming this covers the loss of damaged bricks. The workers, 90% of whom are from the lower castes of India's class system in the case of the kiln's molders, "are convinced that it is really a form of concealed interest" on the money advanced to them.[85] These things considered, if modern slave laborers are less profitable than their free laboring counterparts when it comes to the production of bricks, why would it be that brokers employ a higher proportion of slaves, in the form of migrant bonded laborers, than they do free local laborers? Why even would they claim their businesses cannot operate without the system of advance payments that promotes slavery? One can see from this instance how modern slavery, like the slavery of old, cannot be destroyed by bringing it into competition with free labor. The two are different things. When it comes to the laborers themselves, free laborers and slave laborers, the two work side-by-side in this instance, and it is the bonded laborers who represent the greatest proportion.

The sector is subject to regulation, but as Mr. Yadav points out 50 *per cent* of the kilns are thought to be illegal operations. Lax monitoring is part of the problem, but the sheer scale of the task is certainly also a contributor. Often the authorities don't have enough inspectors to fulfil all that is expected of them. "This makes inspecting such a large number of small-scale units a daunting task", he reflects. One survey carried out by his organization, the CSE, found that more than 20 kilns in Ghaziabad, Noida and Jhajjar had never been inspected. The CSE's research also found that the states where most of the kilns are located, are the very ones with the severest shortage of inspectors.

There is much contrast between the place where these bricks are produced and the place where they will eventually be employed. The bricks are to be used, Hawksley realizes, to build factories, call centers, and offices at the very heart of India's economic miracle and to be used by multi-national companies of renown.[86] Yet, it is this same miracle that is driving the demand for bricks. With these things considered, namely the combination of the advantage bestowed upon the business through its use of slave labor and the high demand for bricks, one might presume the business of producing bricks must be a profitable one. However, while it may be true to conclude slavery is the more profitable option when it can be employed, the business itself may not be profitable. High demand does not necessarily equate to a high price. Added to this the item being traded is merely a commodity item. Buyers can pick and choose from a variety of producers. As a result, prices are kept low and there is strong competition to win business. By 2007 over-production in Chennai, and an accompanying collapse in prices, reduced profits from 10% to 25% in the 1990s, to below 10% from the decade leading up to 2007. Some brick kiln owners claim they are operating at a loss, as is likely the case, with many actually heavily indebted themselves.[87] Perhaps it is unsurprising then how in one report by the United Nations' International Labour Organisation (ILO), this time on brick kilns in Afghanistan, it is asserted that "[u]nderstanding the low profit margins of the brick industry is essential for understanding why this sector relies so heavily on the use of bonded labour."[88] Increases in the demand for bricks, driven by the country's economic success, not only increases the demand for brick kilns but the demand for bonded laborers.

India, and indeed Afghanistan, are not alone in the exploitative practices that occur in the manufacture of bricks. In neighboring Pakistan the industry appears again as a place where workers are exploited as slaves. Nor indeed is the manufacture of bricks the only place where these practices are to be found in India, or in other countries of the region. The weaving of carpets is an activity one often finds mentioned in reports on slavery.

Some of India's workers may be willing to accept advance payments in the hope of faring well in the country's brick kilns. There are other jobs whose costs, however, transcend reward. Being a victim of human sacrifice is the kind of work persons are unwilling to undertake at any price, that is, if given the choice. The practice features once more, this time as one underpinned by economic motives. A day after India's Maharashtra district passed the *Maharashtra Prevention and Eradication of Human Sacrifice and other Inhuman, Evil and Aghori Practices and Black Magic Act*, human sacrifice was carried out in another district. Kalavati Gupta, a 50-year-old woman, was lured to a place where she was beheaded by an Indian tantrik and several accomplices. The tantrik reportedly later confessed to the crime and to having committed another such sacrifice in the past. It was perpetrated to grant prosperity, wealth, and health upon his visitors, who were also the accomplices to his crime.[89]

In 2010 the *Trafficking in Persons Report* stated how, in the year since its last report, Ugandan police had "investigated hundreds of reports of human sacrifice, many involving forced removal of body parts, and confirmed the validity of 29 cases, 15 of which involved the victimization of children."[90] None of these cases ended in prosecutions. The country's Ministry of Internal Affairs ascribed human sacrifice to the fate that befell 12 victims during 2013. Ten of these victims were children. Ten suspects were arrested, with seven going to trial, resulting in only one conviction and a sentence of 10 years' imprisonment.[91] In 2010 the Ugandan chapter of the African Network for the Prevention and Protection against Child Abuse and Neglect (ANPPCAN), expressed its concerns that periods when elections or festivities are imminent are times when children are at risk of being neglected by parents. They are also times, ANPPCAN states, when traffickers may seize children in the country and use them for human sacrifice.[92] In 2015 reporters from Reuters' Tanzanian bureau noted claims of a link between human sacrifice and elections, but this time for an altogether different purpose. It was claimed that politicians engaged the services of witchdoctors to undertake human sacrifices in rites intended to ensure them a successful outcome to the election.[93]

Albinism, a genetic condition, manifests itself through the absence of pigment in the skin, hair, and eyes. Thus, albinos have a remarkable whiteness of each. It is a difference that sets albinos apart from others in their communities. Globally it occurs at a rate of about one person in every 20,000. In Tanzania instances of albinism are much higher, with rates of occurrence running at about one in every 1,429 people. For albinos in Tanzania and some of its surrounding countries, especially those of Burundi and Malawi, this difference can be fatal. Some believe albinos have supernatural powers, and consequently that these powers can be harnessed by obtaining potions and charms made from the body parts of albinos. In all, 75 albinos are thought to have been murdered in Tanzania during the period 2000 to 2015, though the actual figure is likely higher.[94]

Typically, there are three parties to these crimes. They are the witchdoctor, the client, and the victim. Some clients, in this case, are motivated by the pursuit of money and the belief witchcraft rites involving human sacrifice can bring them fortune. Some engage in it for non-economic reasons. Others believe human sacrifice will protect their worldly belongings from misfortune.[95] Some witchdoctors are willing to accommodate these clients, and to charge a fee for the service rendered. One former witchdoctor in Uganda, who now works to end these deeds, confessed to sacrificing 70 people, including his own son.[96] Such is the seriousness of the problem Uganda has a governmental task force, the Ugandan Anti-Human Sacrifice Taskforce, dedicated to the eradication of sacrifices. In recent years the task force has expressed the belief instances of human sacrifice are on the increase, and expressed concern for some of the children missing in the country, who it believes may have fallen victim to sacrificial rites.[97] There is belief too that the worsening of the problem coincides with improved economic prosperity in the country.[98] A report by Uganda's Human Rights Commission on research it conducted within eight districts of the country, during 2010 and 2011, found children, women and the elderly were the most at risk. It found too how human sacrifice is not confined to Uganda, but that it still occurs across continental Africa.[99] The report noted the opinion of some that the sacrificing of children had in effect become a commercial activity.[100]

Of the situation in Tanzania and the plight of its albino population, a United Nations human rights spokesman told a press conference in Geneva: "This is an incredibly vulnerable population in these countries. And when you hear these kind of details of gangs of men roaming around, literally hunting down people with albinism, simply to make money by cutting off their limbs and killing them, you must question whether enough is being done."[101] If one is left wondering what the price of life is in such instances, this too can be answered, as it is claimed witchdoctors "will pay as much as $75,000 for a full set of albino body parts."[102] Societies that conduct these forms of human sacrifice are not the only ones willing to pay handsomely for body parts or indeed to sacrifice a life, if needs be, in order to obtain them.

Among the greatest advances of modern medicine are those allowing organs and tissues to be transplanted. While most of these developments have occurred over the past several decades, some have their origins in ancient times. The text *Sushruta Samhita* was written by Sushruta around the 6th century B.C., a time when offenders were sometimes punished by amputation of the nose. Among the many medical issues addressed there are surgical methods for dealing with skin grafts. Using this procedure ancient clinicians were able to make further advances, including a surgical method for rhinoplasty (reconstruction of the nose). The surgical procedures described in the *Sushruta Samhita* for grafting and rhinoplasty form the basis for modern procedure, and so the text's author, Sushruta, is considered worthy of the crown of "Father of Plastic Surgery."[103]

Today, the factors making restorative surgery necessary are different to those that drove Sushrata. High blood pressure and diabetes, both of which can be caused by genetic conditions, are two of the most common causes of chronic kidney disease (CKD). The damage caused to the kidneys by CKD may ultimately be irreparable, and eventually that damage may lead to their complete failure. Equally high blood pressure is just one of the factors that may affect the operation of the heart, and which may also lead to its demise. Diabetes features again the reasons why the pancreas sometimes fails.[104] Smoking and chronic bronchitis compromise the operation of the lungs, leading to chronic obstructive pulmonary disease (COPD) and rendering them increasingly ineffective. Hepatitis C, primary biliary cirrhosis (PBC), and the consumption of alcohol have a similar effect on the liver.

In 1933 Soviet surgeon Yurii Voroney completed the first human-to-human kidney transplantation. It would take many years, however, before further advances in medical science would allow the procedure to be made viable. In 1963 Thomas E. Starzl, working at the University of Colorado Medical School, completed the first liver transplant. This time four more years were required before the procedure could be made viable. Also in 1963, James D. Hardy working in the United States, this time at the University of Mississippi Medical Centre at Jackson, completed the first transplantation of a lung. The passage of some 20 more years would be required before this procedure could be completed reliably. In 1967 it was the turn of the heart, and it was South Africa's Christiaan Barnard who completed the world's first human-to-human heart transplant. Today, in addition to the kidneys, liver, lungs and heart, modern medicine holds within its grasp the capacity to transplant the pancreas, intestine and thymus. This last organ, the thymus, is situated in front of the heart and is responsible for the production of T cells, part of the body's immune system. In addition to organs, tissues can be transplanted, including bones, tendons, cornea, heart valves, nerves, veins and even skin. Over the years other great strides have been made to refine the procedures these clinicians pioneered and to improve upon the immuno-suppressant drugs so vital to their success.

Many countries around the world now have long-established legitimate medical programs for organ donation. Usually these programs are altruistic in nature, with no money exchanging hands in return for the organs donated, and for good reason. In the United States the *National Organ Transplant Act* of 1984 (NOTA) strictly prohibits the purchase or sale of human organs. When one considers the relatively short time that these procedures have been available to medical science and the relatively long time that NOTA has been around, it is astounding to see just how quickly government perceived these advances could afford opportunities for abuse. Kidneys, for example, appear to top the list. There is extensive demand for them, and most human beings are born with two but perfectly capable of living with just one. The liver too is much in demand and, although human beings have one liver, it can be split allowing donors to be alive when the donation is made.

Every great medical advancement should be welcome, but each development brings with it aspects both positive and negative. The supply for organs and tissues has never been able to keep abreast of demand. Some 114,000 transplants are estimated to take place around the world each year and yet, despite their number, they are thought to account for only 10% of the actual need.[105] Bridging this gap are the human traffickers, who act as brokers between the demand and a potential supply. Experts from the World Health Organization (WHO) estimate the "illegal trade in kidneys has risen to such a level that an estimated 10,000 black market operations involving purchased human organs now take place annually, or more than one an hour."[106]

In *Transnational Crime In The Developing World*, Haken observes how organ traffickers function in the abyss between the world's impoverished and its most wealthy. He further observes how an ideal space for criminality is created by brokering between economic inertia and poor policing in one part of the world, and another part that is increasingly globalized and enabled by technological improvements in communications.[107] The sentiment is echoed by anthropologist Nancy Scheper-Hughes who says "exchanges tend to be poor-to-rich."[108] She goes further, likening these market transactions to "neo-cannibalism" and denouncing the perspective people "can eye each other greedily as a source of spare body parts."[109] Yet this is exactly what human traffickers do. Alongside the legitimate altruistic and ethical supply of organs there is a black-market catering to those who cannot secure them legitimately, but who would pay for them given the opportunity.

An industry of transplant tourism has grown up on demand of some, who need a transplant, to travel to Third World countries, where First World wealth can be leveraged against Third World poverty. The realpolitik principles of the Melian Dialogue's narrative on international relations remain intact despite the passage of some 2,500 years. In *The History of the Peloponnesian War*, Thucydides captured for the principles for the first time. In a forthright manner the Athenians ominously advised the Melians:

> ... we shall not trouble you with specious pretences ... since you know as well as we do that right, as the world goes, is only in question between equals in power, while the strong do what they can and the weak suffer what they must.[110]

One WHO bulletin noted the emergence on the Internet of transplant packages, ranging in price from US$70,000 to US$160,000.[111] China, it is alleged, conducted 12,000 liver and kidney transplants in 2005, with most of the organs being sourced from executed prisoners and priority given to foreign recipients willing to pay.[112] This represents an obvious conflict of interest, one that has brought international scorn upon the country. In late 2014 the country's state media announced China was bringing the practice to an end.

The prices charged by traffickers, and the price they pay to donors, appears to vary considerably depending on the source referenced. One source notes how a kidney buyer in the United States can expect to pay US$120,000, while the donor on average receives just US$5,000. The same source advises how a liver donor in China will receive, if she or he is fortunate to receive anything at all, US$3,660 for part of their organ, while the buyer can expect to pay US$21,900.[113]

Many stories abound concerning how this illicit industry functions. Inevitably some of the stories leave more questions than they answer, as they are both implausible and untrue. Selling one's organs is not human trafficking of itself, however, and clearly some organs are more readily sold than others. That being so, it is a crime in most jurisdictions to sell one's organs. Some find such prohibitions contrary to conceptions of freedom, and yet the only country where one is free to sell an organ is in Iran. Even then, there are limitations, as the transactions are limited to the sale of a kidney. In recent times a small number of other countries have made changes to their laws to permit some financial compensation to be paid to living kidney donors. The process of retrieving organs, whether those of living donors or of deceased persons, is known as *harvesting*.

Tragically organs too are a crop that has become amenable to acts of slavery. The United Nations Global Initiative to Fight Human Trafficking (UN GIFT) describes three common scenarios of how acts of trafficking persons for the removal of their organs occur most often. In the first instance there are those cases where traffickers use deception or force their victims into giving an organ. In the second, informal or formal arrangements are made with a victim who is subsequently either paid less than was agreed or not paid at all. Thirdly, victims are offered treatment for a medical condition which may or may not exist. During this supposed treatment an organ is removed without their knowledge. Traffickers target vulnerable persons such as homeless individuals, migrant workers and those who are illiterate.[114]

Information on the extent of the trade is scant. One estimate, which could not locate sufficient information on illegal transplantations of the pancreas, heart or lungs ensuring it was conservatively made, nonetheless put the value of the trade at between US$600 million and US$1.2 billion annually.[115]

Even before the earthquake of 2015 laid waste to Nepal, killing thousands of its residents, human traffickers were making a killing of their own exploiting Nepalese citizens. CNN's *Freedom Project* reported the tale of Nawaraj Pariyar.[116] Some years earlier Pariyar was working on a construction site in the country's capital of Katmandu when he was approached by the foreman with the offer of cash in return for some of his flesh. Poor and uneducated, Pariyar was sufficiently desperate to accept and suitably ill-informed to decline. He was brought to a hospital in nearby India where he was told to advise doctors he was related to the person who would be the beneficiary of the surgery. He later learned how a kidney had been removed. He received US$300, just 1% of what he had been promised. Today he lives with the repercussions of the surgery, suffering from urinary problems and ever-present severe back pain. Pariyar's tale is just one of many. The poverty of the exploited and their proximity to others who can exploit them are identified locally as reasons why these people are exploited. One can understand then how, when the earthquake struck, many were added to the ranks of the desperate, swelling the numbers of those who could be exploited for their organs. This was not the only reason for exploitation, however, as human traffickers, who had already been preying upon Nepal's women and children, carried many more away to markets of an altogether different kind.

The *Declaration of Istanbul on Organ Trafficking and Transplant Tourism* defines *organ trafficking* in similar terms to human trafficking. It also defines *transplant commercialism*, which it declares to be the commodification of human organs.[117] By including the commercialism of human body parts it recognizes how, when human beings are commodified, it may truly be said a person can become worth less than the sum of their parts. The opportunity for monetary gain is the reason motivating human traffickers to supply a market hungry for human organs. That being so, traffickers can supply an entire human too if that is the nature of the demand, as those who have lost infants to baby traffickers know all-too-well.

These are only some of the varieties of modern slavery. It is by no means an exhaustive list. People are trafficked too, for example, to work as strippers or in the cyber-sex industry. There is evidence indicating human traffickers exploit individuals as *drug mules*, as trans-national carriers of illicit narcotics, because the risk and the penalty of being caught are both high, so why risk it oneself? There is evidence too of how human traffickers sometimes coerce individuals to work in *grow houses*, or in other even larger facilities, where illicitly grown cannabis or marijuana is cultivated, for the same reason. The practice of commercial surrogacy is increasingly under scrutiny. *Sham marriages*, where one person marries another to circumvent immigration requirements, are themselves under scrutiny as events where human trafficking may be employed. The United Nations Special Rapporteur on Human Rights in North Korea has pointed to that country's exploitation of its citizenry in conditions of *forced labor.* Slavery is to be found in the most surprising and yet in the most ordinary of places amidst the most mundane of activities, even it seems, in the picking of earthworms.[118] The tale this narrative conveys is a global one. Within even at the Earth's tiniest corners there exists suffering of immense depth and enormity, all attributable to slavery. The way in which it manifests itself may be different from place-to-place, its practitioners can have different reasons for exploiting it, and it may take different forms, but the practice is the same. What is important is, no matter what forms slavery takes its forms are all part of the same thing and they are driven by a demand for them.

All of slavery's accoutrements of old are to be found in the modern slave trade. There is no one tale of how they are used, in which order, or any one tale that uses them all, but many of the tales concerning the operating methods share common traits. At the outset human traffickers ensnare their prey by a variety of means. Only the brutish employ the more overt forms of restraint, such as kidnapping or, heaven forbid, chains. The accomplished use methods that attract little attention, such as deception, causing little bother to themselves, while facilitating the greatest number of recruits. The simple offer of a job abroad, or at a place nearby, is sufficient for many. This is always welcome news to the impoverished and the persecuted. It is enough even for them to voluntarily take the first steps towards slavery. To their role of *bringer of good news* the skilled trafficker adds another, that of *benefactor*. For what good is a golden opportunity far away for those who cannot afford the expense of their travel? By funding, and often by exaggerating, the expense of travel with the expectation of being reimbursed, an impossible feat, a weight heavier than the heaviest chains is heaped upon the shoulders of the hapless.

Added to the methods of old there are some new. Witchcraft, in the form of Juju and Voodoo, is an odd thing to read about in a modern report from so eminent an institution as the U.S. State

Department.[119] Yet it is there to be found, and with good cause, for modern traffickers have found opportunities missed even by the slaveholders of old. According to Nigeria's anti-trafficking agency NAPTIP: 'about 90 per cent of [Nigerian] girls ... trafficked to Europe are taken to shrines'.[120] Implicitly, once in Europe these girls find themselves victims of child sexual exploitation. By twisting cultural and supernatural beliefs they can be turned inwards on themselves, and upon those who subscribe to them. A benefactor can play the role of the virtuous, but the less virtuous his beneficiary, the more noble his patronage. To secure the assurance of his money he may reasonably expect the swearing of a Juju oath. The anticipation of a new life and the prospect of comparative prosperity finds the beneficiary rushing to provide her bond and deceived into sealing her fate. Soon after she will learn there is no escape, not from her debt nor from the oath accompanying it. Fear begins to temper her will. If she is astute the true nature of the scheme will begin to unfold before her, but too late, for every treachery is revealed just as it is being harvested.

Violence soon follows. What enters by the ears diminishes. What passes before the eyes brings fear. What enters by the mouth deprives of the mind, and the deprivations of the mouth rob strength. No indignity is spared. Every torment serves its purpose: the use of degrading language; threats against the self and against family; witnessing violence against fellows; being plied with drugs and alcohol; being starved to the point of weakness; and being abused physically and sexually. Each serves to destroy the person, to deprive one of oneself, and to render one unto slavery. The slave's condition is known only to the slave and to their tormentor. Keen to conceal the true nature of their relationship, the modern slaveholder does not brand flesh, mutilate ears, or break teeth, should he find it necessary to mark his property. In place of all these things he simply tattoos his mark upon the skin. Sometimes even it appears in the form of a tattooed barcode. Those who assess the slave only by what they see experience him not as he or she truly exists. The slave remains a mystery to them, and so too do the bonds of slavery. In *A Stolen Life*, Jaycee Lee Dugard, who was abducted as a child, abused, and enslaved for nearly 20 years, writes, "I am in another kind of prison now. Free to roam ... but still prisoner nonetheless. I feel I am bound to these people —my captors—by invisible bonds instead of constant handcuffs."[121] It is why too she later adds, "I am not really here. I am not an actual person. I am nobody. Nobody sees me."[122]

What does it mean to be a victim of human trafficking? What is its reality? Wendy Barnes is a survivor of human trafficking, and the author of *And Life Continues: Sex Trafficking and My Journey To Freedom*. At 11 years of age, she was sexually abused by her stepfather. Later, when she was 15, she encountered Greg, a young man just one year her senior. Initially their meeting seemed to be a positive development, but this changed in time. When she was 17 she had her first child and, shortly after, Greg trafficked her for sex for the very first time. Over the next 13 years she was sold in Seattle, Portland, and in California's Orange County. In an interview she points to how vulnerable she already was from the outset.[123] "[W]hen a girl has already been though sexual abuse, or any type of abuse, as a child her mind ..., her heart, or her soul, is already broken down," she says. She likens the first abuse to a hammer blow upon a ceramic pot. With the first blow the pot is broken into just a few pieces. If an exploiter should happen to come along in the aftermath, he will find it much easier to exert control through the pre-existing vulnerability. She equates her experience of being trafficking with those already-broken pieces of life now being shattered by yet another hammer blow. "That is what happens to your psyche, to your soul, when a ... [trafficker] gets a hold of you. You're already broken and that brokenness almost … [becomes] normal," she shares.

The similarity between tales of survivors of human trafficking has not escaped Ms. Barnes. In a presentation she once declared: "I hear stories … all the time and I wonder where were they trained because it is so the same … they beat you down to nothing … At that point when … a person beats you down to the point where you don't even feel human anymore, there are no choices."[124] In Ms. Barnes' case one of her greatest aspirations was to be a good mother to her children, and to have a nice house for them to grow up in. These are noble aspirations. They are ones familiar to most. Greg made sure he understood this about Ms. Barnes and, once he did, he saw how he could twist these aspirations, so they became something else entirely, a way of inflicting violence upon her very spirit. "[F]or my punishment, he wouldn't beat me … he would go off and destroy the entire house, he would break the TV, he would throw the Christmas tree out of the kitchen window, he would break the windows, he would break the doors down, … [leaving me] for days looking at this destroyed house, which for me was my only escape into normalcy," she shares. Even more poignantly, she shares her sense of self-worth at that time. "I was only worth the amount of money I could make in a night. … If I tried to leave him I was worthless," she adds.

What stands out in what she describes is the profound level of psychological insight exercised by Greg, and by others who use these methods. "Exactly!" she reacts enthusiastically in bewildered agreement, "That's what I just can't figure out. How on earth did these men get so smart at how to control people?" She wasn't the only one exploited as she recounts, "When this first started, girls would come and go in six months to maybe a year. Then after a few years he would be able to keep them under his control for two to three years, and then by the end he would be able to keep control over girls for five to ten years. Each girl was different and he would have to learn how to control and manipulate and brainwash her into staying, into feeling so useless." Her exploiter was learning. Gradually he was honing his approach and improving upon its efficacy with every lesson learned. She countenances the possibility these lessons were not learned in isolation, that they were shared between groups of people engaged in the same activity.

There are other lessons to be learned, and other similarities to be recognized, this time by wider society. She directs attention to the distinction made today between cases of human trafficking and cases of domestic violence. "Human trafficking today is like domestic violence was 40 years ago … there is the stigma, there is the ignorance, there is the 'we don't know what to do' or 'oh, she must want it because she's not leaving' … We need to figure out what we are going to do about it," she says. It is an interesting observation. Few today fail to recognize the deliberate role violence plays in instances of domestic violence, and yet violence occupies the same role in other spheres too, particularly in cases of slavery, where its significance nonetheless remains obscure. Chains aren't the real tools of slavery. She laments the over-use in the media of illustrations showing chains. It is an approach impoverished in its understanding of what slavery truly entails. "We're not handcuffed. We're not chained up. Our chain is around the brain," she adds.

Greg eventually ended up in jail. Has Ms. Barnes' captivity ended? "Healing is going to be lifelong. Will I ever be whole again? No, I don't think so. Still to this day, [about 16 years later at this time,] if I stay up late at night it freaks me out because nighttime is part of that life. … It is extremely, extremely difficult to put your life back together, and to put your mind back together. You never become what you used to be. You actually have to create a new person, which is what I ended up doing. I created who I wanted to be. … You have to literally remake yourself. The old you has been shattered," she advises. She recounts once, after securing her freedom, being asked what she liked to eat. She responded how she liked fish sticks. It was only after she had given the response that she realized that she didn't like them at all. The preference she had expressed was not hers, but Greg's. The question of what she liked to eat was beyond her capacity to answer. She had no preferences. There was no sense of self that permitted her to have them. Ms. Barnes is upbeat all the same about the course of her life in the intervening years. She points to the many ways her life has been enriched, and to the many sources of happiness now within it.

With its new name, and with many similarities, to what degree is modern slavery just same-old slavery? "The main difference is that it is no longer legal. I don't think that it can be overstated how radically different this concept became after February 1865," Ambassador CdeBaca says. On January 31 1865, the House of Representatives passed the 13th Amendment to the U.S. Constitution, which formally abolished slavery. The next day, on February 1, President Lincoln submitted the proposed amendment to the States. Up until this point, the concept of slavery as a legitimate institution of the state had enjoyed a long, yet dark, history, one that encompassed the legal and economic systems of the United States, Britain, France and Portugal, to name but a few, the Ambassador notes. "The difference between now and the 1800s is that … it is now illegal to hold somebody as a slave, so instead of the government giving you the power to do it, the government is supposed to punish you for trying to do it. That shift is one of the reasons why, from a policy perspective, I'm more likely to say 'modern-day slavery,' because this is slavery in the context of a world in which it is illegal to enslave," he observes. Differences aside, the Ambassador notes of his encounters with victims of this modern slavery, of the statements made by other victims, and of the narratives published by former slaves, that if one overlays these with the narratives of pre-Civil War slavery, one finds "they are eerily similar".

Section 3

Chapter 8:

Grasping The Wolf

Sex trafficking, also known as *forced commercial sexual exploitation*, is one of the world's most prevalent forms of human trafficking. Such is its prevalence that human trafficking has become virtually synonymous with it. In the United States the National Human Trafficking Resource Center, run by Polaris (formerly Polaris Project), reports it encountered 5,042 cases of potential human trafficking during 2014.[1] Most (71%) related to the sale of sexual services. Of these (61%) involved adults, predominantly women. Around 2015, Polaris was noting the absence of official estimates for the total number of victims of human trafficking in the United States. However, it also noted how 100,000 children were estimated to be engaged in the sex trade and Polaris extrapolated the total number of victims of human trafficking at hundreds of thousands as the trafficking of children is only part of the complete picture.[2] Polaris also states how individuals in the United States are forced to prostitute themselves in hotels and on the streets, and to meet nightly quotas for their traffickers.[3]

Internationally UNICEF estimated in 2000 the sexual exploitation of 1.8 million children in situations of pornography and prostitution. The organization also figured 1 million children entered the sex trade each year.[4] France's Women's Rights Minister Najat Vallaud-Belkacem called for the eradication of prostitution in France in response to claims

90% of the country's prostitutes were victims of human trafficking.[5] Harvard scholar, activist, and human trafficking expert Siddharth Kara contends that "[i]n most of Europe and Asia, sex trafficking represents 30 to 45 *per cent* of the total amount of human trafficking in a country."[6] In one finding concerning the trafficking of women into commercial sexual exploitation, albeit very cautiously conveyed by its authors, Niklas Jakobsson and Andreas Kotsadam found such trafficking was most prevalent in those places where prostitution had been legalized. Such trafficking was less prevalent in places where prostitution (ie. supply) was legal, but the procuring of sexual services (ie. demand) was made illegal. Its prevalence was least in places where prostitution (ie. supply and demand) was illegal.[7] Swedish-Canadian lawyer Gunilla Ekberg, an expert in human trafficking and prostitution, declares the two issues are "intrinsically linked."[8] The Dutch National Rapporteur on Trafficking in Human Beings states, "[t]here has always been a clear relationship between human trafficking and prostitution in the Netherlands."[9] A Swedish Government report notes "a very strong connection between the incidence of prostitution and human trafficking for sexual purposes."[10] In 2003 the Bush Administration saw fit to issue a National Security Presidential Directive declaring, "[p]rostitution and related activities, which are inherently harmful and dehumanizing, contribute to the phenomenon of trafficking in persons."[11]

In stark contrast to these claims, the Report of the Global Commission on HIV and the Law, entitled *HIV and the Law: Risks, Rights & Health*, states "[s]ex work and sex trafficking are not the same. The difference is that the former is consensual whereas the latter is coercive."[12] In a 2011 publication entitled *The Report of the UNAIDS Advisory Group on HIV and Sex Work*, UNAIDS complains of "persistent confusion and conflation between trafficking in persons and sex work."[13] "In reality," it adds, "trafficking and sex work are two very different things. Trafficking involves coercion and deceit; it results in various forms of exploitation, including forced labour, and is a gross violation of human rights. Sex work, on the other hand, does not involve coercion or deceit. Even when it is illegal, sex work comprises freely entered into and consensual sex between adults, and like other forms of labour, provides sex workers with a livelihood."[14] In case this point remains ambiguous the report adds "trafficking in persons for any distinct purpose, including commercial sexual exploitation, should never be implicitly or explicitly conflated with sex work."[15] In an updated version of the report, UNAIDS defines sex work in the following manner:

> By definition, sex work means that adult female, male and transgender sex workers who are engaging in commercial sex *have consented to do so* (that is, are choosing voluntarily to do so), making it distinct from trafficking.[16]

A similar statement is made by the Global Network of Sex Work Project (NSWP) in its report *Good Practice in Sex Worker-led HIV Programming*. The network seeks the amendment, or removal, of laws targeting human trafficking where those laws intermingle human trafficking and sex work.[17] The *Report of the Global Commission on HIV and the Law* also expresses the Commission's objection to a perspective, held by some, that "links prostitution with human trafficking."[18] Should they be linked? Or do they comprise two different acts and those who participate in them two unrelated groups? Moreover, if they are different, can two things that are different have the same cause? What image, or understanding, of prostitution and sex trafficking do these statements have the effect of conjuring?

This is an important issue, for if indeed prostitution (though some prefer the term *sex work*, while equally others object to it) and human trafficking are not to be confused for one another, what advantage could there be in making policy in one for the benefit of the other? The question is whether the claims made by the Global Commission on HIV and the Law, by UNAIDS, by NSWP and others are correct. Some point to the exploitation of women, as in this instance it is predominantly women who suffer at the hands of merciless traffickers who forcibly sell them into the sex trade, as proof positive not all who work as prostitutes do so consensually. To point this out, it is countered, is merely to ignore the previously asserted points and to conflate prostitution, which is consensual, with human trafficking, which is not. Others point to the fact that some who started out in prostitution through their own volition soon find themselves enslaved by traffickers. Here too the argument finds a counter, for in falling victim to human trafficking one can no longer be classed as a member of the group who are working consensually. Others yet, point to the presence of children, who clearly are in no position to consent, as sufficient proof that prostitution is not consensual. Not so, it is argued. For if children cannot consent then they cannot be among the consensual, and thus they should never be classed as prostitutes in the first place. Agreement appears not to be possible.

What is clear, however, is the existence of two polarized ideas, or conceptions, of prostitution: one narrow and one broad. When people talk about prostitution, often they are talking about these two different conceptions, often without realizing they are doing so. Those who view prostitution in the narrow sense perceive it as comprising only those persons who are consensually engaged in it. The existence of persons who are not so engaged does not challenge this conception, because they are not part of the population of prostitutes. The moment somebody is trafficked means they are no longer prostitutes. The two are not to be conflated. In fact, it is often claimed, for these very reasons, prostitution is a *victimless crime*?[19] What business then does the state have in criminalizing it? Conversely those who view prostitution in a broad sense conceive of the population in a different way, as comprising a wider group, one which includes within it those who are trafficked. Does the state not have an obligation to those within its borders to protect their rights? What business then does the state have in decriminalizing prostitution?

The Report of the UNAIDS Advisory Group on HIV and Sex Work states how trafficking and sex work should never be conflated "because, as the definitions ... show, they are clearly not the same."[20] This is problematic on several fronts. First, the U.S. English version of the *Oxford Dictionary* defines the word *definition* as "an exact statement or description of the nature, scope, or meaning of something."[21] The implication is that the purpose of definition is to describe reality, and not to serve as proof of it. Second, if definition alone is sufficient proof prostitution is consensual, then definition is also sufficient proof it is not. For example, in *Flawed Theory and Method in Studies of Prostitution* Ronald Weitzer scrutinizes the works of three authors who "define prostitution as violence against women."[22] By the same rationale then a different result is produced simply by adapting the definition. Third, the *Palermo Protocol*, which provides the world's only internationally agreed definition of human trafficking, specifically refers to the exploitation that occurs in acts of trafficking as including, among other things, "the exploitation of the prostitution of others."[23] This appears to be a *contradiction in terms*, an oxymoron, if one accepts that trafficking and prostitution are separate. The implications go further for they challenge, in the very same way, the categorization of other acts as either forced labor or slave labor. Such a categorization is itself an oxymoron under the rationale. For if work, or labor, is necessarily consensual, and slavery is not, then how can one combine the two? Fourth, one finds a multitude of references to prostitution in reports, such as the *Trafficking in Persons Report* over its many years. In fact the United States' minimum standards measure countries based on the steps those countries have taken to reduce both customer demand for commercial sex acts at home and participation by nationals in sex tourism abroad.[24] Fifth, if one accepts prostitution is consensual, and that what buyer and sellers are engaging in is the purchase and sale of not just sex but consensual sex, then what are the buyers of services provided by victims of sex trafficking buying? The logic of this scenario implies the market does not obscure the nature of the transaction, but when one seeks to migrate this lesson to the corporate world the logic flows in the opposite direction. When slavery is part of the supply chain, a different defense is offered, that the market serves to obscure the true nature of the transactions. In this way the market becomes a vehicle that is both all-knowing and all-ignorant, depending upon whichever version suits at the time. Finally, and importantly, UNAIDS states "trafficking in persons for any distinct purpose, including commercial sexual exploitation, should never be implicitly or explicitly conflated with sex work."[25] An important distinction is made then between labor and slavery. Amnesty International makes this distinction even more explicitly, stating it defines the term *sex work* as the exchange of money for sex in line with the definition provided by the Joint UN Programme on HIV / AIDS (UNAIDS).[26] It is clear then, according to this statement, all that is consensual is work or labor, and all that is not consensual is not work, at least when it comes to the selling of sexual services. What then is sex trafficking's cause? Is it true that "[s]ex work and sex trafficking are not the same?"[27]

During World War II the United States military encountered a problem. How could the military improve its bombers to maximize the survivability of bomber crews and of aircraft?[28] The losses inflicted upon both were staggering. The odds of surviving a tour of duty during the years of the heaviest losses were no better than 50:50.[29] The military devised a plan: it would reinforce the vulnerable areas of the aircraft with additional material to protect those areas against enemy fire. It was imperative the reinforcing material was added to the proper locations since, owing to the constraint of weight, only a limited amount of reinforcement could be added to an aircraft, while still retaining its capacity to remain airworthy. The approach used was straightforward. A study was conducted. Aircraft were examined upon their return from bombing missions, and notes were made of the locations most heavily damaged by enemy fire. Time and again the results told the same tale. Extensive damage was to be found concentrated along the wings, down the center of the aircraft's body and around the position occupied by the tail gunner.[30] The solution, the study concluded, was to reinforce these areas to increase survivability.[31]

Fortunately for the military, and for the airmen who flew these aircraft, a young statistician examined the study's conclusions before they could be implemented. He argued they should be rejected outright and concluded they would make no difference whatsoever to survivability. Abraham Wald's insight was how the military had unwittingly introduced a fatal flaw into the design of its study. It had studied the wrong aircraft. The group of aircraft it studied had been the ones that made it home; the ones it ought to have studied were the ones that did not survive. Yet this critical group had been excluded from the study. Owing to their fate, the casualties were nowhere to be seen so when it came to conducting the study they were easily omitted. The bias that exclusion brought about is termed a *survivorship bias*. This resulted in another bias, which drew a distinction between success and failure. Contrary to what the military had initially thought their study had clearly shown, it had in fact demonstrated something else entirely. It showed how if severe damage was sustained by all the aircraft, chances were only those that sustained it only along the wings, or down the center of the aircraft's body or around the position occupied by the tail gunner would be the ones making it home. If, on the other hand, severe damage was sustained to other locations on the aircraft, the odds were against its crew making it home. What was required of the analysts doing the study was the ability to see who it was that was before them, and who it was that was not. If the military wanted to improve survivability for those still alive, it must look not to the living, but to the dead.

Each new mission brought with it an opportunity to die. Imagine for a moment a scenario where there are 50 aircraft at the beginning of a tour of duty. Each aircraft represents 2% of the entire population. Now suppose 10 of these aircraft are downed in the first mission, representing a 20% loss. And suppose another 15 are downed in the second mission, presenting a 30% loss. By the end of the second mission combined losses are now 50%. However, if one allows the successes to become synonymous with the population, and one simply brushes aside the losses, as though they were something else, the figures can be presented in another way. At the mission's beginning there are 50 aircraft in the population. After the first mission there are 40 and after the second there are 25. If the rationale of this alternative perspective is followed, the population and the successes now being the same, the population is still 100% when 10 aircraft are lost and it is still 100% despite 25 aircraft, or half of the original group, being downed by the enemy. Even when there are no survivors left, there will be no casualties among them. So long as analyses are limited to those who return, and do not include those who do not, the findings of the original study, despite the flawed logic, will remain unchallenged, and so long as they do, more will perish than should be the case if logic and a scientific approach had been properly applied. Despite its now visible flaws, the strategy employed by the United States military is initially tantalizingly plausible. At first glance it appears almost even to be self-evident. "Language matters," the U.S. State Department warns in the *Trafficking in Persons Report*.[32]

When success and failure are perceived as separate, two groups are created in the mind's eye. In one group there are the failures and in the other the successes. The first contains the victims, while the second appears to be *victimless*. The danger is that one of these outcomes becomes conflated with the action that both were engaged in. One outcome comes to own the action. Why is this dangerous? It is dangerous because it leaves one of the outcomes of the act without a cause, while it equates the other outcome exclusively with the cause. So, while one outcome becomes *victimless*, the other one becomes *causeless*. Those who bravely flew these missions fought to prosecute the war against the enemy. They also fought to preserve their lives. None consented to die, though they knew the peril. Yet die they did, and in great numbers. The tale of their successes and failures is not the tale of two distinct groups, but rather the tale of what is happening within a group at a particular moment. Hence the successes and the failures do not constitute two distinct populations, but a single population engaged in a common activity, with different outcomes. Both groups were airmen, irrespective of their fate. Would it not be strange to conclude that those who made it home and those who did not, were in fact engaged in wholly different activities, and somehow their fates did not stem from some common cause? It amounts to concluding that those embarked on these missions were airmen, until such time as they perished when they ceased to be airmen, and thus being an airman means never to perish.

Oddly something else happens too when success and failure are perceived as two separate groups. It can seem like the problem of the casualties is that they weren't more akin to the survivors when they actually belong to the same group. The aircraft in which the airmen flew were identical. It would be an absurdity then to assert, based on their respective fates, that those who perished could have prevailed had they been more like those who had survived. So, while it is true to conclude that one is not the cause of the other, it is nonetheless also the case that one is not the solution to the other, and it is nonetheless the case too they have a common origin. In *Survivorship Bias* McRaney cautions against "picking apart winners and losers, successes and failures, the living and dead," adding that when "failure becomes invisible, the difference between failure and success may also become invisible."[33] In his own time, Calhoun cautioned against accepting just this kind of presentation, one treating "every addition as a blessing" and "every failure to obtain one as a curse."[34] It is only when the two are united, that one comes to see the situation as it truly is, with a clarity that is both black and white.

Defining prostitution as a necessarily-consensual act, confuses and misleads. The effect is compounded when the terms *sex work* and *sex worker* are applied. The implication of the former is that slavery cannot be part of the trade. Yet slavery has always been associated with certain activities. It is patently so, as developments particular to an industry, such as the arrival of the cotton gin or the development of the AK47 assault rifle or advances in medical science, have created pathways for slavery to be used where it could not be used before. Similarly, developments particular to an industry such as the development of miniature robots to replace camel jockeys, have destroyed or reduced opportunities for its use. If industry and slavery are separate, the developments in one could not produce an effect in the other. For Calhoun the making of this kind of distinction, between the successes and the failures, was enough to judge the situation "the strongest confession that, whatever burden it imposes, in reality falls, not on" those who advocate for the policy's adoption, "but on others."[35]

Consider again the characteristics of those industries in which slavery is found. The population available to carry out the trade must be sparse, or it must be made sparse by a general unwillingness of the populace to carry it out. Consequently, the nature of the work is usually something unappealing. When it comes to trafficking, some talk of 3D jobs, those that are dirty, dangerous, or degrading.[36] To these a fourth can be added, those jobs that are deadly.[37] Where the industry is dependent on the soil, that soil must be remarkably fertile, otherwise the slavery upon it must be migratory. Whether dependent or not, there must be an abundant supply. Additionally, it is work that cannot be subdivided, and it remains intact of itself, often untouched by time. As a result, it is difficult work, and it is often crude in nature. The industry employing slavery must also enjoy a monopoly on the supply of a favorite staple. Consequently, there is a very different interpretation to the statement, so assuredly given, that prostitution is "the world's oldest profession."

Through its association with industry, slavery is confirmed as a form of labor, with industry using the species of labor best suited to the tasks at hand at each stage of the process of production. Thus, there is no reason to suppose that one cannot be a slave, while at the same time being a "sex worker": one can be a laborer, and be a slave laborer, just as one can be a laborer and be a free laborer. Consider for a moment the fact how the United Nations' International Labour Organisation (ILO) "does not draw hard and fast distinctions between trafficking for sexual exploitation on the one hand and for forced labour on the other. For the ILO, forced commercial sexual exploitation is one form of forced labour."[38] A more helpful terminology would acknowledge how being a prostitute can mean being a person who is trafficked. The market transcends matters of consent and non-consent. One can see this is the case. The backbreaking work of picking the South's cotton was done by her slaves, while the manufacturing of the wares of that commodity was done by England's free laborers. Each played their assigned role, and one would have been futile without the other. An interesting question arises. Why credit one as being labor, while depriving the other of its rightful recognition? The reason, Calhoun says, is this: "Men ask not for burdens, but benefits."[39]

To know a market's reality, one must count both its burdens and its benefits. This is the measure of the freedoms it produces, the character of those freedoms, and the true test of the price paid for them. To credit any market with consensual-only outcomes is to credit it undeservedly, for though there is one only market there are always two outcomes, and one is always diametrically the opposite of the other, whether they be success and failure, or winning and losing, or consenting and non-consenting. The market accommodates both, preferring neither, albeit one outcome might be more likely to occur than the other. While it is strictly true that freedom does not cause slavery, it is conversely true that the slavery of some is not lessened by the freedoms of others, just as it is true how they can both share a common origin.

Domestically, no modern and democratic state can make either sound, or legitimate, policy for itself on an approach that counts only the successes, and excludes the failures, particularly when those failures come in the form of slavery. The positive consent of one group is given priority over violations of the other. These are not two different things. As an overarching concept they are the same. Both relate to consent. Aside from issues of legitimacy what good is a policy that deprives slaves of the means to free themselves, and despite what it proclaims by its logic, also deprives those not enslaved of any improvement? It can make nothing safer. Its logic is this: *the safe are safe, and if they were not safe they would not be the safe*. In reality, there is no fidelity to any population for no group is assured of success. In reality too, success always comes at the expense of failure and *vice versa*: one must diminish in order for the other to increase, thus it is only when they are placed side-by-side that one can see the true nature of things. The fidelity of the narrow perspective is to an outcome, in the form of success, and not to a group. It is utopianism, washing its hand of all who fail to conform to its standard. To know what prostitution entails one must look at the results it produces, and not the definition it advocates. For all of these reasons the perspective articulated in the reports of the Global Commission on HIV and the Law, UNAIDS, NSWP and Amnesty International, which prioritizes positive forms of consent, through assent, over negative forms of it, through its violation, puts a modern gloss on an old tenet, which Lincoln, once harshly denounced as a malformed conception of the term, *sacred right of self government* "as to amount to just this: That if any one man choose to enslave another, no third man shall be allowed to object."[40]

"Modern slavery is big business," the Global Slavery Index declares.[41] Siddharth Kara, in *Sex Trafficking: Inside the Business of Modern Slavery,* and Alexis Aronowitz, in *Analysing the Business Model of Trafficking in Human Beings to Better Prevent the Crime*, in *Human Trafficking, Human Misery: The Global Trade in Human Beings* and in *Smuggling and Trafficking in Human Beings: The Phenomenon, The Markets that Drive It and the Organisations that Promote It*, concur as they both point to the economic rationale making the occurrence of human trafficking in prostitution a seemingly foregone conclusion.[42] The Dutch National Rapporteur acknowledges "[t]his exploitation is a highly profitable business."[43] In his address at the launch of the *2015 Trafficking in Persons Report*, U.S. Secretary of State John Kerry uttered his determination "to bring to the public's attention the full nature and scope of a $150 billion illicit trafficking industry."[44] "And it is an industry," he added.[45]

Human trafficking then is a crime of economic benefit.[46] This is true of most of its appearances and, though the manifestation of the exploitation may vary, the economic motive is a prominent feature in disparate instances.[47] Indeed an exploration of instances of human trafficking, and a similar exploration of the associated literature, is necessarily an exploration of the relationship between exploitation and economics.[48] The claims made by Kara and by Aronowitz concerning the business-like nature of human trafficking are echoed elsewhere.[49] In the midst of the literature, and accounts given on cases of human trafficking, one finds a plethora of references to syndicates, organized crime, and mafia-like organizations.[50] Kara identifies "elasticity of demand ... [as] the most powerful driver of the demand side of the sex trafficking industry" since the "cheaper the cost of sex, the more men who ... [can] afford it, or afford it more often."[51] It is interesting Kara should focus so singly on this point. It is interesting, given how it is so profoundly reminiscent of another made long ago regarding the wares of slaves. Recall how Jones, in his *An Address on the Progress of Manufactures and Internal Improvement, in the United States*, also pointed to the criticality of elasticity of demand. He stated how, though the price of a yard of cotton cloth had been higher in the earlier part of the 1800s no money was to be made from it. By the time he was making his remarks, some years later, the price of that same yard of cloth was scarcely 40% of what it had been years before yet "the business of making such goods, though made cheaper than they are made in England, is a good one!"[52]

Fortunately, the business of slavery is now prohibited, and slavery's prohibition is not a matter for individual states to decide. Instead, states have obligations to prevent and to protect potential victims against occurrences of slavery. States also have obligations to prosecute those who perpetrate these deeds. Article 4 of *The Universal Declaration of Human Rights* decrees "[n]obody shall be held in slavery or servitude; slavery and the slave trade shall be prohibited in all their forms."[53] *The European Convention for the Protection of Human Rights and Fundamental Freedoms* pronounces "[n]o one shall be held in slavery or servitude."[54] The primacy given to the issue of slavery within these documents, by those who framed them, demonstrates just how central the issue of slavery is to the project of human rights. The now-former U.N. Secretary General of the United Nations Kofi Annan once described slavery, or human trafficking, to be "one of the most egregious violations of human rights that the United Nations now confronts."[55] It is an issue ever to the fore of the agendas of the United States, the European Union, the OSCE and a great many other international and regional bodies.

Human rights represent, to a degree at least, the interests of individuals. They cannot be justified on prudential, or practical, grounds. In fact pragmatic considerations may run contrary to their interests. Consider for a moment how, though slavery might be the most profitable option in some circumstances, the pragmatism of its use never vindicates its being used. In *Making Sense of Human Rights*, James Nickel foresees "[o]ne problem with prudential arguments for general moral principles is the possibility that a powerful group of people will create a system that serves its interests while victimizing a less powerful group."[56] Indeed when one considers just how readily pragmatic justifications are found, some skepticism is warranted when pragmatic reasons are offered to support actions as being compatible with human rights. Human rights are ends in themselves, and not merely means to some other end. Consequently, human rights are moral rights. Much the same can be said of human beings, who are deserving of treatment not as means to some end, but as ends in themselves. This kind of rationale, of seeing certain elements of reality as ends in themselves, originates in the philosophy of Immanuel Kant. In *Justice: What's the Right Thing To Do?* Michael Sandel notes how this Kantian system of morality entails treating persons as *ends in themselves*. This means persons have an inherent value, and they are not to be treated as means to an end. The same Kantian system, Sandel notes, provided the platform upon which the revolutionaries of the 18th century constructed the rights of man. Today we refer to those rights as human rights.[57] Some may prefer to shy away from moral considerations in favor of some apparently value-free alternative, but Turner gives no quarter, putting it thus in his *Outline of a Theory of Human Rights*: "[o]ne problem for a value-free science of politics is that whoever claims that questions of justice cannot play a part in causal explanation has already committed a value-judgement."[58]

Human rights, like the approach adopted by the United States through its use of minimum standards, are themselves minimal standards. One edition of *The Stanford Encyclopedia of Philosophy* entry on human rights clearly says this is so, describing these rights as *"minimal—or at least modest—standards*. They are much more concerned with avoiding the terrible than with achieving the best."[59] Nickel describes human rights as those things states "'must do' rather than 'would be good to do.'"[60] The *Trafficking in Persons Report 2012* proclaims how the *"Palermo Protocol*'s '3P' paradigm of prevention, prosecution, and protection reflects a comprehensive victim-centered approach" that guarantees "the rights of individuals," forestalls "the violation of rights," and is commensurate with "efforts to seek those whose actions have subjugated the lives of their victims."[61] So, even minimum standards require that they be successful.

However, a dilemma arises as only three years earlier the *Trafficking in Persons Report 2009* visited the issue of economics, doing so implicitly, by invoking the facets of supply and demand. The report maintains "[a]ny successful effort to combat human trafficking must confront not only the supply of trafficked humans, but also the demand for forced labor and commercial sex that fuels it."[62] In fact the United States' own minimum standards specifically incorporate the consideration of whether "the government of the country has made serious and sustained efforts to reduce the demand for ... commercial sex acts."[63] In contrast to the emphasis placed on economics by the United States, the internationally agreed *Palermo Protocol* makes no specific reference to tackling the role of demand in the measures it lists as necessary for preventing human trafficking. The *Palermo Protocol* appears to focus more on what is done, in the form of exploitation, rather than on why it is done, as though exploitation were an end in itself. It does say governments should "adopt or strengthen legislative or other measures, such as educational, social or cultural measures, ... to discourage the demand that fosters all forms of exploitation of persons."[64] Can a state truly fulfill its international obligations to human rights by pursuing a minimal approach, which need not of itself address the economic underpinnings of the violation, while at the same time being cognizant of how "[a]ny successful effort ... must confront ... the demand ... that fuels it?"[65]

Chapter 9:

A Safe Bastion?

The year 2000 was a landmark year for efforts to combat human trafficking. The *United Nations Convention against Transnational Organized Crime and its Protocols* was agreed and one of its protocols, the *Palermo Protocol*, provided the very first internationally agreed definition of human trafficking. In that same year the United States government passed The *Victims of Trafficking and Violence Protection Act* (TVPA), initiating a system of worldwide reporting in the form of the annually published T*rafficking in Persons* (TIP) *Report*.[1] Also in 2000, the Netherlands embarked on a policy of legalizing and regulating part of its sex industry.[2] Only one year prior, in 1999, Sweden had undertaken a very different approach to prostitution, by proscribing the purchase of sex. In 2003 New Zealand adopted yet another approach, decriminalizing prostitution and imposing no regulation upon it. Another option exists in the form of criminalization, where those selling or soliciting sexual services are prosecuted. For a variety of reasons this option is not *en vogue* among the various debates between advocates. The approaches adopted by the Netherlands, New Zealand and Sweden reflect an age-old dilemma of whether it is better to abolish, decriminalize or to legalize prostitution, albeit in this instance it is a question posed from the perspective of ending modern slavery in the sector. Many years have now passed since these measures were instituted, and the passage of time may now permit the evidence of those years to settle the matter. The question now at heart of this exploration is whether the internationally agreed 3P approach, which does not require economic factors to be addressed, can be successful in their absence.

Human trafficking is not a new phenomenon to the people of the Netherlands. The Dutch criminal code has long contained measures aimed at tackling human trafficking, with specific measures implemented in the country's legislation in 1911.[3] That being said, it may be the case it was not always fully comprehended how some of what was occurring in prostitution was slavery. An illustration of this point is provided in the *Report of the Dutch National Rapporteur on Trafficking in Human Beings* in the form of an account of the experiences of a Dutch police inspector who went undercover in 1900 to tease out the nature of the relationship between prostitute and prostitution.[4] Inspector Balkestein sets about interviewing prostitutes in Amsterdam. He notes the priority for a researcher is "not to learn how the interviewees feel about their own lives, but only how they have become who they are."[5] In his account he emphasizes the need to interview the women (he makes no mention of male prostitutes) "as far as possible beyond the influence of the brothel owner or madam."[6] Many of those he finds engaged in prostitution are not victims of human trafficking, but there are some who most certainly are trafficking's victims. The description he offers, of the phenomenon he seeks, resounds with contemporary observations: "[w]hat one should search for is the following: are a series of acts of indirect compulsion and deception committed by a large number of persons acting in concert against women and girls, whose lives may not be unimpeachable, but who without these acts of indirect compulsion and deception would still never have accepted the life of a prostitute."[7] The practice he describes seems to be comprised of three parts: "a series of acts of indirect compulsion and deception," undertaken by "persons acting in concert" by various means, for the purpose of exploiting victims who would "never have accepted the life of a prostitute."[8] The significance of this three-part definition of acts, means and purpose is clear. The motive for trafficking these women and girls into prostitution is not specifically addressed in the account given by Inspector Balkestein. What then can the motive be? The financial reward, taken by the "brothel owner or madam" he mentions, offers the obvious and most plausible explanation.[9]

Today the Netherlands is different to Balkestein's time. The country, bordering Belgium and Germany, is a member of the European Union. It is also party to the Schengen Agreement, meaning it is effectively borderless for citizens of countries also party to the agreement. Human trafficking is a problem in the country. In 2015 the *Trafficking in Persons Report* described the Netherlands as "a source, destination, and transit country for men, women, and children from the Netherlands, Eastern Europe – including Roma – Africa, and South and East Asia subjected to sex trafficking and forced labor."[10] In its 2014 report the State Department states how "a significant number of underage Dutch residents continued to be subjected to sex trafficking in the country. Identified trafficking victims primarily originated from within the Netherlands and from abroad, including from Romania, Hungary, Bulgaria, Nigeria, Guinea, Sierra Leone, China, the Philippines, and Vietnam in 2013; victims are also from other countries in Africa, Europe, and South and East Asia."[11] The burden of these crimes falls particularly, as they often do, upon women and children.[12] That burden does not necessarily all fall at home, however, for it is noted how some Dutch nationals travel for the purpose of exploiting children in foreign jurisdictions, a phenomenon known as *child sex tourism*, where protections against such exploitation may be more lax.[13] The *Global Slavery Index 2018* estimates there are 30,000 victims of slavery in the country, 1.8 persons per 1,000 population, ranking the Netherlands 143rd by prevalence by population.[14] The country has performed well in the rankings of the United States' *Trafficking in Persons Report*, consistently being designated a Tier 1 country. To their credit the Dutch were among the first European countries to have a National Rapporteur on Trafficking in Human Beings, with the establishment of the position in the year 2000.[15] The position is a wholly independent one. The very first *Report of the National Rapporteur*, published in 2002, declares how, for as long as human trafficking "has had a place in Dutch criminal law, this is associated with prostitution."[16] The ninth *Report*, issued a decade later, continues to maintain the "prostitution sector has always been susceptible to human trafficking."[17]

A clear objective of the legalization of prostitution entailed improving the overall situation of prostitutes.[18] In *Human trafficking and legalized prostitution in the Netherlands* Dina Siegel expands on this objective, explaining "[t]he main aim was to legalize the adult, voluntary prostitutes (male and female) who possess a valid municipality permit, certifying that … [the business] has fulfilled the legal requirements to operate."[19] Other objectives are also clearly discernible. Two stand out. The first of these sought to "contribute to the governmental efforts for combating organized crime by introducing harsh punishments for offenders, who use violence, who exploit minors and who are involved in trafficking of humans for sexual exploitation."[20] The second objective "was to offer European sex-workers social security and protection from criminal gangs."[21] The measures also sought "to protect foreign nationals who are illegally prostituting in the Netherlands."[22]

Overall, it was hoped the new legislation would fulfill six objectives. First, it was hoped legalization would protect prostitutes from being commercially exploited. Second, the legislation was intended to fight sex trafficking in prostitution. Third, it was intended juveniles would be protected from sexual abuse. Fourth, it was hoped the legislation would advance the cause of those working as prostitutes.

Fifth, the law was intended to "eliminate criminal involvement in the prostitution industry." [23] Finally, it was an objective of the law that it would "limit the number of non-European Union (EU) residents working as prostitutes in The Netherlands."[24]

In the 2004 *Report of the Dutch National Rapporteur* a robust defense of legalization was offered, suggesting those "who do not seek a solution to the problem of ... [human trafficking] by prohibiting the buying and selling of sexual services are criticised, often through the use of suggestive or incorrect information."[25] The Rapporteur of the time also restated the objectives of legalization:

> The aim of lifting the general ban on brothels was, from a pragmatic point of view, to achieve a better control and regulation of the prostitution sector without moralising. For this purpose, six objectives were formulated that aim on the one hand to turn the prostitution sector into a normal sector of business, freed of marginal criminal elements and to which the existing rules of labour and tax apply, and on the other hand to make it easier to tackle undesirable forms of prostitution (exploitation) more firmly. The lifting of the general ban on brothels thus led to a separation of the prostitution sector into a legal sector and a sector prohibited under criminal law. The legal sector is (the organisation of) voluntary prostitution among adults and subject to conditions. The 'illegal' sector consists of all other forms of (organisation of) prostitution, usually typified by exploitation.[26]

Voluntary prostitution would receive an implicit endorsement from the state in return for the delivery of the six objectives set forth.

In an article entitled *The Fine Art of Regulated Tolerance: Prostitution in Amsterdam* written in 1998, two years before prostitution was legalized in the Netherlands, Chrisje Brants makes two observations. The first of these entailed an idiosyncrasy of the Dutch state and

Dutch society: "much of what goes on is not regulated by law, but by an informal system of hierarchical guidelines and unwritten rules that may eventually be elevated to proper legal status. Formally, the execution of such policies is a matter for the public prosecution service in co-operation with the police, but it usually also involves close co-operation with (local) authorities and other law enforcement agencies, and even with the group of potential offenders."[27] This phenomenon, which is known as *gedogen* in Dutch, translates as "pragmatic tolerance."[28] It often leads to the matters dealt with under *gedogen* later becoming legalized, even if legalization "is not seen as the preferred solution."[29] The second observation made by Brants relates to legalization itself. She observes "[t]here is a tendency in the Netherlands to use this option in matters of morality and personal autonomy on which no political consensus can be reached (consensual sexuality, abortion, drugs, pornography, prostitution, euthanasia), or if important vested interests stand in the way of political agreement (certain types of economic and corporate crime)."[30] Brants cautions, however, against misconstruing this pragmatic tolerance as some form of social approval.[31] It is not. In *The Dutch Myth of Tolerance* Rade and Shah claim Dutch tolerance is a fabrication. They attribute part of the myth's rise to foreign preconceptions of the country. The other part they attribute to deliberate political manipulation by external actors who paint the country in utopian terms to creatively further their own agendas. Indeed, the myth may be more tangible abroad than it is for those who reside in the Netherlands.[32] Instead pragmatic tolerance is a permission bestowed grudgingly by a democratic society that feels it has no choice in the face of pragmatic considerations. Kelly *et al.* echo this sentiment, saying the "prostitution regime in the Netherlands is frequently cited as the archetypal example of legalisation, but this misrepresents law and policy at national and local levels."[33] One former Rapporteur has acknowledged how "it would be desirable in a civilised society to completely prohibit vice, but because the incentive was felt to be stronger tha[n] the fear of punishment for vice, this was not thought to be expedient."[34]

In the 1960s prostitution in the Netherlands was a comparatively small-scale affair, albeit even then it was not impervious to coercion and violence. Its nature was forever transformed by events in the following two decades. These transformations would have implications for policy, some of them not immediately comprehended. The transformation was brought about by the arrival of heroin, hardcore porn cinemas and shops, AIDS, Third World immigrants, and other immigrants from former Dutch colonies.[35] Conditions worsened in line with increased opportunities to make money from the sex trade as power gradually coalesced in the hands of criminal operators.[36] Brants labels the response as a comprise typical of what one would expect of Dutch politics, one in which human trafficking penalties were increased but prostitution remained tolerated.[37] Even reluctant tolerance required full compliance with the law governing taxation and any moral value associated with disapproval lost its significance.[38] An account, contemporary to 1998, given by Brants, concluded "new policies in Amsterdam have taken regulated tolerance to its extreme limits and there is now very little, if any, difference between this and legalization. Indeed, when legalization comes, this is very much what it will look like."[39]

Legalization did finally come. Some point to Winnie Sorgdrager's 1997 Bill, which sought to end the prohibition on brothels as a critical moment, while conceding that others attribute the change to the relentless pressure of prostitute advocacy groups.[40] It is clear a critical motivating factor was "the assumption that repeal would provide better protection for vulnerable women."[41] Even so, economic considerations were not overlooked. According to a contemporary account given by Brants:

> The new policy in Amsterdam, which, the municipal authorities claim, will barely have to change when

legalization goes through, is founded on two basic ideas. The first is that prostitution is a fact of life and must be regarded as a normal profession, operating according to supply and demand in a market economy. It is because of the illegal aura that has always surrounded it that it attracts other forms of illegality, which lead to an excessive concentration of power in the hands of criminals and criminal organizations, extreme dependence of vulnerable individuals, and the corruption of public authority. The second is that these problems can only be addressed by bringing acceptable forms of prostitution into the open, protecting them through a system of licensing and putting into effect a comprehensive policy that will both ensure that legal prostitution does not lapse into illegality and that criminal activities can be dealt with effectively.[42]

Policy, then, was informed by an idiosyncrasy of Dutch culture, which combined skepticism concerning the role of the law in addressing issues perceived to be matters of public morality, a reluctant acceptance of the consequences of these matters and a tradition of legalizing at a later juncture. In the opinion of the Dutch National Rapporteur, "[t]he choice made by a country [with regards to policy] depends partly on the culture of that country and how prostitution is regarded there."[43] Success in tackling human trafficking *via* forced commercial sexual exploitation would be delivered through legalization, which would reduce the numbers exploited.

The general ban on brothels had stood in the Netherlands since 1911 with the passage of *Wetsvoorstel tot Bestrijding van de Zedeloosheid*, which translates in English as the *Suppression of Immorality Bill*.[44] Even at this early juncture it included provisions to tackle the trafficking of women and girls.[45] Prostitution itself was not made illegal by the ban, but rather the activities associated with it.[46] The bill led to the introduction of two Articles: 250*bis*, which introduced a general ban on brothels, and 250*ter*, which criminalized the trafficking of women.[47] It is clear from the development of legislation how understanding of the phenomenon of human trafficking has been gained slowly and incrementally, over generations. The form of exploitation envisaged in the legislation of this period entailed obtaining women and girls from abroad to be handed over into prostitution.[48] In time two further realizations would be made: human trafficking can occur within national borders; and males could be exploited for the same purpose.[49] This legislation remained in place for many years, but with the passage of time prostitution was increasingly tolerated and the law was seldom enforced.[50] Up until 1994 human trafficking was punished under Article 250ter of the Criminal Code and limited to the trafficking of women and male minors.[51] In 1994 this changed when the law was modernized and penalties were increased.[52] Significantly the next change came when the ban on brothels was removed from Dutch law on October 1, 2000 when Article 250*bis* was removed.[53] The Netherlands thus legalized prostitution, making it a profession, becoming the first European country to do so.[54]

Many other changes were made over the intervening years culminating in the arrival of Article 273f. Importantly a review of Dutch legislation (see appendix) reveals how, as far as the phenomenon of sex trafficking is concern, it has largely been consistent with the Palermo Protocol since prior to 2005. Protection against victimhood was afforded to foreign witnesses and victims of human trafficking through the measures labelled B-9 regulations. They permit access to protective facilities, including temporary stay.[55] They also "placed the central weight" for the operation of legal "prostitution in the hands of the municipalities," which were "designated as the major designers and upholders of the new policy."[56] This was supposed to mean brothels, as places where sex was sold, would be restricted in number and by location.[57]

Sweden, bordering Norway and Finland, is a member of the European Union. It also enjoys a connection with Denmark, *via* the Oresund Bridge, which traverses the straits between them. Like the Netherlands, Sweden is party to the Schengen Agreement, meaning it too is effectively borderless for citizens of countries party to the agreement. The Swedish approach to prostitution is to prohibit the purchase of sex.[58] The approach is described as abolitionist. It views prostitution as being harmful, and it directs all efforts towards its eradication.[59] The approach itself is comparatively straightforward. The purchase of sexual services is prohibited, although, perhaps surprisingly, the sale of such services is legal. In this way the focus of the approach is squarely upon the demand-side of prostitution, which it seeks to lessen.[60]

Human trafficking is a problem in Sweden. The *Trafficking in Persons Report* has described Sweden as "a destination and, to a lesser extent, source and transit country for women and children subjected to sex trafficking, and a destination country for men, women, and children subjected to forced labor."[61] Like the Netherlands, it too has a problem with citizens travelling abroad for the purpose of child sex tourism. In Sweden's case it is possible to quantify the extent of those perpetrating this abuse, Horrifyingly, between 4,000 to 5,000 Swedes are estimated to travel abroad each year to avail of child sex tourism.[62] The *Global Slavery Index 2018* estimates there are 15,000 victims of slavery in the country, 1.6 persons per 1,000 population, ranking Sweden 152nd by prevalence by population.[63] The country has performed well in the rankings of the United States' *Trafficking in Persons Report*, consistently being designated a Tier 1 country. The country appointed its national rapporteur in 1998.[64]

In *Targeting the Sex Buyer: The Swedish Example,* by Kajsa Claude and the Swedish Institute, two goals are identified for the country's approach. Firstly, an attempt would be made to deter buyers of sexual services from purchasing those services.[65] Secondly, the Swedes sought to create a societal norm, one condemning of the sale of any person for sexual purposes and condemning too of the sexual abuse of any person.[66] Culture most certainly played a role in the formulation of their policy. In contemporary Swedish philosophical ideas of gender equality find their roots in radical feminist thought, which has been foremost in Sweden among other feminist lines of thought since the mid-1990s.[67] A Canadian parliamentary subcommittee examining prostitution law decided the Swedish approach "argues that prostitution promotes the commodification of women and strips them of their human dignity," thus also presenting "an obstacle to sexual equality."[68] Prostitution is viewed as "a form of violence, and by extension, that one can never choose to sell sexual services. As a result, the law must strive to eliminate all forms of prostitution."[69] Put another way, the Swedish approach views prostitution as gender-based violence.

This is not to say the Swedes were confined in their decision-making process to cultural considerations alone. Human rights played a role. Gunilla Ekberg, Special Advisor on Issues Regarding Prostitution and Trafficking in Human Beings to the Government of Sweden, lends credence to this assessment in stating how "any society that claims to defend principles of legal, political, economic, and social equality for women and girls must reject the idea that women and children, mostly girls, are commodities that can be bought, sold, and sexually exploited by men."[70] This is consistent with a Kantian perspective of human dignity. It values people as ends in themselves, and not means to some end. It holds that since human beings are not property, they may not be sold, even by themselves. It is in keeping with the understanding of human dignity the project of human rights seeks to uphold.[71] However, it is in keeping too with an appreciation that if one is to have access to the fruits of society, one cannot be subservient to those fruits. One cannot be a commodity and at the very same time possess equality. Commodities are always priced, and the difference in their price illustrates their inequality.

The Canadian parliamentary subcommittee investigating these matters concluded "that creating harsh penalties for clients will reduce demand and thus reduce prostitution in the long run, while strengthening the law against pimps will reduce the supply side of the equation in an attempt to eliminate organized crime and trafficking in persons."[72] By viewing women and girls as victims of male violence the focus naturally falls "on the root cause, the recognition that, without men's demand for and use of women and girls for sexual exploitation, the global prostitution industry would not be able to flourish and expand."[73] For the Swedes then, any fight against sex trafficking necessarily involved a fight against prostitution. By reducing prostitution, the human trafficking that is part of it must also be necessarily reduced. Success then, for the Swedes, required that prostitution be curtailed.[74]

In contrast to the comparatively hardline approach witnessed in Sweden today, in the 19th century prostitution was seen as a "socially necessary phenomenon."[75] In 1964 street prostitution was decriminalized, though little consideration seems to have been given to other forms of prostitution.[76] With the passage of time, circumstances changed. A series of events, including the emergence of human trafficking and the prospect of an influx of foreign women arising from European Union membership, altered perceptions of the prostitution sector.[77]

The work of two 1995 commissions, one on prostitution and the other on violence against women, proposed the criminalization of acts of purchasing sexual services through the *Act on Violence Against Women (Kvinnofrid)*.[78] In 1999 Sweden introduced the *Act that Prohibits the Purchase of Sexual Services*, alongside the aforementioned Act to combat violence against women, becoming the first country to prohibit the purchase of sex.[79] The approach earned itself the moniker of the *Swedish Model*.[80] It is sometimes also known as the *Nordic Model* or the *Equality Model*. Prostitutes and other "victims of male violence, are not subject to any kind of criminal or other legal repercussions."[81] Hence while it is a crime to purchase sexual services in Sweden, it is no longer a crime to sell those services.[82] The law is gender neutral as "buyer and seller can be either man or woman."[83] In practice, though, it is most often men who buy sexual services and women who sell them.[84] One need not actually be successful in one's attempts to purchase sexual services to violate the law, as attempts to purchase sexual services are also a violation.[85] In July 2004 "the range of punishment was expanded to include human trafficking that is not transnational, as well as human trafficking that relates to types of exploitation whose purpose is not sexual, for example, forced labor or organ trafficking."[86] The Act was revoked in April 2005 and made part of the Swedish Penal Code.[87] Violators of the law face a fine or a term of imprisonment of up to six months, subsequently extended to one year. The fine is an amount equivalent to the earnings accrued from 50 days of the offender's work.[88] Where an offender has repeated their offence the fine can be as high as the equivalent earnings from 150 days of their work.[89]

In 2002 human trafficking for the purpose of sexual exploitation became a criminal offence in Sweden.[90] The definition used to create the offence is based on the *Palermo Protocol*.[91] The minimum penalty imposed under the legislation is two years' imprisonment, although a maximum penalty of 10 years' imprisonment may be imposed if appropriate.[92] Additional measures were introduced in 2004 to "extend the criminalisation of trafficking to all forms of human trafficking, even within national borders."[93] These new measures provide temporary residence to foreign victims of human trafficking.[94] In 2005 the offences of procuring and grave procuring were united under the same section, though they remain distinct offences.[95] Temporary residence was granted to persons whose stay in the country would facilitate the prosecution of cases.[96] In 2010 additional legislative measures were introduced.[97] Swedish law has been consistent with the offence described in the *Palermo Protocol,* as it applies to sex trafficking, for about 15 years.

New Zealand adopted a different approach to those of the Netherlands and Sweden, when it opted to decriminalize prostitution. The difference between regulation and decriminalization can be a source of confusion. The former is a license-based system, one which strives for stringent government control. The latter is more of a hands-off approach, likely with no, or very few, government controls. The Dutch National Rapporteur says in her *Report*: "New Zealand's policy on prostitution is based on the belief that a combination of improving the position of prostitutes, through sex workers' collectives, and decriminalization is an effective instrument in the fight against human trafficking."[98] In *The Sex Myth: Why Everything We're Told is Wrong*, Brooke Magnanti extols New Zealand as the only state to prioritize the safety of female and male prostitutes over relative moral values, adding that the country's decriminalization of sex work has been a tremendous success.[99]

In August 2015 at a meeting of Amnesty International's decision-making forum, the International Council Meeting (ICM), a resolution was passed calling upon the organization to develop policy that underpins the complete decriminalization of all elements of consensual prostitution.[100] In effect, it was calling for a replication of the approach adopted in New Zealand, as the country is hailed not only as a place where prostitution has been decriminalized, but as a place where decriminalization has worked. Implicit to the approach is the belief it is state interference and moralizing, which are the problem's source. Also implicit to the approach is the belief slavery is not the result of rational action, and consequently how if market forces are allowed to prevail slavery will be eradicated when free laborers are allowed to compete with slave laborers.

New Zealand is an island nation comprised of two main islands, and some smaller ones. As an island nation it shares no borders. In fact, its nearest neighbor is the small Norfolk Island, more than 900 miles away. Farther away again is the Republic of Fiji. Its most obvious neighbor, continental Australia, is approximately 1,300 miles away. The capitals of New Zealand and Australia share the distinction of being the next closest cities having the longest distance between them. New Zealand has political and economic ties aplenty, but none permitting either the kind of unrestricted travel, or the comparative ease of travel, possible within Europe's Schengen Area.

What strikes about New Zealand immediately is its remoteness, but then again that shouldn't be a factor, as neither travel nor movement are prerequisites for human trafficking. One *Trafficking in Persons Report* describes the country as "a destination country for foreign men and women subjected to forced labor and sex trafficking and a source country for children subjected to sex trafficking within the country."[101] The report states how a "small number of Pacific Islands and New Zealand (often of Maori descent) girls and boys are at risk of sex trafficking in street prostitution, and some are victims of trafficking in gangs. Some children are recruited by other girls or compelled by family members, into prostitution."[102] The report notes other forms of human trafficking, such as the exploitation of foreign victims in the agriculture, construction and hospitality sectors. It also notes the presence of foreign fishing vessels in New Zealand's waters on which slavery is used. The *Global Slavery Index 2018* estimates there are 3,000 victims of slavery in the country, 0.6 persons per 1,000 population, ranking New Zealand 164th by prevalence by population.[103] New Zealand too has been consistent in attaining a Tier 1 ranking in the *Trafficking in Persons Report* up to the year 2020 inclusive.

Decriminalization commenced in June 2003 with the passage of the *Prostitution Reform Act*.[104] Pimping became a legal activity. Some restrictions were imposed such as ones which act to curtail some aspects of the advertising of commercial sexual services. Coercive elements of prostitution were prohibited. Business operators were required to hold a valid certificate. Restrictions were imposed too on ability of authorities to inspect brothels which, aside from exceptional circumstance such as criminal proceedings, they could now only carry out to ensure compliance with health and safety requirements.

For all the country's attempts to normalize prostitution parts of its law reveal just how defiant prostitution can be of such attempts. Exceptions had to be made, distinguishing prostitution from other legal activities. Paragraph 18 of the law for example, specifies social benefits "may not be cancelled or affected in any other way by ... refusal to work, or to continue to work."[105] Moreover a "person's entitlements under the *Injury Prevention, Rehabilitation, and Compensation Act 2001* may not be lost or affected in any other way by his or her being capable of working as a sex worker if he or she refuses to do."[106] The "fact that a person has entered into a contract to provide commercial sexual services does not of itself constitute consent for the purposes of the criminal law" as a person might later wish to withdraw that consent.[107] Persons entering the country, under the conditions of a visa, are prohibited from entering into prostitution, from being an operator of a place of prostitution, or from investing in it.

The *Prostitution Reform Act* maintains that while it neither endorses nor morally sanctions prostitution it aims: to protect the "human rights of sex workers", to protect such persons from being exploited, to promote the "welfare and occupational health and safety of sex workers," and to prohibit "the use in prostitution of persons under 18 years of age." [108] Having instituted these changes in law, the Act compelled the country's Prostitution Law Review Committee to immediately ascertain the numbers working in prostitution, and to do the same again between three and five years later.

Sarah Scott-Webb is a manager with Hagar International, an organization supporting women and children in Afghanistan, Vietnam, and Cambodia whose lives have been torn asunder through their experiences of human trafficking and gender-based violence. Hagar International has been doing this work for over 20 years now and over this time it has pioneered a model for assisting victims of these forms of abuse. Ms. Scott-Webb works from the organization's New Zealand office. Aside from work done internationally, she and her colleagues undertake work within New Zealand on these issues. Increasingly she is seeing how New Zealand is not as far removed from these issues as some might contend, or others might have hoped. In an interview given late in 2015, she points to a culture among New Zealand's people that takes pride in the integrity of its people, the beauty of its countryside and in its accomplishments. "Human trafficking is such an affront to the values so deeply cherished by New Zealanders that many believe it simply could not happen within its borders," she maintains.[109] She observes how in her everyday conversations with people, when the issue of human trafficking is broached, the reaction is the same, with people expressing their gratitude "that sort of thing" does not happen in New Zealand. "Well, actually, it does," she responds. While there are many who do not know, there are some who apparently do not want to know. She points to the attitudes of the country's government, which rather than seeking to explore the possibility of human trafficking within the country has instead opted to put the burden of proof on advocacy groups, such as Hagar International, to prove its existence.

Hagar International is responding to the challenge. It has partnered with five other non-governmental organizations and is actively funding research into trafficking in New Zealand. The first results of its study into worker exploitation came within only a few months of its commencement. It found evidence of the exploitation of fishermen aboard boats in the country's waters. Other industries are now being explored, including the country's horticulture, viticulture, and hospitality sectors. There is evidence to show that, of the workers brought to New Zealand to work in its horticulture sector, more than 2,000 have been exploited in this area alone, she says. At present Hagar International's researchers are screening this group to assess how many of these cases constitute human trafficking. After the earthquake struck New Zealand in 2011 there was increased demand for laborers to expedite rebuilding. A considerable portion of this labor was sourced from abroad. Migrant laborers are a group vulnerable to exploitation. Spurred on by the early successes of its researchers Hagar International is now beginning to focus on the problem of sex trafficking. Researching sex trafficking in New Zealand is "very difficult," she says, pointing to the country's "extremely powerful prostitutes collective," which she asserts is dismissive of the problem.

Human trafficking is prohibited in New Zealand by the *Crimes Act of 1961*. As the date suggests, the Act, as it was originally framed, could not have been developed in response to the *Palermo Protocol* which, in 1961, was still four decades away. Several amendments have been made to the Act over the years. Nonetheless, a distinction is made in the Act between slavery (Section 98) and human trafficking (Section 98D). It was not until early November 2015 that the law was changed to state an offense of human trafficking was committed by an individual who "arranges the entry of a person into New Zealand or any other State by one or more acts of coercion against the person, one or more acts of deception of the person, or both."[110]

It is also an offence to arrange, organize or procure "the reception, concealment, or harbouring in New Zealand or any other State of a person, knowing that the person's entry into New Zealand or that State was arranged by one or more acts of coercion against the person, one or more acts of deception of the person, or both."[111] It is clear New Zealand's previous definition of human trafficking did not conform to the *Palermo Protocol*, as the protocol does not make travel a requirement, let alone a prerequisite. In a seemingly innocuous statement made before the country's law was changed, the *2014 Trafficking in Persons Report* recommends New Zealand "redefine 'trafficking' … to fit international law definitions, and implement action plan items consistent with the new definition."[112] A year later the State Department repeated the recommendation, this time stating how New Zealand should "update the national action plan to address current trafficking trends in the country by redefining 'trafficking' to conform to international law."[113] It also points to how "New Zealand statutes define human trafficking as a transnational offense akin to smuggling and do not include exploitation as an element of the crime".[114] It further adds while slavery is criminalized in New Zealand, it is of a form limited "to situations of debt bondage and serfdom; this prohibition does not cover forced labor obtained by means other than debt, law, custom, or agreement that prohibits a person from leaving employment."[115] In 2010 New Zealand's Justice Susan Glazebrook, who today serves on that country's Supreme Court, penned *Human Trafficking and New Zealand*. In it she notes how, when it comes to recognizing instances of human trafficking, a "fundamental requirement of the offence is that of entry into New Zealand. Thus New Zealand's trafficking provisions are focused solely upon external trafficking."[116] Consequently, committing an offence of human trafficking within New Zealand was not legislatively possible until November 2015 when the country's law was brought into line with the *Palermo Protocol*.[117] Until then, only the human trafficking of people to New Zealand, a daunting challenge given the combination of its geography and the restrictions upon travel to the country, was an offence under its law.

Children, it seems, do not fare much better in New Zealand. The *2020 Trafficking in Persons Report* recommends New Zealand improves front-line training to ensure "officials understand that children in commercial sex are victims of trafficking."[118] The government's 2002 document *Protecting Our Innocence: New Zealand's National Plan of Action against the Commercial Sexual Exploitation of Children*, published just prior to decriminalization states: "Children or young people often do not identify themselves as either sex workers or prostitutes, nor do they view their actions in the context of those terms."[119] Should this be a consideration? Estimating "the true nature and extent of child prostitution in New Zealand is difficult due to the clandestine nature of the activity. However, research and anecdotal evidence suggest child prostitution is a growing problem in New Zealand," it adds.[120] Yet under no conception of prostitution, neither broad nor narrow, or indeed under the *Palermo Protocol*, is the prostitution of children considered anything other than human trafficking! Not so in New Zealand it seems for the same plan explains how, for human trafficking to occur, even in the case of children, there must be "the transporting of a person from one place to another."[121] There are other places where the human trafficking of children is hiding in plain sight. A 2012 parliamentary research paper published figures for prosecutions and convictions supplied by the country's Ministry of Justice on what it terms "under-age prostitution."[122] From 2004 to 2011 inclusive there were 133 prosecutions resulting in 57 convictions, the figures reveal. The country's prostitutes collective openly states how, among its objectives, it seeks to support those individuals providing sexual services who are *not yet 18 years old*, to help them avail of their options, including if wished to exit the sex trade.[123]

This is evidence of human trafficking, is it not? "Yes, it is," Ms. Scott-Webb responds. "There are some parts of New Zealand where this is a known problem, particularly in South Auckland, which traditionally has been a lower socio-economic area … and there are parts of it where it is known under-age prostitutes work on the streets. … One of the other things that is known to be happening here in New Zealand is there is a lot of trafficking between the [biker] gangs of young women and girls, and I'm assuming young boys as well … to the extent that when the Rugby World Cup was held here … years ago there were gangs from the South Island who were trafficking kids up to work in prostitution in Wellington around the big matches. Because we have no legislation that can capture that as trafficking it all gets watered down," she says. Long after Ms. Scott-Webb shared her assessment, the *2021 Trafficking in Persons Report* announced it was lowering New Zealand's tier ranking. The country was now designated as Tier 2. Numerous reasons were given. The report noted while "government convicted offenders in more cases of child sex trafficking than in previous years, it did not identify any victims in these cases as trafficking victims, as it did not use a system to specifically designate individuals as trafficking victims".[124] The problem was once again one of definition. It was recommended the country "[a]mend the trafficking statute to explicitly define the sex trafficking of children as not requiring the use of deception or coercion".[125]

At the time of the interview, Hagar International had recently responded to claims of two women being held against their will in an apartment in Auckland, allegedly for the purpose of sex trafficking. The organization was vehemently opposed to the way in which the matter was treated by authorities. Instead of treating the women as possible victims of human trafficking, police were more intent on treating the pair as violators of the country's immigration rules, the organization protested.[126] Their deportation from the country may be the only outcome of the case. It is "so typical of what happens in New Zealand," according to Ms. Scott-Webb. "They kind of missed the point that somewhere in there are women asking for help and I find that quite distressing," she says.

All factors considered, it was apparent prostitution was only decriminalized for those who, under the law, could never have been classed as victims of human trafficking. So how then should one treat claims that New Zealand's decriminalization has been a remedy to human trafficking in the sex trade? This was a question about which journalist Lincoln Tan was concerned in his article *NZ's Sex-Slave Cases 'Slip under Radar'* for the *New Zealand Herald* when he reported how no "one has been prosecuted in New Zealand for human trafficking but critics say that is only because a difference in definition is allowing cases to slip under the radar."[127] He recounts the experience of one Malaysian prostitute who claimed she was "lured here with a $4,500 cash offer, plus airfares, but was later told that it was a loan she had to repay. Her passport was also taken from her soon after she arrived."[128] She also complained at how she "had been made to work 16-hour shifts with few breaks on most days."[129] She was told this did not constitute human trafficking. In 2006 eight people were prosecuted and duly convicted for prostituting persons under 18 years of age. Additionally, one brothel client and three brothel operators were prosecuted for similar offences. They were subsequently convicted. One of the brothel owners was given just 300 hours of community service, while his secretary received 180 hours. Another was imprisoned for 21 months. The client received a period of detention of between one and two years. It was an outcome the U.S. State Department deplored as being inadequate, given the gravity of the offences.[130]

In 2008 the *Prostitution Law Reform Review Committee Report*, mandated by the *Prostitution Reform Act*, was published. It expressed its concern at how "there are still some managed sex workers who are being required by brothel operators to provide commercial sexual services against their will on occasion."[131] The plight of those working in decriminalized prostitution remained a harrowing one. According to the *Report*, of 760 prostitutes surveyed, 10% reported they had been physically assaulted in the past 12 months, 3% admitted to being raped by a client during that time, 17% had received abusive messages from a client and 5% had been held against their will in the 12-month period.[132] In 2011 the *Trafficking in Persons Report* noted anecdotal evidence of how "women, including some from Malaysia, are recruited by labor agents, but upon arrival in New Zealand, are handed over to brothel owners, who confiscate their passports and force them into prostitution for up to 18 hours a day to repay the 'loan' of recruitment and transportation costs."[133]

New Zealand's first conviction for human trafficking was secured in September of 2016 when Faroz Ali was convicted in Auckland of multiple charges of human trafficking and exploitation. He was found guilty of luring 15 Fijian workers to the country on the pretext of their being able to earn NZD900 ($640) weekly while working as fruit pickers. When the workers arrived in New Zealand they were forced to work illegally, leaving them open to being exposed to deportation from the country if they made any objections. They were indeed threatened by Ali in this manner. A few months after being convicted, Ali was given a sentence of nine years and six months and ordered to pay reparation to his victims. In *Exposed: The dark underbelly of human trafficking in New Zealand*, investigative reporter Olivia Carville asserts her newspaper has learned of instances of passports being confiscated, false promises being made, threats of deportation, "and people caught up in modern day slavery since 1990."[134] She has some tough questions. "The US Government identified New Zealand as a destination for human trafficking in 2004. So why did it take 12 years for authorities here to secure a conviction?," she asks.[135] She identifies a new-found focus on the crime of human trafficking as a factor leading to the conviction. She attributes the 2015 amendment of the country's law as another factor. There is more. Echoing the sentiments expressed by Hagar International's Ms. Scott-Webb some months before, Ms. Carville writes:

> As an isolated and supposedly clean, green and pure island in the South Pacific, one does not usually correlate the dark and sordid crime of human trafficking with the Land of the Long White Cloud. [136]

Chapter 10:

The Modern Civil War

There is appeal in trying to mentally compartmentalize certain facets of prostitution. The compartmentalization exists solely however in the mind's eye, and though it is seemingly plausible it disappears quickly when confronted by reality. The Dutch soon saw this for themselves. Ask what it was the Dutch sought to regulate and the answer is invariably *prostitution*, but the reality is more complex than the answer reveals. The legalized sector was envisaged as a sector where abuses would not, and could not, occur. In 1998 Brants gave a contemporary account of the thinking. The policy, as mentioned earlier, envisaged prostitution as "a fact of life" that "must be regarded as a normal profession, operating according to supply and demand in a market economy" and which attributed the problems of prostitution to an "illegal aura that has always surrounded it that ... attracts other forms of illegality."[1] In 2004 the Rapporteur of the time restated this ethos, advising how the lifting of the ban on brothels had separated the prostitution sector into two parts. One of these was the legal part, which the Rapporteur described as being voluntary and permitted only under particular conditions; the other was the illegal part, which was visualized as being exploitative.[2] In 2007 the Rapporteur said of the illegal sector how owing to the fact "no administrative checks are made there ... [this] makes it a suitable refuge for human traffickers."[3] The Dutch, it seemed, were trying to divide the market into consensual and non-consensual parts. Contrary to what these statements proclaim and envisage, human trafficking was not confined to the illegal sector, as was learned from the *Sneep Case*.

The case traverses the first eight years of legalization in the Netherlands. It begins in 1998, two years before the legalization of prostitution, and continues until 2008 when the perpetrators were sentenced.[4] Two aspects make it remarkable. The first is how the victims, all women, were not hidden from sight, but rather hidden in plain sight as they were sold openly in licensed window prostitution.[5] The second lies with the number victimized, which was put at 120 women.[6] Dutch Public Prosecutor Schepers states:

> As a society, we made window prostitution a licensed branch to be able to control and counter situations of abuse. But in spite of it, licensed window prostitution is the very branch in which everything went as terribly wrong as Operation SNEEP demonstrated. In licensed window prostitution human trafficking was daily practice: manipulation, coercion, exploitation, even brute forces were the order of the day. Victims were dehumanized and degenerated into mere production factors. The lifeless victims were working as mechanical devices, often even up to 12 hours or more a day, day in day out, throughout the year. The fact that the victims will then cut off their emotions and resort to their survival instinct, makes the phenomenon human trafficking so horrible, so objectionable.[7]

The scale and sophistication of the crime is proof of the level of organization that sustained it.[8] From humble beginnings a Turkish criminal group developed into an organized network, with parts of it specializing in different facets of the network's activities.[9]

The evolution of these activities meant the network became an organized criminal group. As an organized crime the implications are immediately apparent, and they point once again to the economic underpinnings of sex trafficking. The group was able to extort significant monies, purportedly as much as €1,000 daily, from their victims.[10] Moreover they were also able to work these women long hours each day, every day of the week, thus maximizing the sales made. Dutch police estimated monthly revenues at €400,000.[11] The total profit accumulated by the group over the years of its operation was estimated to be €19 million.[12] Despite encountering difficulties in gathering evidence from witnesses, Dutch police nonetheless managed to secure convictions.[13] Aside from the significance attached by Dutch police to the economic aspects of the case they also noted the significance of the violence used against the women.[14] The victims were raped, forced to undergo breast enlargements, and forced too to undergo abortions.[15] The six defendants were all found "guilty of trafficking in women with respect to one or more women."[16] The defendants were given sentences ranging from eight months to in excess of seven years.[17]

If one measures the premise for legalization, which advocated it was prostitution's illegal status rather than its economics that incentivized exploitation, against its own yardstick then the premise is found wanting. Even when prostitution was legalized, much of what went on in it remained immersed in criminality.[18] In 2008 *Trafficking in Persons Report* noted how Amsterdam's authorities had closed one-third of the red light district about that time due to illegal activities and how overall "legalization and regulation have not dried up sex trafficking, which has continued apace."[19] In 2009 the Dutch Rapporteur pointed to the closure of licensed window prostitution in Amsterdam, Arnhem and Alkmaar under the *BIBOC Act*, which sought to curtail serious crime.[20] In 2015 Utrecht's city council approved the opening in about

2017 of a new prostitution district not far from the old district of the Zandpad.[21] Only two years earlier the local authority had withdrawn the license of the only remaining legal operator, amidst claims of human trafficking.[22] At about the same time brothels in another of Utrecht's districts, this time Hardebollenstraat, were also closed and, despite an appeal, the decisions to close were upheld. Some who decried the closure of the Zandpad were prostitutes who had worked for a legal operator. They claiming they were happy with the way that the operator had conducted the trade. The Rapporteur notes:

> A number of prostitutes did indeed clearly state that they were independent, were not forced to become prostitutes and would now lose their livelihood. They also said they were satisfied with ... [the legal operator]. However, they only represented a small proportion of the women, and it is highly questionable whether they were speaking on behalf of the entire population of women working on the Zandpad. The notion that all of the women working on the Zandpad were independent and working voluntarily was, in any case, contradicted by the facts.[23]

Since 2006 the role of the Dutch National Rapporteur on Trafficking in Human Beings and Sexual Violence against Children has been occupied by former district court judge Ms. Corinne Dettmeijer. Through numerous reports she, and her team, have painstakingly recounted the experience of her country's policy approach. As a resource, there is scarcely anything that comes close by comparison. In a 2012 interview with the Rapporteur she states how "crime hasn't really diminished. So on that account it hasn't really worked so well."[24] She points to the licensed window prostitution sector, where "it is mostly Hungarian, Romanian, Bulgarian women ... and many of them are coerced or forced or misled into prostitution." This is despite the fact licensed window prostitution forms part of the licensed legal sector. In her 2013 report the Rapporteur observes:

> The romantic ideal of articulate men and women who choose to work in prostitution entirely voluntarily is refuted by the harsh reality – a reality in which human traffickers deceive, abuse, threaten and exploit the vulnerable position of men and women, minors and adults, Dutch and non-Dutch.[25]

Operation Koolvis had its humble origins in a May 2006 report made to police by a lawyer who suspected her Nigerian client might be a victim of human trafficking.[26] In time the operation expanded to include authorities in other European countries and in Nigeria.[27] At the outset it was discovered how between 2005 and 2006 a large number of unaccompanied minors had arrived from Nigeria.[28] Soon after, the nature and full scale of the crime being perpetrated became evident, with the Netherlands being used as a transit country for Nigerian children destined to other European countries such as Spain, Italy and France.[29] Traffickers are known to have brought more than 100 girls to Europe to sell them into prostitution.[30] The girls were told to apply for asylum immediately upon arrival in the Netherlands and to escape from their place of detention at the first opportunity. To ensure their compliance Voodoo, or African witchcraft, was one of the coercive elements employed.[31] Upon escape some of them were put to work, for a time, in the country's legalized window prostitution.[32]

Unfortunately, when these matters came before the court it found the burden of evidence too heavy to allow for a trafficking conviction, despite the enormity of the crime perpetrated. It "found that it could not be concluded that the suspects had knowledge of the things that had happened to the girls in Nigeria or the things that would probably happen to them in Italy and/or Spain, including forced prostitution."[33] The sentences handed out ranged from one to four-and-a-half years, with some of the defendants being acquitted.[34] In commenting on the scale of the offence Hans Gaasbeek, Vice-President for the organization Lawyers without Borders, pointed to the fact that those being trafficked were mere children. He decried that it wasn't considered a priority issue and pointed to the fact that had the case involved more than 100 Dutch girls public indignation would have been uncontainable.[35] Ineke van Buren, a coordinator with the Fier Fryslan network on human trafficking, felt no lessons had been learned from Operation Koolvis. Despondently she pointed to the amounts of money being made from trafficking in human beings as the reason why the problem was growing.[36] There is good cause to suppose that van Buren was correct in that assessment, as police estimated trafficking activities in the Koolvis case generated profits of €4 million.[37]

Children are exploited in the Dutch prostitution sector by other means too. One particularly resilient mode of recruitment of girls is the *Loverboy Method*, by which a male romantically woos his prospective victim. In time he betrays her trust, and she is either enticed or forced, into prostitution. Either way, she is now a victim of human trafficking. In the 2013 report of the Dutch Rapporteur, she says:

> Underage Dutch victims are too often seen as girls with "a loverboy problem" rather than as victims of human trafficking. As I said in my report *Trafficking in Human Beings: Visible and Invisible*, this group comprises a substantial number of girls. My earnest desire is for the term "loverboy problem" to be abandoned altogether and the phenomenon to be referred to by its proper name: human trafficking ... The perception of this group, as adolescents with a problem, is persistent. We also see this phenomenon in other countries, although the situation does seem

> to be changing as it becomes increasingly evident that young girls are easy prey and generate a lot of money for human traffickers.[38]

One seemingly unintended consequence of legalization, and with hindsight a significant one at that, was how the Dutch expectation of prostitution did not envisage all who were actual participants. The vision could not be inclusive of all of those engaged in prostitution, as not all who were prostitutes were citizens of the European Union. Those who were not EU citizens had no automatic legal right to work in the European Union. Two years before legalization, Brants noted how new laws would not protect highly vulnerable illegal immigrants as deportation was the most likely outcome for those who had been compelled into prostitution. This, Brants cautioned, would have the effect of driving these immigrants into situations where they were entirely at risk from exploitation and further abuse.[39] More than a decade later it was clear how this is indeed what happened.[40] The significance of this oversight cannot be overstated. One estimate put the number of non-EU female prostitutes in the country at 65% to 80%, making them the largest group of prostitutes in the country. Another significant group were children, a group who could never legally work in the legalized sector. A Canadian governmental report concluded, perhaps somewhat overly pessimistically, that six years after the introduction of legalized prostitution "only 4% of individuals selling sexual services in the Netherlands have registered with the authorities."[41] The minority who engaged in the licensed sector was now in effect in competition with a majority in the unlicensed illegal sector. While it is plausible to state the Dutch legalized prostitution, it is nonetheless the case that on the day prior to legalization in effect all prostitution was illegal, while on the day after legalization most of it was still illegal.

Of question too is whether the boundaries of the legal and illegal spheres delineate borders that cannot be crossed. In the U.S. State of Nevada where prostitution in brothels has been legalized, it is nonetheless only permitted in certain counties. A clear effort is made to isolate these brothels to ensure prostitutes cannot work in both the legal and illegal sectors at the same time. To achieve this, prostitutes and brothel operators have been subject to a range of extraordinary restrictions. Brothels must be located within certain counties, particularly in ones isolated from communities. In some instances, the prostitutes working in these brothels have been required to remain within the vicinity of their work even when not working. In other instances, they have been restricted from leaving their county for protracted periods in case they might engage in prostitution's illegal sphere. Prostitutes have sometimes been restricted from leaving the brothel after 5pm, and brothel operators have been required to notify local police of their car's registration plate.[42]

Another problem encountered by the Dutch, one that could have been anticipated, had the relationship between trafficker and trafficked been truly understood, concerned the concept of consenting adults. As tangible as the concept may seem, a challenge is presented when one is asked to discern a consenting adult from a non-consenting one. The control manifested by traffickers is real but the manner by which control is exerted is often less apparent.[43] The Dutch National Rapporteur observed how this presents a very real problem for "[p]rostitution inspectors [who] often cannot identify the signs that women are working involuntarily in the prostitution industry, so criminal investigation does not occur."[44] Thus though there was a legal sector, not all that went on it was actually legal. The seemingly dualistic nature of prostitution, divided into legal regulated *versus* illegal unregulated manifestations, was itself challenged by other events. The Rapporteur later observed how "[t]hree sectors have arisen since the legalisation of prostitution: the illegal, the legal licensed and the legal unlicensed [sector]."[45]

The emergence of this unforeseen third sector was typical of the evolution taking place in the prostitution sector. A key premise of regulation of prostitution entailed its geographic curtailment. Prostitution would be pinned down and, in pinning it down, it would be controlled. In reality, however, the geographical element by which municipalities were supposed to govern prostitution became less relevant.[46] The law seems to have lost a lot of its utility due to a number of factors, some of which were designed to deliberately circumvent it. First, in 2007 the Rapporteur observed how "prostitutes from (previously) significant countries of origin for victims … have apparently found a way to work in the sex industry legally, for instance *via* marriages of convenience or self-employment."[47] Second, the Internet and the mobile phone made new operations, outside the legalized sector, increasingly mobile.[48] Escorting was now a legal activity. In some cases, municipalities imposed no licensing requirement on the escorting businesses based in them so it was sufficient of itself for such businesses to be based in these municipalities to fulfil legal requirements. In other cases, it was difficult to establish where precisely the business should have been based. Nonetheless having attained legal status for their business in one municipality, escorts were now free to roam to other municipalities giving rise to the legal unlicensed sector.[49] In 2004 the Rapporteur acknowledged of businesses in this sector how "it is very complicated in practice to check whether the business makes use of underage or illegal prostitutes, or victims [of human trafficking]."[50] In her 2010 report the Rapporteur noted how the "exclusion of the sector from the licensing system … [meant] no administrative control … [could] be exercised over it. Accordingly, the Rapporteur … expressed concern about the possibility of the banned variants of the exploitation of prostitution becoming rooted in this sector."[51] Third, and finally, the number of licensed businesses and their clients were diminishing by 2006.[52] In an interview with the Dutch Rapporteur, Ms. Dettmeijer, she said, "we do know that we do not have street prostitution anymore and that not all the street prostitutes went into the licensed prostitution area. Some of them stopped [engaging in prostitution entirely]." She comments on how the "prostitution population has changed dramatically" and how "it doesn't look like [it was] fifteen years ago." She attributes the changes in the country's sex industry over this period to the role of the Internet, its participation in the EU, and an influx of non-EU citizens.[53]

To address elements of the legal unlicensed sector in the Netherlands new administrative measures were proposed. Tellingly they had many of the same objectives established for legalization nine years earlier, and one could argue, not achieved through it.[54] Thus one can conclude the effect was derived not from whether the sector was legal or illegal, as established by legalization, but rather from the degree to which measures were enforced.[55] There is ample evidence to show the Dutch struggled heavily in this regard.[56] Overall, the burden placed upon the public prosecution service and the police meant they never had, over the first nine years of legalization at least, sufficient capacity to deal with all that was expected of them.[57] In December 2009 a Dutch parliamentary committee concluded decentralization of the existing administrative arrangements had not worked due to a "lack of uniformity in the rules on issuing licences and the conditions to be attached to them; supervision and enforcement; [and problems with] the registration of sex workers and the criminalisation of prostitutes."[58] The new measures were described as being "intended to create the most comprehensive possible administrative system that by regulating the sector can improve efforts to address abuses in the sex industry, provide better protection for prostitutes and provide better support for combating human trafficking, prostitution by minors and forced prostitution through criminal law."[59] Ultimately these new measures passed. Perplexingly the initiative was entitled *Safety Begins with Prevention*.[60]

In Sweden too prostitution was changing. There too the role of technology was also making itself felt where, by 2006, its Rapporteur was noting how:

> sex buyers can order women to Sweden *via* the Internet by calling a booking centre abroad. Travels and hotel rooms are paid, probably by the booking centre, and then the women are sent to order to Sweden or to some other country. Instructions to the women and the sex buyers about time and place for agreed purchases of sex are given *via* the Internet and SMS. In the advertisement it very often appears in plain text that the sex buyer is to pay a certain part of the purchase sum (often half of it) into an account and pay the rest in cash to the woman.[61]

By 2009 the Rapporteur was observing how "[t]he sale and purchase of sexual services now takes place largely over the Internet."[62] A Swedish government review of the ban also noted the role and growth of the Internet as a factor in prostitution.[63] Reductions in street prostitution did not lead to "a change in arenas," it claimed or in other words, those who once worked as street prostitutes did not migrate into off-street variants.[64] At the outset Sweden, like the Netherlands, experienced difficulties with its law. The Rapporteur noted in 2006 how problems were experienced by police in their efforts to prove the link between buyer and prostitute.[65] By the time of a later review this situation seems to have improved.[66] Eighty per cent of those prosecuted for purchasing sexual services were now admitting to having done so, thus facilitating the case against them.[67] The penalties imposed have been "for the most part, limited to fines."[68]

The legal economies of human trafficking persist, however, and the offence of human trafficking remains a challenging one to prosecute. Prosecutions are likely made more difficult to obtain due to the reluctance of victims to facilitate investigations and trials. Quite simply, victims are too afraid.[69] This is true even when there is no possibility of these victims having committed an offence by selling sex.[70] Instead prosecutors may prefer to seek "convictions for procuring / aggravated procuring."[71] The financial economies of human trafficking are explicitly acknowledged by the Swedes. Ekberg states how, in Sweden, it "is understood that the purpose of the recruitment, transport, sale, or purchase of women and girls by traffickers, pimps, and members of organized crime groups within countries or across national borders is, in the overwhelming majority of cases, to sell these female human beings into the prostitution industry."[72] These realities mean human trafficking continues to exist in Sweden, despite attempts to eradicate it.

A highly organized case of sex trafficking in Sweden involved a large-scale Estonian trafficking network that sold women for sex from 15 addresses.[73] Coercion was evident, with some of the women owing a debt to their trafficker and being expected to work it off. The women were required to hand over 50% of their daily earnings to representatives of their trafficker and, even when they had not worked, monies were still due. Three cases were progressed against the network. In one such case profits were put at €100,000 and in another they were estimated to be €50,000 "for 212 days of work for the women involved."[74] Some insight can be gleaned as to the distribution of the monies earned. In one case police estimated, traffickers earned €80,000 in profits from the work of several women over the course of one year sharing just €24,000 of this with their victims.[75] Thus for every €10 earned, the traffickers were taking €7, while passing along €3 to those they victimized. The Swedish

National Rapporteur references an "Estonian grouping which had been involved in trafficking in human beings for sexual purposes."[76] The report notes how Sweden had since been "abandoned ... as a market" by this group.[77]

On the experiences gleaned from Sweden and the Netherlands, enforcement of the approach is as important as the approach itself. In 2006 Sweden's Rapporteur noticed how "it is very difficult to prove the crime of trafficking in human beings, [with the consequence that] this crime is in many ways also very resource-demanding."[78] The Swedish Rapporteur says, "surveillance for long periods, translations, interpreters, telephone interception, and travels to the countries of origin of the victims to look for evidence make the costs of these cases soar."[79] Thus there is an asymmetric cost element, with traffickers seeking to earn money from their investment, while government is compelled to invest its own money to prevent them from earning. The Rapporteur has vindicated the Swedish Model on the basis it is the "least resource-heavy way to handle prostitution and human trafficking."[80] So if enforcement, rather than administration, is the key to attaining the goals of prostitution policy, the approach maximizing resources for enforcement should be the one that proves most successful.

Detective Sergeant Jonas Henriksson has worked with the Stockholm section of Sweden's Prostitution Unit since it started in 2009, combatting prostitution and the human trafficking he encounters in it. Interestingly the detective notes how, though the Internet offers unparalleled opportunities to advertise women for sexual services, the women advertised are often not those shown in the adverts. "The buyer is buying another body, we can't get away from that, because what we see is that [even when the buyer finds the prostitute isn't the one advertised they will sometimes] go away, but that is one out of ten. Usually they go ahead anyway," he states.[81] Through their actions the buyer demonstrates how, when it comes to buying sex, one person is as good as another, which in turn illustrates the commoditized nature of these transactions. Even when the person who was intended to be purchased is absent there is nothing preventing the transaction from going ahead. There is no value or quality specific to the person meaning they cannot be substituted for something similar, that is, something of a similar price. Does this tally with the daily experience of what the detective sees of prostitution in Sweden? "Yes, yes, absolutely. As soon as we see an advertisement with decent pictures, with a price tag that is a little bit lower than what's usual ... there's a lot more buyers there. Immediately!" he responds emphatically. The full weight of the implication of this economic insight ought to be clear.

Appreciating the opportunity afforded by the heterogeneity of markets, and the willingness of a small number of buyers to pay for commodities of a different ilk, some prostitutes verify their picture is indeed the one advertised. Those who do this capture a segment of the market and charge a premium for doing so, but they are in the minority, and they do not reflect the tale of the population overall. In his experience, Detective Sergeant Henriksson notes, poignantly, how even when it is the case that some are doing better than most others in prostitution, one often finds that "something has happened, ... they have some kind of trauma in the background."

Markets express their diversity in a multitude of ways. The way in which they distribute money is just one of them. In the case of prostitution, gender is another. So too is ethnicity and a great many of those working in prostitution are non-nationals who are even more susceptible to exploitation than their counterparts. Often non-national women are brought to Sweden by boyfriends, and many of them know they are going to be selling sex, but once they have arrived the nature of the arrangement changes into something much more coercive. So prevalent is exploitation among this group the detective is confident 95% of them are trafficked, but even this figure he believes is conservative. Numbers alone don't tell a full story, but they do give some idea of the scale of the suffering. From 2003 to 2012 inclusive, there were 271 reported cases of human trafficking for sexual purposes in Sweden. Sometimes Swedish prosecutors chose to pursue a case of procuring or one of aggravated procuring instead of trafficking. There were 830 such cases during the same period.[82] One edition of the *Trafficking in Persons Report* reported that Swedish police put the number of persons exploited in Sweden annually at 400 to 600. Unsurprisingly prostitution has provided the forum where most have been exploited. More surprising, however, is the disclosure that "in 2011 the number of reported labor trafficking victims was larger than the number of reported sex trafficking victims."[83]

Between 1992 and 1999 inclusive Dutch authorities identified 1,301 potential victims of human trafficking working in its prostitution sector, with 287 of these identified in 1999 alone.[84] From 2000 to 2009 inclusive the total number of victims of human trafficking located in the Netherlands accounted for 5,084 persons, across a variety of forms of exploitation.[85] A breakdown of the figures for the period 2007 to 2009 inclusive reveals sex trafficking accounted for 50% of those exploited. This figure may well be much higher, and it is likely to be, as in the case of 39% of victims the reason for exploitation either could not be ascertained or the person had been recovered before their exploitation could begin.[86] On average, a minimum of 410 victims of trafficking were identified in prostitution each year over this three-year period. In 2012 a total of 1,711 potential victims of human trafficking were registered for just that year alone, with 1,216 (71%) exploited in the sex trade.[87] At first glance it seems human trafficking in the Netherlands is increasing. This may be so, but it is also possible detections are increasing to converge on the real number exploited. Whatever is happening the trend remains unclear, and this too is a problem for legalization.

Years after the approach was introduced even the most fundamental of questions remains unanswered. Nobody can say for sure, for example, how many individuals work in Holland's prostitution sector. In *Does Legalised Prostitution Generate More Human Trafficking?* the Rapporteur says, "an estimated 20,000 people in the Netherlands were working in prostitution in 2012. While a similar estimate has been repeatedly cited, it seems to come from a study carried out in 1999, before the abolition of the ban on brothels. At the moment, there are no reliable figures available for the total number of prostitutes in the Netherlands."[88] The Rapporteur asserts "it is not known how many women are forced to work in the prostitution sector in relation to the number who do so voluntarily … Evidently, some prostitutes are exploited, but because of the hidden nature of both human trafficking and prostitution, it is difficult to say how large this proportion is."[89] Clearly more answers are needed.

In the *Ninth Report on Trafficking in Human Beings*, published in 2013 the Dutch Rapporteur states: "Questions about the effectiveness of measures and moral arguments must be kept separate. Instead of asking 'What is a desirable policy on prostitution for combating exploitation?' the leading question in the debate should be 'What is the most effective policy on prostitution for combating exploitation?.'"[90] If regulation does not command moral strength can it be effective? Much of the advocacy for legalization rests on guaranteeing consent through market regulation, but what happens if those whose consent is to be guaranteed don't consent to be regulated? This is precisely what happened in the Netherlands when it was proposed a register would be introduced to strengthen regulation. The Rapporteur has long advocated for these measures, deeming them to be crucial to regulating the sector.[91] One petition, from the Prostitution Information Center, opposed regulatory measures at the heart of legalization. It denounced the notion that governmental databases are either temporary or secret. Any persons who would register to be included would carry thereafter be labelled a prostitute for the remainder of their days, it cautioned. Reminiscent of the point made by Rade and Shah in *The Dutch Myth of Tolerance*, the petition also cautions how popular perceptions of Dutch tolerance do not match the reality on the ground.[92] The Rapporteur is aware the "most important drawback of the registration requirement, according to various sources who were consulted (from the police, the social services and the municipality, but also among the operators) is that the women themselves do not fully support it. For example, prostitutes feel that registration threatens their privacy and does not contribute to combating human trafficking."[93] The measures for which the Rapporteur had so intensely lobbied, the measures deemed so necessary to regulation, were removed from the Bill.

There were other reasons not to consent to the requirements of regulation. Even in the run-up to legalization concerns arose about *competitive advantage*. It was felt the introduction of licenses would result in small brothels being priced out of the market by high costs. It was further felt the decline of these operators would be accompanied by a concentration of money and power in fewer hands.[94] Those who worked in the legal licensed sector now found themselves competing against a greater number who were neither licensed, nor legal. The Rapporteur points to the conundrum of "unfair competition: if the licensed – and *bona fide* – sector is subject to regulation and / or monitoring but illegal operators are allowed to operate relatively undisturbed, legitimate operators are at a disadvantage."[95] A campaign run by a union for prostitutes exemplified the situation when it claimed Dutch prostitutes were having to compete with others coming to the Netherlands from Russia, the Dominican Republic, and Eastern Europe.[96]

There are several resources indicating what prostitutes in the Netherlands charge per hour, but hourly charges are not the same as actual earnings. One online article advised prostitutes around 2012 how research into the trade's earnings, when all forms of the activity were combined, averaged €15 per hour. The article noted however how this was an average figure and net income for some may be as low as €5 per hour, with others getting €25 hourly.[97] In contrast to the diminishing licensed sector "[i]llegal prostitution in hotels ... [appeared] to have increased since the ban on brothels was lifted, due to technological developments and other factors."[98] An assortment of businesses "such as massage parlours, beauty parlours, tanning salons, couples' clubs, saunas and erotic cafes" provided cover for illegal prostitution.[99] By 2013 Dutch police were pointing to the trend of prostitutes migrating from regulated brothels to illegal home-based ones to escape the restraints imposed.[100] In their 2010 article *The Audacity of Tolerance: A Critical Analysis of Legalized Prostitution in Amsterdam's Red Light District* Cruz and van Iterson reveal how in Amsterdam one witnesses a situation where many prostitutes select to operate outside the legal sector simply because there are more benefits.[101]

In Germany too, where prostitution has also been legalized, the tale is much the same. Business is thriving, but the fate of those working in prostitution is not. In its 2013 article, entitled *Unprotected: How Legalizing Prostitution Has Failed*, Germany's *Der Spiegel* spoke to Andrea Weppert, a social worker in Nuremberg, where the number of prostitutes has tripled over the past 20 years. As the numbers grew, working conditions declined. Across all of Germany, Weppert added, prostitutes were providing increasingly more services for less money than they were getting a decade before, and under more dangerous conditions.[102]

In the U.S. state of Nevada a downturn in the economy, combined with rising costs, the perpetual outlay of monies to middlemen, and the lure of revenue from Internet-based business meant legal prostitution was proving less alluring. In a report by Chris Morris for CNBC entitled *Brothel or Bust: Hard Times at Nevada's Bordellos*, a lobbyist for the Nevada Brothel Owners Association advised how a decline in business led to a migration by many prostitutes from legal brothels to illegal prostitution. The lobbyist advised too how the rise of technology had provided attractive opportunities in the illegal sector.[103]

Disrespecting prostitutes was tantamount to disrespecting all women, the leader of a labor union for prostitutes in the Dutch red-light district, once reportedly proclaimed.[104] It may seem counterintuitive but, in legitimizing the activity of prostitution, priority may have been given to the activity rather than to the individuals engaged in it. The closure of brothels in the Netherlands by the authorities led to a lessening of supply, but not of demand, thus it was the operators of the sex businesses who benefitted through elevated rates of utilization of their facilities and employees.[105] There were now more prostitutes than there were licensed premises in which to work. With their bargaining power diminished, few had opportunities to run their own business and "[t]he prostitute's position ... deteriorated as a result."[106] The pragmatic implications of these points go much further however, and they have a resounding impact upon assessing just how pragmatic Dutch policy proved to be.

Did the Dutch regulate prostitution? Ostensibly the answer is yes. They certainly legalized it under specific conditions, and it was most certainly the intent this would result in regulation, but regulating an industry entails much more than intent. Regulation necessitates some form of control, including control by bureaucratic measures and auditing the application of those measures. Transparency then is not only an outcome of regulation but a prerequisite, for how can one regulate what is wholly opaque? Yet at least 18 years after legalization, by which time further information becomes comparatively scant, the transparency once promised as an outcome of legalization and consequently of regulation, is nowhere to be seen. At what, precisely, could one look today to conclude the trade is transparent? Instead, the lack of transparency now shrouding the sector is used to defend it against failures, even against failures to attain the goals it had once set for itself. Most of the sector remains in the illegal sphere where there is no regulation. Paradoxically when one compares what is known about human trafficking in the country's prostitution sector to what is known about the sector overall, the trove of information produced by Ms. Dettmeijer and her team on trafficking, amounting to thousands of pages, stands in stark contrast to any tangible information on a sector supposedly legitimate and regulated. It once again illustrates how legitimacy does not necessarily result in transparency but in privacy. Dutch policy has never been able to establish a sizeable footprint for itself in the prostitution sector. What little it initially managed to establish has been diminishing ever since. So, the question remains: did the Dutch regulate prostitution? Or did their policy mean the Dutch merely entered the market, as a competitor among many others, imposing controls with varying degrees of success on what little they managed to secure?

Linda Watson knows prostitution better than most having spent 20 years in the sector in Australia. She started out as a prostitute before also becoming a madam. In time she founded her own escort agency. At one time she had 35 women working for her on any given day. Over the years she encountered many women, hundreds of them in fact, engaged in prostitution. Now she encounters them in a differently. In 1997 she experienced a change of heart and she established *Linda's House of Hope* in Australia to help women escape from prostitution. Her organization provides a variety of services, including counseling and a range of practical supports. In late 2013 she provided an interview for this research. Why the change of heart? "I saw so much damage – to myself and the women I employed – caused by prostitution. There is drug addiction, mental and physical pain that you do not realize when you start", she conveys.[107] She knows the realities of prostitution personally: "Most prostitutes say they have been raped by customers. I was, more than once – and bashed," she shares.

Fully cognizant of how foreign migrants have shaped prostitution, and indeed how they have been shaped by it, she pointed to the many Asian prostitutes working in Perth. Many of these she believed may have been trafficked into the sector. She believed the situation to be the same in Adelaide from accounts imparted to her from a reliable source. Contemporary to the interview, she noted how of 120 brothels visited "90 have Asian workers – out of all proportion to the number of Asians in the population generally". When asked whether, in her experience, prostitution can be regulated she replied, "No – I tell MPs who think it can be that they're dreaming. Look at Amsterdam – they legalized and regulated it and now it's out of control."

Within Sweden the law is credited with curtailing the number engaged in prostitution. Estimates around 2015, according to Detective Sergeant Henriksson, put the number of prostitutes in Sweden at approximately 1,000 working in the trade. They are not all active at the same time, he cautions, but over the course of year there may be this many engaged in prostitution. In the 1970s estimates put the figure at about 3,000, and by the 1990s this figure was 3,500, he recounts. The comparatively small number estimated to be working in prostitution in Sweden today "correlates with what I see," he says. A 2010 review concluded street prostitution has about halved since the law was introduced, and "that is also what I see, that street prostitution is more or less gone." Overall Detective Sergeant Henriksson is content Sweden's law has kept prostitution to a minimum, certainly in comparison "to the other countries where it has flourished." The law has achieved its aim by targeting the buyer. On a rare occasion the police find they have arrested a buyer who they had arrested before, but this is not predominantly the case. The detective's team is small, however, numbering only six police officers for all of Sweden, so those they arrest are only a portion of those patronizing prostitution. While other sections of Sweden's police force also tackle buyers of sexual services, Detective Sergeant Henriksson's team is the only one dedicated to the issue. Yet there is no reason to believe those they arrest are not representative of the population of buyers. The detective believes the law is an effective deterrent against patronizing sexual services.

Economics are inherent to Sweden's approach. The approach targets the demand side of a market relationship founded upon supply and demand, so the question then is whether policy on human trafficking can be effective in the absence of its addressing monetary considerations? He answers, "I think that the most important thing when talking about this is that first you have to agree on the fact that when it comes to prostitution ... the absolute majority of prostitution involves human trafficking ... and when you look at human trafficking there is money for criminal organizations, and when you look at criminal organizations as [ones existing to acquire] money, they look at demand and supply, so if you want to defeat them, you need to focus on what they are focusing on. They are working in economics," he says. So, what does success look like? "We know what we do has an effect. Success to me ... is pushing down demand by arresting sex buyers. ... Equally important is what [Sweden's police force's] human trafficking section does in figuring out the networks and targeting them," he says. There is more, for there must be success too in helping victims of human trafficking. "We are trying to protect this massive group of people who are being used," he says.

Survivor Wendy Barnes has her own harrowing experience to look to in formulating her views. Should the buyers of sexual services be criminalized? "Yes, definitely, it should be a crime for those who buy sex," she responds, adding how over the many years of her victimization she encountered a broad spectrum of punters.[108] At one end of this spectrum there are some who are naive, and who thought they were actually doing her a favor by paying her for sex when in fact her predicament was the result of their willingness to pay. At the other end of the spectrum there are some who are brutish individuals. This latter group she thinks would be less inclined to be deterred by criminalization, but the former group most certainly would be deterred resulting in a reduction in demand overall. Ms. Barnes doesn't subscribe to the contention consensual sex is being purchased. It is a characteristic credited to the transaction that is entirely outward-looking. She does not believe it reflects reality, however. The buyer is concerned only with one thing and that is inward-facing: "their sexual satisfaction is what is being bought," she asserts.

Clearly in making these efforts the Swedes do not make a distinction between legal and illegal forms of prostitution, and they may well be justified in their assessment for it may indeed be the case there is not a corresponding difference in levels of trafficking within them. When this question was put to the Dutch Rapporteur in an interview she remarked: "I would, first of all, not say that there is less trafficking in the licensed sector than there is in the illegal sector."[109] In their journal article *Does Legalized Prostitution Increase Human Trafficking?* Cho *et al.* compare prostitution in Denmark, where self-employed prostitution is permitted but brothels are not, with Sweden, where prostitution in all its forms is criminalized. They find the distribution of trafficked persons among their respective prostitute populations is roughly equal, despite their legislative differences.[110] In their research they look at the inward flows of victims of human trafficking over a global sample of 150 countries, spanning the years 1996 to 2003. They conclude international traffickers are disinterested in countries with low incomes.[111] In constructing their research Cho *et al.* assume the market for prostitution exists as a single market and not as two markets: one legal and the other illegal.[112] Significantly in analyzing their findings they conclude they are justified in their assumption of their being a single market.[113]

Cho *et al.* argue the theory for legalizing prostitution, and the theory against legalizing it, are based on two opposing effects. These they call the *substitution effect* and the *scale effect*. Proponents of the former argue coercive forms of prostitution are substituted for less coercive forms, making prostitution a comparatively safer activity. Proponents of the latter argue that human trafficking accounts for a proportion of the population of prostitutes, and that consequently when the demand for prostitution is legitimized the population of prostitutes is enlarged, and so too, consequently, the number of victims of trafficking. Cho *et al.* state their observed analysis, spanning 150 countries, demonstrates the dominance of the *scale effect* over the *substitution effect*.[114] They also conclude countries where prostitution is legally tolerated report larger inflows of human trafficking.[115] They find the type of legalization does not matter. What does matter is whether prostitution is legal or whether it is not.[116] If Cho *et al.* are correct then it is the size of the market that matters, for according to their conclusions, the bigger the market the greater the number of slaves there must be. Moreover, if Cho *et al.* are correct their study of legalized prostitution is a vindication not of the policy approach adopted by the Dutch, but rather of the one adopted by the Swedes.

There is, however, another possibility and it too is problematic for proponents of legalization. In contrast to the illegal prostitution sector, which was increasing in the Netherlands, it was noted by 2006 how the number of licensed businesses, and their clients, was diminishing.[117] The Dutch Rapporteur was asked about these events. She confirms that by 2006 it was evident the number of licensed businesses in the Netherlands was declining and that six years later, in 2012, this was still the case.[118] The "amount of business in the licensed window prostitution area is diminishing and that it is also shifting because one of the complaints of the licensed" prostitutes is how they feel "they are being scrutinised all the time, which makes it harder for them to work, while the illegal sex worker is being left alone."[119] There has been a preference then to move to less regulated forms. A 2010 report by Humanity In Action, was emphatic that government attempts to introduce improved conditions for those in the sex trade and remove exploitation by criminals had yielded a regime where their business operations could not be successful.[120] In 2021, it was reported that the brothel windows of Amsterdam's red light district would be closed and those operations would be moved away from the city's center.

The legal licensed sector is only part of the legal sector. Nonetheless its decline is problematic for proponents of legalization who support it on the basis it is less coercive than its legal unregulated and illegal counterparts. Presume for a moment this is the case. As more and more migrate to legal licensed prostitution, they become safer than they were in the legal unregulated and illegal spheres. Suppose however the trend was to work in reverse, that over the course of time the legal licensed sphere diminished, while the unregulated and illegal spheres flourished, then the logic works in the opposite direction, with more coercive forms of prostitution becoming representative of the sector. Problematically the legal licensed sphere has not only decreased, but the illegal sphere has increased. If proponents are to accept the tenet of their own argument they must correspondingly conclude, on the evidence available, prostitution in the Netherlands has become more, and not less, coercive.

Conclusions

Long even before the shores of the Americas were sighted for the very first time there was slavery in the world. Years later, by the time the Founding Fathers were readying themselves to put quill pen to the parchment of the Constitution of the United States slavery was an old practice in the Americas. When the North finally acceded to the South's demands that slavery should be permitted in the fledgling United States, those in the North consoled themselves in the confidence it would die out of its own accord. Soon, they thought, slavery and free labor would be in competition. Market rationale would win the day and slavery would perish. Yet slavery did not die out. From humble beginnings it expanded. It even diversified until, after decades of use, as the sun rose on the Civil War, there were 4 million slaves in the South. By the time the dust had settled on the war, and upon the more than 600,000 who perished in it, slavery was no longer an instrument of the States. Yet today, more than 150 years after the ending of Civil War, slavery afflicts many more millions globally than it did in the United States at its highest point. Even within the confines of modern-day America, slavery although now illegal, is still found in every State. The institutionalization of slavery in the South, in the form of chattel slavery, was merely the formalization of a tradition already ages old. The legal position occupied by slavery prior to the Civil War was not slavery's source, but merely the reflection of its underpinnings. Slavery is not contingent on legal ownership, even if some of its forms are so contingent, and the law is not its source.

Across the broad spectrum of labor, slavery is the exception rather than the norm. Slavery does not thrive under most forms of labor. Only where labor possesses amenable characteristics can slavery be employed successfully. The work must be of a crude form making it defiant of a division of labor, or there must be insufficient labor available to allow for the work's division. If slavery is to endure the soil where it is practiced must be extraordinarily fertile, otherwise its practice must be either wholly independent of the soil or slavery must instead migrate to farther fields. Either way, the issue of fertility will not be permitted to compromise its plentiful supply. There must too be some form of monopoly acting to restrict the possibility of slavery's produce being sourced elsewhere. In comprehending the role played by these characteristics it becomes possible to predict where slavery will be found in future, and to understand why it was to be found where it existed in the past. It becomes clear too how, where the nature of an activity's labor remains unchanged, and where slavery was to be found in the activity in the past, slavery will continue to thrive in that activity's present. It is no coincidence, no unfortunate twist of fate bedeviling certain forms of labor, that slavery is found time and again in close association with them. In contrast to the North, when the demands of the South were acceded to its confidence was in a different direction. By the time of the Constitutional Convention the slaveholders, and their representatives, comprehended how their slavery would not be extinguished by the labor of the North, for they were well-acquainted with the crops they grew, crops different to those in the North, and they were well-acquainted too with the nature of the labor most suited to cultivating them. Slavery is a form of labor, one whose roots are found in the very crops it produces.

The characteristics of the labor demanded by those crops for their cultivation is of the kind most human beings would rather not provide. There are various reasons why most do not wish to engage in slavery's activities. Much of it involves hard work, exhaustingly long hours, and innumerable days. Some of it is dirty and degrading. Added to this the benefits may be so low, to the point of being almost non-existent, and the costs to human well-being so high, that participating in these activities makes little sense. At its extremity, slavery involves the kind of activities whose costs are so high, including even death, that no person would contemplate them under any circumstance. What benefits do amass may be substantial only when accumulated, benefitting not the individual laborer, but the enslaver who gathers them cumulatively. Of course, not all slavery involves the growing of an actual crop. The term can be used euphemistically for other activities. The same is true too of the terms: *costs* and *benefits*. This being so, economics often play a role in slavery's motives. Some of it is cost-reducing, enabling the enslaver to acquire services at prices lower than they could otherwise be secured. Much of it, however, is profit-making. Even when this is the case the issue of cost remains at its core. Slavery's wares are sold for their low price. It cannot tolerate cost. When viewed from the perspective of the slaveholders anything serving to contravene this tenet might be considered a "tariff of abominations." Where it can be used, slavery is cheaper than free labor.

Slavery's ambition is not to complete jobs well, but to bring them to the nearest point of completion where might be said to be done. It can afford none of the extravagances of free labor, but it has little need of them either. It matters little to the slaveholder whether the work is done freely or by slaves as the work's nature imposes an equality of its own. The laborer working freely adds no value to the work above what might otherwise be obtained from the use of slaves. Such a laborer is deprived of the advantages work amenable to free labor normally bestows. She or he cannot work any faster than the slave, only as fast as the slave, but it is the slave who works longer, and who costs less to maintain. If value could be added to the work it could only come through the destruction of the form of labor required, bringing the work's nature into the realm of free labor. This is a critical point, and one likely not comprehended by the North when it acquiesced to slavery. Free labor and slavery cannot be brought into competition.

Owing to the limitations of slavery's labor what it produces is invariably a commodity. Yet for all its limitations, the slaveholders saw slavery as such a necessity to the cultivation of the abundance of the world's staples that contemplating a world without slavery was an absurdity. Key to understanding the economics of slavery's profit-making powers is the priority given to *volumes of sales* over *margin of sales*. Counterintuitive perhaps but, by pushing the price of its wares ever-downward a disproportionate increase in profits is reaped through the corresponding explosion in volume of sales this produces: each small loss of margin on any given sale is handsomely rewarded by bigger gains on the number of sales made. The fluidity in the nature of the relationship between price and volume is known in economics as *elasticity of demand*. Crucially slavery must drive prices so low that those goods become everyday items, so low that the expense of consuming them becomes hardly worthy of thought. In this way the hard work required to furnish slavery's produce is rewarded with an upward spiraling demand for more hard work, and consequently for more slaves. In this way too slavery perpetuates slavery. Slavery is a rational, albeit an immoral, economic response to certain types of labor.

Where slavery and free labor can be separated from one another on the content of their labor and the distinctiveness of their economic approaches they can be united again on the benefits one provides to the other. Slavery is employed, as free labor is employed, to provide a profit. To conduct their business, the slaveholders found uses for the North. Drawing upon the capital reserves of the North they found banks to fund the cost of their slaves and their slavery. They found in the North finished goods they could never have manufactured in the South, goods they needed to transact the business of slavery, and at prices cheap enough to satisfy. As well as providing supplies to the South, the North proved to be a good customer. Goods produced by slaves were shipped a long way to the markets of the North where value could be added to them by the North's manufacturers. Other goods were shipped abroad, as was the case of the immense volumes shipped to England's markets, where these goods were consumed by her manufacturers in the production of finished goods. Free trade is not impervious to slavery: what matters is not how freely trade is conducted but the nature of the crops being traded.

Even if distinct, free labor and slavery are often linked. Aptly, in the case of slavery, this relationship in which successive customers become suppliers to other customers is known as *the supply chain*. When slavery forms part of the supply chain, it will be found at its first link. As one follows the chain from start to finish its first link will always be a supplier and its last link always a customer. With their exception, the first and the last links, every link plays two roles. Initially it is a customer of the one preceding it, and then it is a supplier to the one following it. The relationship between any two links on the chain is the same as that between any two prior to them. This is the supplier-customer relationship. Hence, the chain, though often long, is just a repetition of same supplier-customer relationship. It follows then how, if long supply chains serve to make the presence of slavery in the supply chain opaque, the relationship between supplier and customer may itself be opaque, as from start to finish the supply chain is merely a repetition of this relationship. There is no element of the supplier-customer relationship requiring it to be either transparent or consensual.

Slavery exists not to add value, but to extract it, and do so at the lowest possible cost to itself. Rather than create something anew it must exploit a thing already in existence. Natural resources are an obvious target for its application. Humankind, being part of this realm, is also a target. As slavery bears no costs of its own, it can afford to spare no person, not even its laborers, and no resource, in foisting the full cost of its practice. This does not injure slavery, but it does injure its slaves. The role of violence in slavery cannot be overstated. The potency of the image of the slaveholder leading his chained slave, or of the image of the slaveholder whipping his slave, are images deeply ingrained in the minds of the sympathetic. Nevertheless, to understand slavery solely by its physical restraints or by its visible punishments is not to understand it at all. In the hands of the slaveholder violence is the instrument used to produce slaves and it takes many forms. Through violence, little by little the slaveholder chips away at the fabric of Man until, having ravaged him in body, mind and soul, having stripped of all humanity, the slave emerges. Violence is the tool by which slaves are made.

It must have been a perplexing thing for Northerners to see the South's landscape itself so ravaged. Everything they saw in the South was so contrary to what they understood about how their own interests were fulfilled. The land was poorly maintained. The equipment was of the poorest kind, and it too was poorly kept. The same was true of the livestock. If the soil was not abundantly fertile, slavery soon broke its back. The slaveholders would have to move to new pastures, while at the same time leaving the ones departed unfit for sale. Too much was being paid for labor, it must have seemed to the Northerner, and the slave was such an expensive commodity that paying for him could not have been economically viable. Added to this, the goods slavery produced were cheap, so cheap that producing them scarcely seemed worthwhile, especially given the immensity of effort required for their production. It appeared to be entirely irrational, contrary even to profitability and to the interests of the South, Northerners could conclude. The South was proud enough that these sentiments could only have served to deepen the divide between it and the North. Where the crops in the North rewarded investment, those in the South punished it. Destruction is inherent to slavery's practice.

The purpose of any lens is to bring something into focus or to view the thing it seeks to enlighten from a different perspective. There is absolutely nothing wrong with trying to analyze a phenomenon through a variety of lenses. Each view may glean something new. What is problematic, however, is the employment of a lens in such a way as to compromise its transparency or the use of a distorted lens that alters what it views. When this is done, the image it reflects is inherently flawed. In attempting to understand slavery through the lens of free labor the Northerner introduced biases ensuring slavery's opacity. For this reason, slavery's true nature probably remained hidden from many. The same, however, appears not to have been true of the South, which appears to have appreciated the virtues of the North's economic ways, but which appears also to have appreciated how they could not be applied to the labor of the South. What is clear is the importance given by the South to the relationship between labor and freedom. Surprisingly perhaps, but free labor can be distinguished from labor freely given. Certainly, in the South such a distinction was made and there is evidence aplenty to give it substance. Free labor, properly understood, is not labor freely given, but labor incompatible with slavery: it is labor not possessing those characteristics which make it amenable to slavery.

One could take an alternative view and view these matters through a different lens, equating free labor with any work done freely. Scientifically this is problematic, however, because it breaks the link between cause and effect. Not all work done freely possesses characteristics making it amenable to slavery, and yet some of the work done that might be done freely does possesses these characteristics. When viewed in this manner, slavery becomes an effect without a cause, and the view offers no explanation of why slavery is found repeatedly in association with certain forms of labor. This alternative view may have utility for freedom, but it can be of little use in ending slavery or making sound policy. From what has been gleaned about slavery, knowing what it rewards, knowing whom it rewards, and knowing too how those rewards are attained, could slavery ever truly reward those it commoditizes, even if the commoditization is self-imposed? In a market whose wares are compatible with the interests of slavery success appears in the form of low margin and high volume. Overwhelmingly a market founded on slavery is more likely to benefit those who gather the rewards cumulatively than those who gather them individually, even if the labor is given freely. Whether given freely, or otherwise, labor amenable to slavery is unlikely to be rewarding for those who carry it out.

There will be exceptions, of course, as there always are. With their own eyes visiting Northerners saw the condition of the slave before them, and from what they saw they extrapolated this to be the condition of all. They were deceived by the slaveholder, who knew precisely how to warm their hearts to his cold profession. He did not show them the posts where the slaves were whipped or the markets where families were torn apart. Doubtless he did not show them the advertisements seeking the return of escaped slaves. He certainly did not bring them to the jails where escaped slaves were deposited upon capture. He did not take them into the fields to see the many who labored there, exhausted by endless toil, naked, and emaciated by hunger. Instead, he kept them close to the house and close to the slaves of the house whose innate characteristics made it desirable for him to have them about it. Even slavery has those who might reluctantly be called its winners, those who carve out a niche for themselves, and who fare better than their counterparts. The illusion would have been seen for what it was had the Northerners realized how life, like markets, is not uniform. It would have been shattered had they thought to ask just how representative those at the house were of the many absent from it. No market is comprised solely of success. To survey slavery, one must view the full range of results it produces, those few it readily parades as its successes and those many it fervently conceals as its failures.

Slavery was not agreeable to the North all the same. It was not a necessity for its economy and its very presence was a refutation of the North's sense of freedom. Slavery was the very thing the Founding Fathers had fought against and the inheritance they bestowed was freedom from slavery. Freedom and slavery simply could not co-exist. The labor of the North was shared by all. The character of its freedom was one of union. No burden was placed upon the shoulders of human beings to prove their minimal right to equality. It was a notion presumed, a thing held as being self-evident even if given grudgingly in some quarters, a form of secular faith, and a necessary starting point for a just democratic society. Economic factors ensured the necessity of slavery in the South. Necessity too ensured that the South fashioned a model of freedom uncontradicted by the presence of slavery. Thus at the South, the relationship between slavery and freedom was itself a confederate one. Of equal necessity to the South was a class of workers to furnish the produce of the South's labor. Those upon whom this labor fell were the slaves, and those who were exempt from the South's labor were its People. In this way all who were equal in the South were the People, and though the South was fervently for equality, even more so in some instances than those in the North, not all who were people were equal. In the North all the People were equal, while in the South all who were equal were the People.

Generations of Southern slaveholders and advocates of slavery were able to profess their self-evidential equality, only after it had been secured for them by their antecedents. Yet those same slaveholders and advocates were unable to extend to others the very principles others had so generously extended to them. Instead, they heaped upon the shoulders of their slaves, as they had heaped a great many other burdens, the burden of proof, and in so doing they deprived those slaves of the same starting point from which they themselves had benefitted. The proclamation of the self-evidential equality of Mankind may have more of a moral basis than it has an evidential one. When, in all human history, has it been proven? Who has ever proven it so they might be spared from slavery and injustice? What is patently evident is of how little use the self-evidential proved to be to the Founding Fathers in advance of their winning freedom, and of how little use it proved to be to America's slaves after it had been won. What is evident too is how the self-evidential offered as little prospect of the North securing freedom for slaves in the United States without force of arms, as it did to the Founding Fathers securing their own freedom by the same means in their own time. The virtue of its proclamation may be, not in its pointing to something so evident as to be scarcely worthy of mention, but in its courage and its generosity, for through the proclamation an insurmountable burden is lifted from the shoulders of all Mankind. In this way too the labor of North and South was different. From their polarized starting points, North and South imposed different burdens.

If slavery is principled, it is principled only in this: slavery acts only to serve its own self-interest. In every other regard its principles can be put aside as suits its need. When it suited slavery to deprive human beings of the benefits of their labor and of their freedom the South showed neither hesitation nor remorse in treating them as mere property. At the same time a slave was recognized to be enough of a person, even constitutionally so, to secure partial votes for his Southern owner. A slave then was a member of a group so long as it met slavery's needs, not a member of it the moment non-membership fulfilled another, and a member of it once again when the demands of non-membership were met. Group membership was not quite so fixed as slavery portrayed and this played out in other ways too. The South was to be found unwaveringly in support of the Union so long only as it suited its slavery. When economic factors threatened to undermine the viability of South's slavery, secession was conspicuous among the options it touted. When the crisis passed the South was once again firmly established in the Union, until many years later when the time came its slavery was threatened once more, it finally acted to secede. Under slavery, group membership is fixed not by fidelity to a group, but by fidelity to an outcome. Equally the language used to describe a group may be as empty, or as full, as suits slavery's need at the time. In analyzing slavery, one cannot be guided by the compass of its principles or by the presentation of its language, simply because neither represent a fixed point. Slavery's compass has no North.

That slavery may well have been the most profitable option, or the least expensive depending on the application, for the South to pursue does not excuse its use. All it truly illustrates is how what might find a justification in economics, or in even pragmatism, might not find a counterpart in moral behavior. Slavery is wrong. Slavery is wrong because it treats fellow human beings as means to an end, and not as ends in themselves. Treating persons in this manner leaves them and their most fundamental rights exposed to the whims of others. It imposes all sorts of cruelties and inhumane treatment. It is a gross violation of human dignity. The nature of the objection to slavery cannot be one rooted in purely economic or pragmatic considerations because slavery itself can be grounded economically and, through it, pragmatically. The objection to slavery is a moral one. It is one rooted in justice. The fight against slavery, and the fight for the cause of its slaves, must be a moral one.

The crux of the war between North and South lies in their diametrically opposite relationships with the concepts of freedom and slavery. If there was to be freedom in the South, there must be slavery; the crops demanded it. If there was to be freedom in the North, there could be no slavery; it was not a necessity of its labor and slavery's presence was repugnant to the North's very sense of freedom. Having established slavery as a matter private to the affairs of the South, it nonetheless became a policy for all the States, whether they subscribed to it or not, *via* the Union. Through the Supreme Court's ruling in the *Dred Scott Decision* slavery was unshackled from the South to the effect that, to a degree at least, it might spread northwards. The whole character of the Union was to be shaped by slavery in other ways too. The economic agenda of the North was incompatible with that of the South. So, while the North might pursue a private economic agenda of its own it would nonetheless impinge upon the South through its association *via* the Union. In this way, though slavery was a matter private to the South, the needs of its slavery went far beyond itself. Without even a glint of appreciation for the irony of this predicament, or the injustice of it as an arrangement between the states and the Union, the South never missed an opportunity to defend slavery. Under slavery, all costs or failures accrue to the North and all benefits or successes to the South.

What began as the South's *peculiar institution* contaminated the Union, and the North wished to be free of it. Ending slavery was in keeping with its worldview. However, ending slavery in the South, whose very freedom was dependent on it, was tantamount to ending its freedom. One could get rid of the institution to be sure, but the crops would linger, and so too would the demands those crops exacted of their cultivators. From the Southern perspective, ending the institution of slavery in the South was not the end of slavery, but merely the transference of its labor onto the people of the South, and their enslavement as a result. Their respective positions can be viewed another way too. Their freedom was contingent on their consent. The South consented positively, asserting the rights conferred upon it, to slavery. The North consented negatively, asserting its right to withhold its assent to slavery, to be free of it. In this way the consent and the rights of the two were brought into conflict as the interests of each lay in opposite directions. So, though North and South fought for very different reasons on the issue of slavery, they fought for the very same reason on the issue of freedom. North and South fought one another to preserve their freedom.

Edmund Ruffin, the confederate wrongly credited with firing the Civil War's first shot, was correct. Describing slavery is difficult. In truth describing slavery is extremely difficult. So too is tackling it, and many mistakes have been made. Ruffin's three-part definition, given 140 years before the *Palermo Protocol*, could readily have served as a template for the internationally agreed protocol's three-part definition. A decade was lost to many of the world's nations when the protocol's definition was incorporated *verbatim* into their law. This was never the intent. The purpose of the definition was to encapsulate the activity its convention's signatories wished to curb. When the definition was assimilated it was efforts against slavery that were curbed. Globally prosecutors found themselves confronted by a complex definition whose three parts imposed an often-insurmountable burden. Simpler approaches, using discrete offences, compatible with the aims of the protocol would surely have been more productive. Where this lesson has been learned changes have been made. Where they have not yet been made, the lesson has not yet been learned.

Broadly, to make sense of slavery it can be reduced to three considerations: the suitability of slavery to certain forms of labor; the economics underpinning slavery's application; and the role of violence in making slaves. To make sense of the politics of slavery one must add to the previous three considerations a fourth: the role of definition in assigning or manipulating group membership. Though Ruffin and his ilk are now long-gone, and a chasm of time now separates them for the contemporary, this chasm has its uses. Their frankness about the business of slavery, which was legal in their own time, is scarcely possible today. Their insights into the nature of the slavery are untainted by the biases of modern philosophical and political debate. For all the passage of time, it is difficult to conceive the slaveholders of old would find much in the modern practice of slavery that would render its appearance different from its old self.

Environmentalism is a term that would have meant little to the slaveholders of the South. Yet they were well-acquainted with problems the term seeks to address. Through is experiments on fertilization of the soil, Edmund Ruffin attempted to put right some of the injury slavery perpetuated upon the South's land. Few today are likely to claim Ruffin as an *eco-warrior* or as an environmental pioneer. They would probably be right. Ruffin's concerns about the environment were not solely for the environment's sake. Nonetheless in a world increasingly conscious of environmental degradation there is much to be learned from the past. The connection between environmentalism and slavery may not at first be apparent. It is no accident, however, how those who campaign to protect the environment sometimes encounter slave labor at locations, or in activities, of priority. Owing to slavery's destructive nature and to its focus upon natural resources, it is understandably so. Modern slavery is an environmental issue.

The most striking difference today between the slavery of the South and how of the modern day is slavery's illegality. It is specifically prohibited under the very first articles of the *Universal Declaration of Human Rights*. The slaveholders would never have agreed to the term *human trafficking* because, in viewing the modern as a continuation of the slavery of the past and they understood there must be a continuation, the term acknowledges the humanity of those they once deprived. Modern slavery is partially redeemed for if today it continues to conceal the reasons underpinning slavery, it nonetheless acknowledges the humanity of those it enslaves. Modern slavery does indeed conceal the reason behind enslavement, but only in certain instances as suits its need. The term *sex worker* is one used, seemingly innocuously, to evoke the image of consensual workers engaged in a field of legitimate labor. There is a flip side to its use however, for it monopolizes ownership of labor, and in doing so it implicitly suggests work not done consensually is not labor. While the slaveholders of old were content to resign themselves, and the fate of their slaves, to the use of slavery as a matter of necessity, the modern slave is sometimes robbed even of ownership of the cause of her enslavement in a way that could never have been so in the South. While the term *sex worker* may be used out of a sense of respect, in preference to *prostitute*, it is disrespectful of those whom it excludes, those who know all too well the source of their enslavement. If the rationale depicting labor as an endeavor necessarily carried out consensually were applied retrospectively, the term's proponents would quickly find themselves on untenable ground. Could one genuinely believe slavery in the South had nothing to do with the business of picking cotton, on the basis that it was not done consensually, and that its slaves could not be described as cotton pickers for the same reason? The South's slaveholders knew better. So too did the South's slaves. The slave, it might be said, has much to fear from the *new paradigm*, and more particularly those forms of it that, through their flawed logic, deprive him of the cause of his slavery, while necessitating his enslavement all-the-same. The term *sex worker* is a politically-charged one, it is a misnomer, and a dangerous one at that.

Implicit to the policy approach adopted by New Zealand is the assertion that prostitution's illegal status is the source of the human trafficking within it. Prostitution's frequent status in law is not the cause of the slavery the industry contains; it is the effect of it. That decriminalizing prostitution, an act that leaves it legal and unregulated, would be a remedy for slavery is itself flawed, when one considers how most of the industries where slavery occurs globally (for example, agriculture, horticulture, fishing, mining, forestry, brick making, carpet weaving, and others) are already legal and unregulated. There is evidence of human trafficking within the country's decriminalized prostitution sector. New Zealand's definition of human trafficking has not complied with international standards and traditionally it has not conformed to the *Palermo Protocol* definition. For almost the entirety of the period scrutinized under this work, human trafficking in New Zealand was confined to a phenomenon requiring international movement. The country's remoteness made such an occurrence highly unlikely, although not impossible. Of much more likelihood was the probability that human trafficking would be encountered as an internal phenomenon. Yet the law precluded any possibility a person trafficked internally could ever be classed by law as a victim of human trafficking. Even when the country decriminalized prostitution it refrained from doing so in every instance. Foreign students, for example, who might be classed as victims of trafficking, despite the law's narrow application, were prohibited from entering the sex trade. Prostitution was decriminalized in such a way as to ensure those working in it could never be classed as victims, no matter the reality of their situation.

In finally making changes to its law, to bring its definition of human trafficking into conformance with international standards, after years of pressure, New Zealand has acknowledged the problems previously implicit to those laws. Its problems are compounded by its tendency to classify young people in the prostitution sector as child prostitutes, when as a matter of fact they should be classified as victims of human trafficking. This demonstrates how what was cast as a labor rights violation should have been cast as a human rights violation, and this may be the case with New Zealand's decriminalization policy overall. Advocating decriminalization as an approach to slavery is not wholly without precedent. Legitimizing prostitution in the narrow belief it constitutes free labor, and in the belief free labor can be brought into competition with slave labor, so that the former can triumph over the latter, bears striking similarities to a rationale once held by the North. There is nothing in the approach adopted by New Zealand, when properly understood, that challenges the rationale behind slavery. Decriminalizing prostitution provides no remedy for the human trafficking it contains.

Explicit to the policy approach adopted by the Netherlands when it legalized prostitution in particular circumstances are six objectives. Of these, the third and sixth objectives are similar, as they seek to prevent the entry of certain groups into the sex trade. The third was aimed at protecting children from sexual abuse by excluding them from the market, and the sixth aimed at excluding the entry into the market of non-European Union (EU) residents. There is a contradiction, of course, as legality was advocated as a necessity for control so even by the yardstick of its own logic, what cannot be legalized cannot be controlled. How then could these two be objectives, for they would never fully fall within the remit of legalization's sphere? When the law was changed, those who were in the majority were non-EU residents and many too were mere children. Immediately after legalization neither group was more advantaged or disadvantaged by the passage of the law than they had been prior to it, and the demand for their services was much the same after legalization as it had been before it. The fight against illegal prostitution was precisely the same, requiring its curtailment through police enforcement. The first and fourth objectives are also similar. The first sought to protect prostitutes from their being exploited commercially. The fourth hoped to advance the cause of those working in prostitution. Little consideration appears to have been given what success, in the form of a thriving prostitution sector would resemble. Had the economics of labor amenable to slavery been considered, even in the face of success the sector was certainly never going to attain the first and fourth objectives. There would be exceptions of course, those niches where some fared better than others, simply because they were able to distinguish themselves as exceptional. Overall though a thriving competitive prostitution sector would tend towards deflating prices, while increasing volumes of transactions. If the benefits were not all that might have been expected the same could not be said of the costs. Regulation imposed the very thing this form of labor could ill-afford. It imposed a tariff upon the finances and time of those whose activities it sought to regulate. In this way the Dutch may have unintentionally instituted some of the very conditions the law hoped to avert. The second objective sought to combat sex trafficking in prostitution but here too such an objective must necessarily be limited to the realm the policy set for itself. In this case that realm was quite small, encompassing the minority in fact, so even from the outset such an objective could not be met in full. Dutch policy did not colonize prostitution. Instead, it established a small and tenuous bridgehead from which the state became a market participant, one among many, through its association with legalized business operators. From this vantage point it would need to gain ground against the illegal sector to accomplish the objectives of the fifth objective, to eliminate criminality in the prostitution sector. The prospects were not good however as economically the minority legal sector, bearing all the costs of regulation, was pitched against the majority illegal sector, which bore none of legality's expense, in a battle where volume of work and low cost prevail. On one hand serious doubts exist as to whether a real distinction can be made between the levels of trafficking in the legal licensed sector and those of its illicit counterpart. On the other, the legal sector has declined, and its borders have been pushed back. Societal pragmatism may have led the Netherlands to legalize prostitution, but it did not recognize the pragmatic business-like nature of the trade. Even so, the fate of Dutch policy was bound by this business-like pragmatism. There is nothing in the approach adopted by the Netherlands, when properly understood, that challenges the rationale behind slavery. Legalizing prostitution is not a remedy for the human trafficking it contains.

Few of the borders the country's policy constructed around sections of prostitution proved to be as rigid as their presentation first seemed. When it sought to construct a border around the legal sector, it learned that border could be subdivided in ways its policy had not anticipated. Unexpectedly for the Netherlands, its policy brought it a legalized licensed sector and a decriminalized unlicensed one. Later it also learned the borders it had seemingly constructed around the legal sector were not as impervious to human trafficking as it had anticipated. Policy borders were enough however to curtail the reach of its policy, which would be limited at the very most to the extent of what it could ostensibly establish as legitimate. The objectives of policy decisions must themselves be limited to the confines of those borders, and so they could never attain what they had aspired to achieve. Certainly, legality did not yield transparency. Indeed, much more is known today about human trafficking in the country's legal prostitution sector through the steadfast work and voluminous reports of the country's Rapporteur than is known about activities supposedly regulated. The shroud of transparency which once surrounded the whole sector, and which once served as a reason to promote legalization, now serves to protect the legalized part of it from criticism now that it has been legalized. The continued lack of transparency in the legalized prostitution sector is itself a critique of the effectiveness of the policy.

If regulation is to be meaningful it must first be ascertained whether a regulatory regime holds within its grasp the capability to deliver upon the goals it promises to deliver, and it must deliver upon them within a timeframe that is not open-ended. It must be wary not to exclude the possibility of failure, otherwise all shortcomings risk becoming attributable to *failures to regulate* rather than countenancing some of them, as they ought to be countenanced, as *failures of regulation*. The problems in this instance may not be ones of regulation at all, but ones of presumption. Regulation may indeed result in the control of an industry, but that is not to say regulation is suited to every type of industry. It was never in the self-interest of the country's sex trade to be regulated. It did not suit those who had no rights to work in the country to declare their involvement. It did not suit those who had pimped children into the trade to declare what they had done. The economics themselves made it counterproductive. So too did other facets of regulation make it objectionable to, and incompatible with, the interests of those engaged in the sector. When this proved to be the case it was the requirements of regulation which were compromised, and not the requirements of those whom regulation required to be regulated. Measures long deemed key to regulating the sector, and particularly to combatting human trafficking, have been abandoned. One could question whether the Netherlands truly regulated prostitution. Whatever the case, one thing is clear. The success of a policy is achieved not by its enactment, but by its timely attainment of the objectives it once established for itself.

Sweden, in contrast, constructed no such borders. Its policy on prostitution is made for all, and can reach all, and through its homogeneity it encompasses all the intricacies of slavery's heterogeneity. The country's approach recognizes prostitution's true nature, as a business activity amenable to slavery, and as incompatible with freedom. It comprehends too how markets founded on prostitution are incompatible with the interests of a free, just, and democratic society. Certainly, states can raise up markets but the outcomes of those markets, both the successes and the failures, must be in line with the commitments incumbent upon states to guarantee fundamental human rights. The successes do not vindicate the failures, and anything professing otherwise is merely sectionalism. The approach scorns a perspective that promotes freedom as an inevitability. It recognizes how the converse may be more likely, especially in those cases where the nature of the labor is more likely to produce slavery. That some might extract utility from those circumstances is no vindication of them in the eyes of human rights, or in those of the Swedish policy approach. It recognizes how the role of slave is confined to the supply chain's first link. Correspondingly it recognizes how the role of customer is confined to the links that follow the first link, and particularly to the last link that embodies it exclusively. In this way customer and slave are always linked. While the enslaver dictates the slave's place on the chain, only the customer can dictate his or her own. In this way the Swedish approach upholds the rights of the slave by punishing the customer for patronizing the slave's services. In turn by focusing upon the customer and diminishing his patronage it seeks to strike at the very thing slavery needs in abundance: its volume of sales. Markets alone, where all parties pursue their self-interest, where the interests of some are pitted against the more fundamental interests of others, cannot be the guarantors of freedom.

The Swedish Model (or Nordic Model or Equality Model) finds no contradiction of its approach in the fruits of decriminalization or in those of regulation: slavery is viable when a market is decriminalized and it even more viable in a legalized market where some of its competitors are burdened with costs. Neither approach challenges slavery's economic rationale. Something then of a *Greek tragedy* is played out in the character of policies not incorporating an economic approach to the problem of slavery, depriving those policies of the very possibility of success even before they have set foot onto the stage. The brunt of this tragedy is borne by people whose pre-existing hardships have made them vulnerable to exploitation. Among these people are those from the Third World who have escaped calamities of all kinds at home only to find slavery in markets abroad. Those who stay at home may fare no better. In a world increasingly committed to markets, to the globalization of markets, to their freedom, and to free trade, care is needed to ensure all these things are compatible with human rights, and with human dignity. Other perspectives may yield their own conclusions on other matters pertaining to markets, but from the point of view of slavery what may matter most is not the freedom of the market, or the extent of its reach, but the nature of the labor it shares, and the capacity of those who receive that labor to process it without recourse to slavery.

For all their flaws, the approaches adopted by the Netherlands and by New Zealand prove invaluable in one regard. Their outcomes affirm the central role of economics, and consequently those of *supply and demand*, and of *risk and reward*. Their current policies present their respective states with the quandary of laying claims to objectives without having means of their attainment, as their legislation is oriented to support, and not to hinder, prostitution. Only Sweden's model leverages such an approach. It answers the question central to this work. A state cannot fulfill its international obligations to human rights simply by pursuing a minimal approach of the type prescribed under the *Palermo Protocol* and its 3P paradigm, as such an approach need not address the economic underpinnings of slavery, and if it does not do so it cannot yield success. This conclusion echoes Ruffin's sentiment that "[w]ithout the existence of such a demand for the services of slaves as will induce and compensate ... slavery cannot be begun."[1] More importantly it echoes the assertion of the U.S. State Department's *Trafficking in Persons Report* that if efforts to combat human trafficking are to be successful, even minimally, those efforts must "confront ... the demand ... that fuels it."[2]

All is not lost for the *Palermo Protocol*, however. Whatever its deficiencies in tackling the roots of slavery, it has an importance transcending even that role. For slavery's importance lies not in itself, but in those whom it trades, those many millions across the globe today who live under the tyranny of its relentless regime. The *Palermo Protocol* has a vital role to play in alleviating the suffering of those enslaved, who are trying to escape this tyranny. Pensively now, with forethought given to the utterance of every word, as he seemingly surveys in his mind's eye the landscape of his experience as United States Ambassador-at-Large to Monitor and Combat Trafficking in Persons, Ambassador CdeBaca cautions prostitution's policymakers how their decision:

> ... does not obviate their responsibilities to help victims ... If you think that having the right answer on whether or not one of the parties to that transaction should be criminalized ... and yet you are not screening trafficking victims in immigration detention; if you are not allowing trafficking victims who face the risk of harm if they were returned home, if you are not allowing them to stay in your country; if you are not allowing trafficking victims to have access to social programs; if you are not setting up social programs that recognize the particular trauma; if you are not doing all of those things your magic bullet that you were hoping for, as a result of whatever direction you're changing your ... policy, then you are totally missing the point of the Palermo Protocol, which was that victim care matters just as much as prosecution.[3]

As citizens there is a part to play. As citizens we alone decide the character of the world's freedom. Is freedom then an inheritance flowing from the Founding Fathers, who through force of arms, secured it solely for themselves, for their descendants, for their section, and therefore rightfully belonging to a few alone? Is freedom only a small stride forward, a thing itself enslaved, dependent upon and hemmed in by the decrees of slavery? Is freedom consequently only to be found in confederation with slavery, with each in pursuit of their respective interests, and with each tending to their profits by the means best suited to them? If this is the character of the world's freedom, it is the one found in the despondent words of pro-slavery writer David Christy. His invitation to the free is not to spread freedom, but to accept the way of the world, to accept slavery as an inevitability and, as a free citizen, to join in the fruits of slavery's bounty. His pre-Civil War penmanship conveys in black and white terms the co-existence of slavery and freedom, and as inescapable the contest between the interests of some with the more fundamental interests of others: consumers *versus* consumed; state *versus* Union; winners *versus* losers; free *versus* slave; a global war for freedom and a global war against it; an eternal and universal Civil War.

There is another possibility, of course, that through the struggles of the Founding Fathers something greater was attained, a form of freedom capable of overwhelming slavery and standing in defiance of its professed inevitability, a form of freedom transcending even sectional interests, and assures as one of the most basic rights of humanity the freedom of all Mankind. Was it this kind of freedom that compelled the Founding Fathers to make so bold and determined a declaration that they held as self-evident, and by so holding to make certain, without compelling proof, the equality of Mankind? Was this the vision of freedom Jefferson enslaved eternally by the stroke of his quill pen in the Declaration of Independence? Surely it was this vision inspiring his indictment of England's king, one only America's own slavery deprived him of delivering, one declaring how her king had:

... waged cruel war against human nature itself, violating its most sacred rights of life & liberty in the persons of a distant people who never offended him, captivating & carrying them into slavery ... to keep open a market where MEN should be bought & sold.[4]

Was this the blow for freedom Lincoln struck when he took up a pen of his own and signed the Emancipation Proclamation? Is freedom to be found then in the simple terms, possibly in the words of William Henry Singleton? Having escaped from the exertions of slavery Singleton took upon himself the burdens of a citizen to serve with honor in the Union Army. He declared how, when on January 1 1863, Lincoln "signed the Emancipation Proclamation, which made me and all the rest of my race free. We could not be bought and sold ... We were not to be treated as things without souls any more, but as human beings."[5]

There has never been an easy remedy to slavery, one attainable without sacrifice, courage, generosity, faith, and wisdom. In Major Anderson's time he saw how this was so, when he witnessed how readily Fort Sumter might be defended in support of the cause of slavery, but how readily assailed she was when in opposition to it. The freedom espoused by Jefferson, Lincoln, Anderson, and Singleton was never secured solely by the position it took, but on the willingness of the people to support it. The world today stands, as it ever does, at freedom's crossroads, at a place where freedom and slavery meet. Along one route, at one end of it, there is free labor as embodied by labor incompatible with slavery, and at the other, free labor as labor freely given by laborers. In two places along this route, near each end, there is a crossroads where it meets another. At one end of this new route there is unrestrained consumerism and self-interest. At the other there is citizenry, restraint, and selflessness. The character of the world's freedom, whether it perceives slavery as co-existing alongside freedom, or as negating freedom, is discerned by the path taken. History will record the destination reached, but only the world's citizens can determine it. The true measure of freedom lies not in what can be secured for ourselves, but instead in what we must sometimes secure for others.

Reflection

King Cotton cares not whether he employs slaves or freemen. It is the cotton, not the slaves, upon which his throne is based. ... He receives no check from the cries of the oppressed, while the citizens of the world are dragging forward his chariot, and shouting aloud his praise!

King Cotton is a profound statesman, and knows what measures will best sustain his throne. He is an acute mental philosopher, acquainted with the secret springs of human action, and accurately perceives who can best promote his aims. He has no evidence that ... men can grow his cotton, except in the capacity of slaves. ... It is his policy, therefore, to defeat all schemes of emancipation. To do this, he stirs up such agitations as lure his enemies into measures that will do him no injury ..., and sustains the supremacy of King Cotton in the world.

In speaking of the economical connections of slavery, with the other material interests of the world, we have called it a tripartite alliance. It is more than this ..., the abolitionists do not stand in direct contact with slavery; they imagine ... But they, no less than their allies, aid in promoting the interests of slavery. Their sympathies are with England on the slavery question, and they very naturally incline to agree with her on other points. She advocates Free Trade, as essential to her manufactures and commerce; and they do the same, not waiting to inquire into its bearings upon American slavery. ... The free trade and protective systems, in their bearings upon slavery, are so well understood, that no man of general reading, especially an editor, or member of Congress, who professes anti-slavery sentiments, at the same time advocating free trade, will ever convince men of intelligence, pretend what he may, that he is not ... woefully perverted in his judgment ... England, we were about to say, is in alliance with the cotton planter, to whose prosperity free trade is indispensable. Abolitionism is in alliance with England. All three of these parties, then, agree in their support of the free trade policy ... slavery and free trade nationalized!

David Christy, *Cotton is King*

Bibliography

African Network for the Prevention and Protection against Child Abuse and Neglect. (2010) 'Child Sacrifice epidemic during festival and election period: Urgent need for cautiousness towards child protection during the Election and Festive season' (16 Dec) Available: http://www.anppcanug.org/wp-content/uploads/press_releases/PR_Child_Sac_epid_fest_elect_period.pdf [Accessed 19 March 2015].

Agence France Presse. (2009) 'Nigerians jailed in Dutch 'voodoo curse' prostitution trial ' *AsiaOne News* (4 Dec) Available: http://news.asiaone.com/News/AsiaOne%2BNews/World/Story/A1Story20091204-183926.html [Accessed 25 July 2012].

Agence France Presse. (2010) 'Trio arrested over suspected human sacrifice' *ABC News* (20 Apr) Available: http://www.abc.net.au/news/2010-04-20/trio-arrested-over-suspected-human-sacrifice/404204 [Accessed 20 March 2015].

Agence France Presse. (2014) 'Mikhail Kalashnikov, AK-47 Inventor, Repented Killings In Letter To Church: Report' *The Huffington Post* (13 Jan) Available: http://www.huffingtonpost.com/2014/01/13/mikhail-kalashnikov-repented_n_4587462.html [Accessed 9 March 2015].

Agence France Presse. (2015) 'ICC Prosecutor Fatou Bensouda in Uganda urges LRA rebel chief Joseph Kony to surrender' (28 Feb) Available: http://www.standardmedia.co.ke/article/2000153181/bensouda-urges-lra-rebel-chief-joseph-kony-to-surrender [Accessed 10 March 2015].

Agency Reporter. (2012) 'Nigerian jailed for trafficking 17 women to Holland' *Punch* (14 March) Available: http://www.punchng. com/news/nigerian-jailed-for-trafficking-17-women-to-holland/ [Accessed 25 July 2012].

AllAfrica. (2012) 'Nigeria: Police Smash Human Trafficking Syndicate, Rescue Five Children' *AllAfrica* (25 April) Available: http:// allafrica.com/stories/201204260320.html [Accessed 28 June 2012].

Almelo District Court. (2008) 'The Sneep Case' Available: http:// ec.europa.eu/anti-trafficking/download.action;jsessionid= QyQPPlGbGQdKSTsXh6Bj61WdDBSkC0Gmzfs4zx2QLcclmP QHQHn8!511069867?nodeId=e8620d9a-a2d2-4fa9-bfe0-4cf21cc085db&fileName=The+SNEEP+case_en.pdf [Accessed 28 May 2012].

Amnesty International. (2014) 'Summary: proposed policy on sex work' (2 Apr) Available: https://www.amnesty.se/upload/ files/2014/04/02/Summary%20of%20proposed%20 policy%20on%20sex%20work.pdf [Accessed 12 May 2015].

Amnesty International. (2015) 'Global movement votes to adopt policy to protect human rights of sex workers' (11 Aug) Available: https://www.amnesty.org/en/latest/news/2015/08/global-movement-votes-to-adopt-policy-to-protect-human-rights-of-sex-workers/ [Accessed 26 October 2015].

ANSA. (2013) 'Police arrest 4 forcing 65-year-old to beg, house them' *ANSA.IT* (12 Sept) Available: http://www.ansa.it/web/notizie/ rubriche/english/2013/09/12/Police-arrest-4-forcing-65-year-old-beg-house_9290560.html [Accessed 10 October 2013].

Anti-Slavery International. (2015) 'Forced labour in the brick kiln sector in India' (Jul) Available: http://www.antislavery.org/ includes/documents/cm_docs/2015/f/forced_labour_in_ brick_kilns_in_india_august_2015_briefing.pdf [Accessed 13 January 2017].

Anti-Slavery International & International Trade Union Confederation. (2011) 'Never work alone: Trade Unions and NGOs joining forces to combat Forced Labour and Trafficking in Europe' (February) Available: http://www.ituc-csi.org/IMG/pdf/Forced_labour_EN_FINAL.pdf [Accessed 22 July 2012].

Araujo, A. L. (2014) *Shadows of the slave past : memory, heritage, and slavery*, New York: Routledge.

Armstrong, K. (2014) 'Staff at United Arab Emirates embassy in Dublin were treated like slaves, tribunal hears' (26 Nov) Available: http://www.irishmirror.ie/news/irish-news/staff-united-arab-emirates-embassy-4696255 [Accessed 12 March 2015].

Aronowitz, A., Theuemann, G. & Tyurkanova, E. (2010) *Analysing the Business Model of Trafficking in Human Beings to Better Prevent the Crime,* OSCE Office of the Special Representative and Co-ordinator for Combating Trafficking in Human Beings [Online], Available: http://www.osce.org/cthb/69028 [Accessed 15 Sept 2012].

Aronowitz, A. A. (2001) 'Smuggling and Trafficking in Human Beings: The Phenomenon, The Markets that Drive It and the Organisations that Promote It', *European Journal on Criminal Policy and Research* 9(2), 163-195.

Aronowitz, A. A. (2009) *Human trafficking, human misery: the global trade in human beings*, Westport, Conn.: Praeger.

Asghar, S. M., Farhat, S., Niaz, S. & Save the Children Sweden-Pakistan. (2005) *Camel jockeys of Rahimyar Khan : findings of a participatory research on the life and situation of child camel jockeys,* Save the Children Sweden [Online], Available: http://lastradainternational.org/lsidocs/351%20Camel-jockeys_of_rahimyar_khan.pdf [Accessed 10 October 2013].

Associated Press. (2012) 'Police: Indian child killed as human sacrifice' *CBS News* (2 Jan) Available: http://www.cbsnews.com/news/police-indian-child-killed-as-human-sacrifice/ [Accessed 20 March 2015].

Biaudet, E. (2009) 'Speech of Ms. Eva Biaudet, OSCE Special Representative and Co-ordinator for Combating Trafficking in Human Beings' *In:* BIAUDET, E., ed. *18th Baltic Sea Parliamentary Conference, Session 3: New Threats to Security*, Nyborg, 1 September 2009 Nyborg: Organization for Security and Co-operation in Europe (OSCE), 1-5.

Bordewich, F. M. (2011) 'Fort Sumter: The Civil War Begins' *Smithsonian Magazine* (April) Available: http://www.smithsonianmag. com/history/fort-sumter-the-civil-war-begins-1018791/?no-ist [Accessed 6 May 2014].

Brants, C. (1998) 'The Fine Art of Regulated Tolerance: Prostitution in Amsterdam', *Journal of Law & Society,* 25(4), 621.

Brook, P. (2015) 'The DIY Robots That Ride Camels and Fight for Human Rights' *Wired* (3 Mar) Available: http://www.wired. com/2015/03/diy-robots-ride-camels-fight-human-rights/ [Accessed 20 March 2015].

Bucken-Knapp, G., Karlsson Schaffer, J. & Persson Strömbäck, K. (2012) 'Security, Equality, and the Clash of Ideas: Sweden's Evolving Anti-Trafficking Policy', *Human Rights Review,* 13(2), 1-19.

Bunker, R. J. (2013a) 'Santa Muerte: Inspired and Ritualistic Killings (Part 2 of 3)', *FBI Law Enforcement Bulletin,* 82(2), 1-4.

Bunker, R. J. (2013b) 'Santa Muerte: Inspired and Ritualistic Killings (Part 3 of 3)', *FBI Law Enforcement Bulletin,* 82(2), 1-3.

Burns, K. (1990) *The Civil War: The Cause (1861) Episode 1* [film], USA: PBS Distribution.

Cairnes, J. E. (1862) *The slave power: its character, career, and probable designs: being an attempt to explain the real issues involved in the American contest*, New York: Carleton.

Calhoun, J. C. & Lence, R. M. (1992) *Union and liberty : the political philosophy of John C. Calhoun*, Indianapolis: Liberty Fund.

Campbell, D. & Davison, N. (2012) 'Ilegal kidney trade booms as new organ is "sold every hour"' *The Guardian* (27 May) Available: http://www.theguardian.com/world/2012/may/27/kidney-trade-illegal-operations-who [Accessed 5 May 2015].

Carville, O. (2016) 'Exposed: The dark underbelly of human trafficking in New Zealand' *New Zealand Herald* (22 Sept) Available: http://www.nzherald.co.nz/nz/news/article.cfm%3Fc_id%3D1%26objectid%3D11711211 [Accessed 10 October 2016].

CdeBaca, L. (2014) 'State's CdeBaca on Combating Forced Labor in East Asia' (8 July) Available: http://iipdigital.usembassy.gov/st/english/texttrans/2014/07/20140708303533.html?CP.rss=true#ixzz37RaQ6qxs [Accessed 14 July 2014].

Champaneria, M. C., Workman, A. D. & Gupta, S. C. (2014) 'Sushruta Father of Plastic Surgery', *Annals of Plastic Surgery,* 73(1), 2-7.

Cho, S.-Y., Dreher, A. & Nuemayer, E. (2013) 'Does Legalized Prostitution Increase Human Trafficking?', *World Development,* 41, 67–82.

Christy, D. (1856) *Cotton is King*, New York: Derby & Jackson.

Claude, K. & Swedish Institute. (2010) 'Targeting the Sex Buyer: The Swedish Example' Available: http://www.si.se/upload/Human%20Trafficking/Targeting%20the%20sex%20buyer.pdf [Accessed 15 August 2012].

Collins Jenkins, M. (2011) 'Fort Sumter: How Civil War Began With a Bloodless Battle' *National Geographic* (April 12) Available: http://news.nationalgeographic.com/news/2011/04/110412-fort-sumter-civil-war-nation-150th-anniversary-first-battle/ [Accessed 9 May 2014].

Conrad, A. H. & Meyer, J. R. (1958) 'The Economics of Slavery in the Ante Bellum South', *Journal of Political Economy,* 66(2), 95-130.

Cooper, W. J. (1978) *The South and the politics of slavery, 1828-1856,* Baton Rouge: Louisiana State University Press.

Council Framework Decision 2002/629/JHA of 19 July 2002 on combating trafficking in human beings.

Council of Europe. (1950) 'European Convention for the Protection of Human Rights and Fundamental Freedoms' (4 November 1950) Available: http://www.unhcr.org/refworld/docid/3ae6b3b04.html [Accessed 22 June 2012].

Crimes Act 1961. New Zealand: Parliamentary Counsel Office.

Cruz, J. & van Iterson, S. (n.d.) 'The Audacity of Tolerance: A Critical Analysis of Legalized Prostitution in Amsterdam's Red Light District' *Humanity In Action* Available: http://www. humanityinaction.org/knowledgebase/312-the-audacity-of-tolerance-a-critical-analysis-of-legalized-prostitution-in-amsterdam-s-red-light-district [Accessed 29 August 2015].

Daalder, A. (2007) *Prostitution in the Netherlands since the lifting of the brothel ban,* Boom Juridische Uitgevers [Online], Available: http://wodc.nl/images/ob249a_fulltext_tcm44-83466.pdf [Accessed 22 June 2012].

Dettmeijer-Vermeulen, C. E., Boot-Matthijssen, M., van Dijk, E. H., de Jonge van Ellemeet, H., Koster, D. A. C. & Smit, M. (2007) 'Trafficking in Human Beings: Fifth Report of the Dutch National Rapporteur' Available: http://english.bnrm.nl/ Images/NRM%20Fifth%20Report%20Rapporteur%20def_tcm64-102040.pdf [Accessed 25 January 2012].

Dettmeijer-Vermeulen, C. E., Boot-Matthijssen, M., van Dijk, E. H., de Jonge van Ellemeet, H. & Smit, M. (2008) 'Trafficking in Human Beings: Sixth report of the Dutch National Rapporteur' Available: http://english.bnrm.nl/Images/6e%20engels_tcm64-135704.pdf [Accessed 25 January 2012].

DeWan, J. & Lohan, D. (2012) *Open Secrets: An Irish Perspective on Trafficking & Witchcraft,* Cois Tine [Online], Available: http:// www.amazon.com/Open-Secrets-Perspective-Trafficking-ebook/dp/B0084ZZFQW [Accessed 28 May 2015].

Dickens, C. (ed.) 1852. *Household words,* London.

Ditmore, M. (2009) 'Sex and Taxes' *The Guardian* (16 Apr) Available: http://www.theguardian.com/commentisfree/ cifamerica/2009/apr/03/nevada-prostitution-tax [Accessed 1 September 2015].

Doherty, B. & Whyte, S. (2014) 'India's mica mines: The shameful truth behind mineral make-up's shimmer' *Sydney Morning Herald* (19 Jan) Available: http://www.smh.com.au/national/indias-mica-mines-the-shameful-truth-behind-mineral-makeups-shimmer-20140118-311wk.html [Accessed 12 March 2015].

Doty, F. A. (1956) 'Florida, Iowa, and the National "Balance of Power," 1845', *The Florida Historical Quarterly,* 35(1)**,** 30-59.

Doubleday, A. (1876) *Reminiscences of Forts Sumter and Moultrie in 1860-'61*, New York: Harper & Brothers.

Douglass, F. (2014) *Narrative of the Life of Frederick Douglass, an American Slave,* HarperTorch [Online], Available: http://www.amazon.com/gp/product/B00LSSH718/ref=docs-os-doi_0 [Accessed 15 November 2014].

Drury, P. (2009) 'Tarts 'n Army' *The Scottish Sun* (24 Mar) Available: http://www.thescottishsun.co.uk/scotsol/homepage/news/article2337077.ece [Accessed 27 July 2012].

DubaiCity. (n.d.) 'What to Do in Dubai - Sports' Available: http://www.dubaicity.com/what_to_do_in_dubai/camel-racing-championship.htm [Accessed 12 August 2011].

Dugard, J. L. (2011) *A stolen life: a memoir,* Simon & Schuster [Online], Available: http://www.amazon.com/dp/B005BQNC44/ [Accessed 13 November 2015].

Dunne, L. (2009) 'Smugglers but not traffickers' *Radio Netherlands Worldwide (RNW)* (3 Dec) Available: http://www.rnw.nl/africa/article/smugglers-not-traffickers [Accessed 25 July 2012].

DutchNews.nl. (2013) 'Forced prostitution shifts to unsold homes in residential areas' (17 Jun) Available: http://www.dutchnews.nl/news/archives/2013/06/forced_prostitution_shifts_to/ [Accessed 21 October 2015].

ECPAT International. (2011) 'The Netherlands' *Global Monitoring status of action against commercial sexual exploitation of children* Available: http://www.ecpat.nl/images/13/1610.pdf [Accessed 29 July 2012].

Egizi, A. (2013) 'Should Prostitution Be Legal?' *News Junkie Post* (8 Oct) Available: http://newsjunkiepost.com/2013/10/08/should-prostitution-be-legal/ [Accessed 1 September 2015].

Ekberg, G. (2004) 'The Swedish Law That Prohibits the Purchase of Sexual Services: Best Practices for Prevention of Prostitution and Trafficking in Human Beings' *Violence Against Women* 10 (10) Available: http://www.turnofftheredlight.ie/wp-content/uploads/2011/02/Ekberg-The-Swedish-law-that-prohibits-the-purchase-of-sexual-services.pdf [Accessed 22 January 2012].

Ekberg, G. S. & Wahlberg, K. (2011) 'The Swedish Approach: A European Union Country Fights Sex Trafficking' *The Solutions Journal* (March) Available: http://www.thesolutionsjournal.com/node/895 [Accessed 27 May 2012].

Elliott, E. N. (ed.) 1860. *Cotton is king, and pro-slavery arguments; comprising the writings of Hammond, Harper, Christy, Stringfellow, Hodge, Bledsoe, and Cartwright, on this important subject,* Augusta, Ga., Pritchard, Ga.: Abbot & Loomis.

Encyclopaedia Britannica & Urofsky, M. (2014) 'Dred Scott decision' (25 Mar) Available: http://www.britannica.com/EBchecked/topic/171273/Dred-Scott-decision [Accessed 6 June 2014].

Englund, C., Viuhko, M., Jokinen, A. & Aromma, K. (2008) *The Organisation of Human Trafficking: A Study of Criminal Involvement in Sexual Exploitation in Sweden, Finland and Estonia,* Report 2008-21, Stockholm: Brå (The Swedish National Council for Crime Prevention).

Environmental Justice Foundation. (2015) 'Pirates and Slaves: How Overfishing in Thailand Fuels Human Trafficking and the Plundering of Our Oceans' Available: http://ejfoundation.org/sites/default/files/public/EJF_Pirates_and_Slaves_2015.pdf [Accessed 10 March 2015].

EUROPA. (2011) 'Combating trafficking in human beings' (3 Mar) Available: http://europa.eu/legislation_summaries/justice_ freedom_security/fight_against_trafficking_in_human_ beings/l33137_en.htm [Accessed 13 July 2012].

EUROPA. (2012) 'Together against Trafficking in Human Beings: Koolvis case' (11 June) Available: http://ec.europa.eu/anti-trafficking/ entity.action?id=861811e6-b0e7-40fe-87e4-571f83e47098 [Accessed 25 July 2012].

European Commission. (2012a) 'Netherlands' *Together against Trafficking in Human Beings* (11 Jun) Available: http://ec.europa.eu/anti-trafficking/showNIPsection. action?country=Netherlands [Accessed 13 July 2012].

European Commission. (2012b) 'Sweden' *Together against Trafficking in Human Beings* (11 Jun) Available: http://ec.europa.eu/ anti-trafficking/showNIPsection.action?country=Sweden [Accessed 7 August 2012].

Finkelman, P. (2006) Fugitive Slave Law of 1850. *In:* FINKELMAN, P. (ed.) *Encyclopedia of African American history, 1619-1895 : from the colonial period to the age of Frederick Douglass.* New York: Oxford University Press, 74-78.

Fogel, R. W. & Engerman, S. L. (1989) *Time on the cross : the economics of American Negro slavery*, New York: Norton.

France24. (2012) 'French minister wants prostitution to 'disappear'' (24 Jun) Available: http://iphone.france24.com/en/20120624- france-women-rights-minister-najat-vallaud-belkacem-ban- prostitution-sex-trade-trafficking [Accessed 6 July 2012].

Genovese, E. D. (1965) *The political economy of slavery; studies in the economy & society of the slave South*, New York: Pantheon Books.

George W. Bush Administration. (2003) 'National Security Presidential Directive 22: Trafficking in Persons' (25 February) Available: http://www.fas.org/irp/offdocs/nspd/trafpers.html [Accessed 6 July 2012].

Glazebrook, S. (2010) 'Human Trafficking And New Zealand' *In: AGM of the New Zealand Women Judges Association*, Auckland, 2010: Courts of New Zealand.

Global Commission on HIV and the Law. (2012) 'HIV and the Law: Risks, Rights & Health' (July) Available: http://www.hivlawcommission.org/resources/report/FinalReport-Risks,Rights&Health-EN.pdf [Accessed 6 Oct 2013].

GlobalSecurity.org. (n.d.) 'Avtomat Kalashnikov AK-47' Available: http://www.globalsecurity.org/military/world/russia/ak-47-spec.htm [Accessed 10 March 2015].

Gluckman, R. (n.d.) 'Death in Dubai' Available: http://www.gluckman.com/camelracing.html [Accessed 22 August 2011].

Governor of Maharashtra. (2013) 'Translation in English of the Maharashtra Prevention and Eradication of Human Sacrifice and other Inhuman, Evil and Aghori Practices and Black Magic Act, 2013' Available: http://www.bombayhighcourt.nic.in/libweb/acts/Mah.Ord.2013.14.PDF [Accessed 13 March 2015].

Grenier, J. (1997) Illegal Slave Trade. *In:* RODRIGUEZ, J. P. (ed.) *The Historical encyclopedia of world slavery.* Santa Barbara, California: ABC-CLIO, 363.

Guérin, I., Augendra, B. & Parthasarthy, V. G. (2007) 'Labour in Brick Kilns: A Case Study in Chennai', *Economic and Political Weekly,* 42(7), 599-606.

Hagar International. (2015) 'Press Release: Korean sex workers held against their will in Auckland is human trafficking - isn't it?' (12 Oct) Available: https://hagarinternational.org/new-zealand/press-release-korean-sex-workers-held-against-their-will-in-auckland-is-human-trafficking-isnt-it-2/ [Accessed 13 November 2015].

Haken, J. (2011) *Transnational Crime In The Developing World,* Washington DC: Global Financial Integrity.

Hammond, J. H. (1866) *Selections from the letters and speeches of the Hon. James H. Hammond, of South Carolina*, New York: J. F. Trow & Co., printers.

Hammond, M. B. (1897) 'The Southern Farmer and the Cotton Question', *The Academy of Political Science,* 12(3)*,* 450-475.

Hardaway, R. M. (2003) *No price too high : victimless crimes and the Ninth Amendment*, Westport, Conn.: Praeger.

Harper, W., Dew, T. R., Hammond, J. H. & Gilmore Simms, W. (1853) *The pro-slavery argument; as maintained by the most distinguished writers of the southern states*, Philadelphia: Lippincott, Grambo, & Co.

Harress, C. (2013) 'The Economics Of Slavery: Centuries-Old Debate Surfaces Again In The Economist' *International Business Times* (30 Sept) Available: http://www.ibtimes.com/ economics-slavery-centuries-old-debate-surfaces-again-economist-1412802 [Accessed 18 July 2014].

Hatcher III, R. W. (2010) 'The Problem in Charleston Harbor', *Hallowed Ground Magazine,* 11(4).

Havocscope. (n.d.) 'Organ Trafficking Prices and Kidney Transplant Sales' Available: http://www.havocscope.com/black-market-prices/organs-kidneys/ [Accessed 26 October 2015].

Hawksley, H. (2014) 'Why India's brick kiln workers 'live like slaves'' *BBC News India* (2 Jan) Available: http://www.bbc.com/news/ world-asia-india-25556965 [Accessed 20 March 2015].

Helper, H. R. (1857) *The impending crisis of the South; how to meet it*, New-York: Burdick brothers.

Hergesheimer, E. 1861. *Map showing the distribution of the slave population of the southern states of the United States. Compiled from the census of 1860.* Washington: Henry S. Graham.

Hindle, K., Barnett, L. & Casavant, L. (2008) 'Prostitution: A Review of Legislation in Selected Countries' (19 Nov) Available: http://www.parl.gc.ca/Content/LOP/ResearchPublications/ prb0329-e.htm#Netherlands [Accessed 13 July 2012].

Hodal, K. & Kelly, C. (2014) 'Trafficked into slavery on Thai trawlers to catch food for prawns' *The Guardian* (10 Jun) Available: http://www.theguardian.com/global-development/2014/jun/10/-sp-migrant-workers-new-life-enslaved-thai-fishing [Accessed 4 March 2015].

Hodal, K., Kelly, C. & Lawrence, F. (2014) 'Revealed: Asian slave labour producing prawns for supermarkets in US, UK' *The Guardian* (10 Jun) Available: http://www.theguardian.com/global-development/2014/jun/10/supermarket-prawns-thailand-produced-slave-labour [Accessed 4 March 2015].

Howard, O. O. (1886) *A Brief History of the Mexican War,* A. J. Cornell Publications [Online], Available: http://www.amazon.com/Brief-History-Mexican-War-ebook/dp/B007OLYLE4/ref=sr_1_1?s=digital-text&ie=UTF8&qid=1401899865&sr=1-1 [Accessed 3 February 2014].

Hubbard, P., Matthews, R. & Scoular, J. (2008) 'Regulating sex work in the EU: prostitute women and the new spaces of exclusion', *Gender, Place & Culture: A Journal of Feminist Geography,* 15(2), 137-152.

Hughes, D. M. (2005) 'The Demand for Victims of Sex Trafficking' (June) Available: http://www.uri.edu/artsci/wms/hughes/demand_for_victims.pdf [Accessed 15 August 2012].

International Labour Organization (ILO). (2014) 'ILO says forced labour generates annual profits of US$ 150 billion' (20 May) Available: http://www.ilo.org/global/about-the-ilo/newsroom/news/WCMS_243201/lang--en/index.htm [Accessed 23 January 2016].

International Organization for Migration. (2005) 'Awareness raising of judicial authorities concerning trafficking in human beings: Handbook' 1 Available: http://ec.europa.eu/anti-trafficking/download.action;jsessionid=TC41NsdNky22vb4vjJBhWK9h7hnwy9y38KSvYWmy9XBJmjGvyZZJ!855818409?nodeId=5239e3a8-6374-46dd-a4ea-78d46b3fe7c0&fileName=AGIS_2004_1-93_1+Handbook.pdf [Accessed 22 July 2012].

Jacobs, H. A. & Child, L. M. (1861) *Incidents in the life of a slave girl*, Boston: Pub. for the author.

Jakobsson, N. & Kotsadam, A. (2011) 'The law and economics of international sex slavery: prostitution laws and trafficking for sexual exploitation', *European Journal of Law and Economics*, 1-21.

Jefferson, T. (1820) 'Thomas Jefferson to John Holmes' (22 Apr) Available: http://www.loc.gov/exhibits/jefferson/159.html [Accessed 22 April 2014].

Jefferson, T. (1853) *Notes on the state of Virginia*, Richmond, Va.: J. W. Randolph.

Jefferson, T. & Boyd, J. 'Jefferson's "original Rough draught" of the Declaration of Independence' Available: http://www.loc.gov/exhibits/declara/ruffdrft.html [Accessed 5 December 2014].

Johnston, J. F. W. (1853) 'Slavery and the Slave Power in the United States of America', *Blackwood's Edinburgh Magazine,* LXXIII(January - June)**,** 1-20.

Jones, T. P. (1827) *An address on the progress of manufactures and internal improvement, in the United States; and particularly, on the advantages to be derived from the employment of slaves in the manufacturing of cotton and other goods. Delivered in the hall of the Franklin Institute, November 6, 1827*, Philadelphia: Judah Dobson.

Kabuye, D. B., Ndyabagye, E., Nnanyonjo, R. & Okurut, B. (2014) *Child Sacrifice in Uganda and its Human Rights implications*: Uganda Human Rights Commission.

Kamyotra, J. S. (2015) 'Brick Kilns in India' (11 Mar) Available: http://www.cseindia.org/docs/aad2015/11.03.2015%20Brick%20Presentation.pdf [Accessed 13 January 2017].

Kara, S. (2009) *Sex Trafficking: Inside the Business of Modern Slavery,* Columbia University Press [Online], Available: http://www.amazon.com/Sex-Trafficking-Inside-Business-Slavery-ebook/dp/B003UNK26G [Accessed 1 July 2012].

Kelly, L., Coy, M. & Davenport, R. (2009) 'Shifting Sands: A Comparison of Prostitution Regimes across Nine Countries' Available: http://www.cwasu.org/filedown.asp?file=shifting%20 sands%20published%20version.pdf [Accessed 22 January 2012].

Kerry, J. (2015) 'Remarks at the 2015 Trafficking in Persons Report Ceremony' (27 Jul) Available: http://www.state.gov/secretary/ remarks/2015/07/245298.htm [Accessed 28 July 2015].

Kloer, A. (2010) 'The Mafia Caught Prostituting Kids on Craigslist' Change.Org (21 April) Available: http://news.change.org/ stories/the-mafia-caught-prostituting-kids-on-craigslist [Accessed 28 June 2012].

Konrad, H. (2005) 'Assessment of the human trafficking situation and anti-trafficking activities in the Netherlands' (Dec) Available: http://www.osce.org/cthb/18839 [Accessed 22 July 2012].

Korvinus, A. G., van Dijk, E. M. H., Koster, D. A. C. & Smit, M. (2004) 'Trafficking in Human Beings: Third report of the Dutch National Rapporteur' Available: http://english.bnrm.nl/Images/ Rapportage%203%20(Eng)_tcm64-83607.pdf [Accessed 25 January 2012].

La Strada International. (2008) 'Trafficking in Human Beings: Trafficking in Europe' Available: http://lastradainternational. org/?main=traffickinghumanbeings [Accessed 10 October 2013].

Lancaster, J. (2003) 'In India, case links mysticism, murder' The Boston Globe (29 Nov) Available: http://www.boston.com/news/ world/articles/2003/11/29/in_india_case_links_mysticism_ murder/ [Accessed 20 March 2015].

Lebby, R. (1911) 'The First Shot on Fort Sumter', The South Carolina Historical and Genealogical Magazine, 12(3), 141-145.

Lewis, J. (2005) 'Robots of Arabia' Wired (13 Nov) Available: http:// www.wired.com/wired/archive/13.11/camel.html [Accessed 14 October 2013].

Library of Congress (1861) *Map showing the distribution of the slave population of the southern states of the United States. Compiled from the census of 1860* [image online], Available: https://www.loc.gov/item/ody0314/ [15 August 2016]

Library of Congress (1885) *[Theodore Dwight Weld, 1803-1895, bust portrait, facing slightly left] digital file from b&w film copy neg.* [image online], Available: https://www.loc.gov/resource/cph.3a49911/ [16 August 2016]

Lincoln, A. (1858) 'House divided speech' (16 Jun) Available: http://www.abrahamlincolnonline.org/lincoln/speeches/house.htm [Accessed 5 June 2014].

Lincoln, A. (1861) 'Inaugural Address' (4 Mar) Available: http://www.presidency.ucsb.edu/ws/?pid=25818 [Accessed 14 April 2014].

Lincoln, A. (1863) 'The Gettysburg Address' (19 Nov) Available: http://www.abrahamlincolnonline.org/lincoln/speeches/gettysburg.htm [Accessed 7 May 2014].

Magnanti, B. (2012) *The Sex Myth: Why Everything We're Told is Wrong*, London: Hachette UK.

Mangel, M. & Samaniego, F. J. (1984) 'Abraham Wald's Work on Aircraft Survivability', *Journal of the American Statistical Association,* 79(386), 259-267.

Marinova, N. K. & James, P. (2012) 'The Tragedy of Human Trafficking: Competing Theories and European Evidence 1', *Foreign Policy Analysis*, 1-23.

Mayo Clinic Staff. (2015) 'Pancreas transplant' (27 Jan) Available: http://www.mayoclinic.org/tests-procedures/pancreas-transplant/basics/definition/prc-20014239 [Accessed 27 March 2015].

McClure, J. M. (2014) 'Edmund Ruffin (1794-1865)' *Encyclopedia Virginia. Virginia Foundation for the Humanities* (4 Jan) Available: http://www.encyclopediavirginia.org/Ruffin_Edmund_1794-1865#start_entry [Accessed 28 January 2015].

McDonald Beckles, H. & UNESCO. (2002) *Slave voyages : the transatlantic trade in enslaved Africans*, Paris: UNESCO.

McRaney, D. (2013) 'Survivorship Bias' *You are not so smart: A celebration of self delusion* (23 May) Available: http://youarenotsosmart.com/2013/05/23/survivorship-bias/ [Accessed 6 May 2015].

Michaud, H. (2009) 'Dutch tribunal to rule on sex trafficking case' *Radio Netherlands Worldwide (RNW)* (3 Dec) Available: http://www.rnw.nl/international-justice/article/dutch-tribunal-rule-sex-trafficking-case [Accessed 25 July 2012].

Michaud, H. (2012) 'Nigerian trafficker convicted after anti-voodoo move' *Radio Netherlands Worldwide (RNW)* (12 Mar) Available: http://www.rnw.nl/english/article/dutch-police-break-fear-juju [Accessed 14 July 2012].

Migiro, K. (2015) 'U.N. condemns surge in hunting and killing of albinos in East Africa' *Reuters* (10 Mar) Available: http://www.reuters.com/article/2015/03/10/us-eastafrica-albinism-idUSKBN0M61I520150310 [Accessed 20 March 2015].

Minister of Integration and Gender Equality Sweden. (n.d.) 'Against prostitution and human trafficking for sexual purposes' Available: http://www.sweden.gov.se/content/1/c6/13/36/71/ae076495.pdf [Accessed 7 August 2012].

Ministry of Justice. (2002) *Protecting our innocence: New Zealand's national plan of action against the commercial sexual exploitation of children*, Auckland: New Zealand Government.

Ministry of Justice. Prostitution Law Review Committee. (2008) *Report of the Prostitution Law Review Committee on the Operation of the Prostitution Reform Act 2003*, Wellington: New Zealand Government.

Moneyhon, C. H. (2012) 'Slavery' *The Encylopedia of Arkansas History & Culture* (2 May) Available: http://www.encyclopediaofarkansas.net/encyclopedia/entry-detail.aspx?entryID=1275 [Accessed 1 July 2014].

Morris, C. (2013) 'Brothel or bust: Hard times at Nevada's bordellos' *CNBC* (28 Aug) Available: http://www.cnbc.com/id/100994185 [Accessed 23 October 2013].

Munro, V. E. (2006) 'Stopping Traffic? A Comparative Study of Responses to the Trafficking in Women or Prostitution', *British Journal of Criminology,* 46(2)**,** 318-333.

National Archives and Records Administration (1861) *Edmund Ruffin. Fired the 1st shot in the Late War. Killed himself at close of War.* [image online], Available: https://research.archives.gov/id/530493 [15 August 2016]

National Archives and Records Administration (1942 - 1945) *Harriet Beecher Stowe, circa 1870s-80s* [image online], Available: https://research.archives.gov/id/535784 [15 August 2016]

National Human Trafficking Resource Center. (2014) '2014 NHTRC Annual Report' Available: http://www.traffickingresourcecenter.org/sites/default/files/2014%20NHTRC%20Annual%20Report_Final.pdf [Accessed 18 May 2015].

National Rapporteur on Trafficking in Human Beings. (2002) 'Trafficking in Human Beings: First report of the Dutch National Rapporteur' Available: http://english.bnrm.nl/Images/Rapportage%201%20(Eng)_tcm64-83603.pdf [Accessed 25 January 2012].

National Rapporteur on Trafficking in Human Beings. (2009) 'Trafficking in Human Beings: Seventh Report of the Dutch National Rapporteur' Available: http://english.bnrm.nl/Images/7e-rapportage-engels-def_tcm64-281585.pdf [Accessed 25 January 2012].

National Rapporteur on Trafficking in Human Beings. (2010) 'Trafficking in Human Beings: Ten years of independent monitoring' Available: http://english.bnrm.nl/Images/8e%20rapportage%20NRM-ENG-web_tcm64-310472.pdf [Accessed 25 January 2012].

National Rapporteur on Trafficking in Human Beings and Sexual Violence against Children. (2013a) 'Does legalised prostitution generate more human trafficking?' Available: http://www.dutchrapporteur.nl/Images/dutch-rapporteur.does-legalised-prostitution-generate-more-human-trafficking.2013_tcm64-558164.pdf [Accessed 30 August 2015].

National Rapporteur on Trafficking in Human Beings and Sexual Violence against Children. (2013b) 'Ninth Report on Trafficking in Human Beings' Available: http://www.dutchrapporteur.nl/Images/national-rapporteur-on-trafficking-in-human-beings-and-sexual-violence-against-children.ninth-report-of-the-dutch-national-rapporteur.2014_tcm64-564024.pdf [Accessed 30 August 2015].

National Rapporteur on Trafficking in Human Beings and Sexual Violence against Children. (2014) 'Factsheet on Trafficking in Human Beings: Visible and Invisible II: A quantitative report 2008-2012' (1 Dec) Available: http://www.dutchrapporteur.nl/Images/dutch-rapporteur-trafficking-in-human-beings-visible-and-invisible-ii_tcm64-573604.pdf [Accessed 21 October 2015].

New Zealand Prostitutes Collective. (n.d.-a) 'The Mission of NZPC is:' Available: http://www.nzpc.org.nz/index.php?page=Home [Accessed 13 November 2015].

New Zealand Prostitutes Collective. (n.d.-b) 'NZPC | Aotearoa New Zealand Sex Workers' Collective' Available: https://www.nzpc.org.nz/About-NZPC [Accessed 21 August 2021].

New Zealand. Parliamentary Library. (2012) 'Prostitution law reform in New Zealand' (Jul) Available: http://www.parliament.nz/resource/en-nz/00PLSocRP12051/c62a00e57bd36e84aed237e357af2b7381a39f7e [Accessed 10 November 2015].

Nichter, L. S., Morgan, R. F. & Nichter, M. A. (1983) 'The Impact of Indian Methods for Total Nasal Reconstruction', *Clinics in Plastic Surgery,* 10(4), 635-647.

Nickel, J. (2010) 'Human Rights' *The Stanford Encyclopedia of Philosophy* (Fall 2010 Edition) Available: http://plato.stanford.edu/entries/rights-human/ [Accessed 6 July 2012].

Nickel, J. W. (2007) *Making sense of human rights,* Blackwell Pub. [Online], Available: http://www.amazon.com/Making-Sense-Human-Rights-Nickel/dp/140514534X [Accessed 12 July 2012].

Nielsen, N. (2012) 'Human traffickers evade conviction' *EUObserver. com* (25 June) Available: http://euobserver.com/22/116750 [Accessed 25 June 2012].

Nigeria. National Agency For The Prohibition Of Trafficking In Persons. (2019) 'Nigeria Country Report on Human Trafficking 2019' Available: https://www.naptip.gov.ng/wp-content/uploads/2020/01/Nigeria-Country-Report-on-Human-Trafficking3.pdf [Accessed 1 June 2021].

Northup, S. (2014) *12 Years a Slave (Illustrated),* Ostrich Books [Online], Available: http://www.amazon.com/Years-Slave-Illustrated-Solomon-Northup-ebook/dp/B00I4YAVJE/ref=tmm_kin_title_12?ie=UTF8&qid=1407696875&sr=1-5 [Accessed 10 August 2014].

NSWP. (2014) 'Good practice in sex worker-led HIV programming: Global report' (16 May) Available: http://www.nswp.org/sites/nswp.org/files/Global%20Report%20English.pdf [Accessed 12 May 2015].

Obaji Jr., P. (2015) 'The Child Soldiers Fighting Boko Haram' *The Daily Beast* (7 Mar) Available: http://www.thedailybeast.com/articles/2015/03/07/the-child-soldiers-fighting-boko-haram.html [Accessed 10 March 2015].

Olmsted, F. L. (1861) *Journeys and explorations in the cotton kingdom. A traveller's observations on cotton and slavery in the American slave states. Based upon three former volumes of journeys and investigations*, London: S. Low, Son & Co.

Opala, J. A. (1987) 'The Gullah: Rice, Slavery and the Sierra Leone-American Connection' Available: http://www.yale.edu/glc/gullah/02.htm [Accessed 16 July 2014].

Organization for Security and Co-operation in Europe (OSCE). (2008) 'Human Trafficking for Labour Exploitation/Forced and Bonded Labour: Identification – Prevention – Prosecution' Available: http://www.ungift.org/doc/knowledgehub/resource-centre/OSCE_Human_Trafficking_for_Labour_Exploitation.pdf [Accessed 22 June 2012].

Oxford Dictionaries. (2013) 'Definition of definition in English' Available: https://www.lexico.com/en/definition/definition [Accessed 15 July 2021].

Palmstrom, B. (2014) 'Forced to fish: Slavery on Thailand's trawlers' *BBC News* (23 Jan) Available: http://www.bbc.com/news/magazine-25814718 [Accessed 9 March 2015].

Parker, T. (1848) *A letter to the people of the United States touching the matter of slavery*, Boston: J. Munroe and company.

Participants in the International Summit on Transplant Tourism and Organ Trafficking Convened by The Transplantation Society and International Society of Nephrology in Istanbul Turkey April 30 through May 2 2008. (2008) 'The Declaration of Istanbul on Organ Trafficking and Transplant Tourism' Available: http://multivu.prnewswire.com/mnr/transplantationsociety/33914/docs/33914-Declaration_of_Istanbul-Lancet.pdf [Accessed 2 November 2015].

Peachey, P. (2010) 'UAE defies ban on child camel jockeys' *The Independent* (3 Mar) Available: http://www.independent.co.uk/news/world/middle-east/uae-defies-ban-on-child-camel-jockeys-1914915.html [Accessed 10 October 2013].

Pedigo, K. (2013) 'Prostitution: A 'victimless crime'?' *Al Jazeera* (19 Mar) Available: http://www.aljazeera.com/indepth/opinion/2013/03/20133187151912199.html [Accessed 9 October 2013].

Persad, R. (2013) 'Prostitution Boats Utrecht Close' *NLTimes.nl* (25 Jul) Available: http://www.nltimes.nl/2013/07/25/prostitution-boats-utrecht-close/ [Accessed 21 October 2015].

Phelan, S. (2014) 'South African diplomat in 'slavery' row departs Ireland' *Irish Independent* (12 Mar) Available: http://www.independent.ie/irish-news/news/south-african-diplomat-in-slavery-row-departs-ireland-30391727.html [Accessed 12 March 2015].

Pieters, J. (2015) 'Utrecht gives green light do [sic] new prostitution district' *NLTimes.nl* (18 Sep) Available: http://www.nltimes.nl/2015/09/18/utrecht-gives-green-light-do-new-prostitution-district/ [Accessed 21 October 2015].

Pogue, Dennis J. (2002) 'The Domestic Architecture of Slavery at George Washington's Mount Vernon', *Winterthur Portfolio,* 37(1)**,** 3-22.

Pokharel, S. (2015) 'Nepal's Organ Trail: How traffickers steal kidneys' *The CNN Freedom Project* Available: http://edition.cnn.com/2014/06/26/world/asia/freedom-project-nepals-organ-trail/ [Accessed 2 November 2015].

PolarisProject.org. (2014) '2014 Statistics' Available: http://www.polarisproject.org/storage/documents/2014statistics.pdf [Accessed 12 March 2015].

PolarisProject.org. (n.d.) 'Human Trafficking' Available: http://www.polarisproject.org/human-trafficking/overview [Accessed 18 May 2015].

Polisen. (2006) *Situation Report 8: Trafficking in human beings for sexual purposes,* Swedish National Police Board [Online], Available: http://www.osce.org/cthb/25186 [Accessed 7 August 2012].

Polisen. (2009a) *Situation Report 9: Trafficking in human beings for sexual purposes,* Rikskriminalpolisen [Online], Available: http://www.polisen.se/Global/www%20och%20Intrapolis/Informationsmaterial/01%20Polisen%20

nationellt/Engelskt%20informationsmaterial/Trafficking_
Lagesrapport_9_ENG.pdf [Accessed 8 August 2012].

Polisen. (2009b) *Situation Report 10: Människohandel för sexuella
och andra ändamål [Trafficking in human beings for
sexual and other purposes]*, Swedish National Police Board
[Online], Available: http://ec.europa.eu/anti-trafficking/
download.action;jsessionid=0L5rT2dQ2ykS1WS85GNyG3L
M41b9zlrk23826nZTcTGLGgvyxz0B!741669820?nodeId=e
a9811f0-33ad-4939-bc46-af76391b55a1&fileName=Traffic
king+in+human+beings+for+sexual+and+other+purposes+
Situation+Report+10_en.pdf&fileType=pdf   [Accessed   8
August 2012].

Polisen. (2010) *Situation Report 11: Människohandel för sexuella
och andra ändamål [Trafficking in human beings for sexual
and other purposes]*, Swedish National Police Board [Online],
Available: http://www.si.se/upload/Human%20Trafficking/
L%C3%A4g%2011%20Fin%20ENG.PDF   [Accessed   29   July
2012].

Polisen. (2011) *Situation Report 12: Människohandel för sexuella
och andra ändamål [Trafficking in human beings for sexual
and other purposes]*, Swedish National Police Board [Online],
Available: http://www.polisen.se/Global/www%20och%20
Intrapolis/Informationsmaterial/01%20Polisen%20nationellt/
Engelskt%20informationsmaterial/Trafficking_1998_/
Trafficking_report_12_20120502.pdf [Accessed 22 August
2012].

Polisen. (2013) *Tillsynsrapport 2013:7: Inspektion av polismyndigheternas förmåga att utreda ärenden om människohandel för sexuella ändamål och köp av sexuell tjänst [Inspection of the police authorities' ability to investigate cases of human trafficking for sexual purposes and the purchase of sexual services],* Rikspolisstyrelsen [Online], Available: https://polisen.se/Global/www%20och%20Intrapolis/Rapporter-utredningar/01%20Polisen%20nationellt/Ovriga%20rapporter-utredningar/Inspektioner-tillsyns%20rapporter/2013/Tillsynsrapp_7_Manniskohandel_13.pdf [Accessed 21 October 2015].

Prabhakar, S. & Raja, A. (2015) 'Bought and Sold Like Cattle Under Law's Nose' *The New Indian Express* (30 Jul) Available: http://www.newindianexpress.com/cities/chennai/Bought-and-Sold-Like-Cattle-Under-Laws-Nose/2015/07/30/article2947816.ece [Accessed 4 August 2015].

Prostitution Information Center. (2012) 'Petition against registration' (4 Jul) Available: http://www.pic-amsterdam.com/wordpress/en/?p=131 [Accessed 31 August 2015].

Prostitution Reform Act 2003. No.28/2003, New Zealand: Parliament Counsel Office.

Rade, M. & Shah, A. (2010) 'The Dutch Myth of Tolerance' *Humanity In Action* Available: http://www.humanityinaction.org/knowledgebase/315-the-dutch-myth-of-tolerance [Accessed 29 August 2015].

Reformina, I. (2011) 'Human trafficking syndicate falls, teen rescued' *ABS-CBN News* (4 April) Available: http://www.abs-cbnnews.com/nation/metro-manila/04/04/11/human-trafficking-syndicate-falls-teen-rescued [Accessed 28 June 2012].

Reuters. (2015) 'Tanzania police arrest 32 witch-doctors over ritual albino killings' *The Guardian* (6 Mar) Available: http://www.theguardian.com/world/2015/mar/06/tanzania-witch-doctors-arrested-albino-killings [Accessed 19 March 2015].

Rogers, C. (2011) 'Where child sacrifice is a business' *BBC New Online* (11 Oct) Available: http://www.bbc.co.uk/news/world-africa-15255357#story_continues_1 [Accessed 19 March 2015].

Ruffin, E. (1857?) *The Political Economy of Slavery*, Washington D.C.: Lemuel Towers.

Ruffin, E. & African American Pamphlet Collection (Library of Congress). (1860) *Slavery and free labor, described and compared*, S.l.: s.n.

Ruhama. (n.d.) 'Analyzing the Swedish Model on prostitution' Available: http://www.ruhama.ie/easyedit/files/analyzingtheswedishmodelonprostitution.doc [Accessed 4 January 2012].

Samuel Hall Consulting. (2011) 'Buried in bricks: A rapid assessment of bonded labour in brick kilns in Afghanistan' Available: https://www.ilo.org/wcmsp5/groups/public/---asia/---ro-bangkok/documents/publication/wcms_172671.pdf [Accessed 29 Jun 2021].

Sandel, M. J. (2010) *Justice : what's the right thing to do?*, New York: Farrar, Straus and Giroux.

Sattler, J. (2013) 'David Vitter Has Already Paid for His Crimes -- Literally' *The Huffington Post* (17 Sept) Available: http://www.huffingtonpost.com/jason-sattler/david-vitter-has-already-_b_3935053.html [Accessed 9 Oct 2013].

Scalise, K. (1999) 'Extreme Research', *Berkeley Magazine,* (Summer).

Schepers, I. (2011) 'Operation Sneep: "The frayed edges of licensed prostitution."' Available: www.osce.org/cthb/84652 [Accessed 15 Sept 2012].

Shimazono, Y. (2007) 'The state of the international organ trade: a provisional picture based on integration of available information' *Bulletin of the World Health Organization* 85 (12) Available: http://www.who.int/bulletin/volumes/85/12/06-039370/en/ [Accessed 5 May 2015].

Siegel, D. (2009) 'Human trafficking and legalized prostitution in the Netherlands' *Temida* 12 (1) Available: http://www.vds.org.rs/File/Tem0901.pdf [Accessed 15 Sept 2012].

Siegel, D. (2012) 'Mobility of sex workers in European cities', *European Journal on Criminal Policy and Research,* 18(3)**,** 255-268.

Singleton, W. H. (1922) 'Recollections of My Slavery Days' Available: http://docsouth.unc.edu/neh/singleton/singleton.html [Accessed 5 January 2015].

Sinha, S. (2013) 'India: Mumbai Woman Beheaded in Gory Tantrik Ritual' *International Business Times* (16 Dec) Available: http://www.ibtimes.co.uk/indian-woman-beheaded-human-sacrifice-black-magic-530535 [Accessed 20 March 2015].

Skinner, J. S. (ed.) 1827. *The American Farmer, containing original essays and selections on agriculture, horticulture, rural and domestic economy and home improvements with illustrative engravings and the prices of country produce,* Baltimore, Maryland.

SlaveryFootprint.org. (n.d.) 'About' Available: http://slaveryfootprint.org/about/#aboutus [Accessed 27 February 2015].

Smith, A. (2012) *An inquiry into the nature and causes of the wealth of nations,* [Online], Available: http://www.amazon.com/Inquiry-Nature-Causes-Wealth-Nations-ebook/dp/B00847CE6O/ref=asap_B00KD0BXRQ_1_1?s=books&ie=UTF8&qid=1416750888&sr=1-1 [Accessed 23 November 2014].

SOAIDS. (n.d.) 'Money Matters' Available: http://www.prostitutie.nl/index.php?id=11&L=1 [Accessed 3 August 2012].

Spiegel Staff. (2013) ' Unprotected: How Legalizing Prostitution Has Failed' *Spiegel Online International* (30 May) Available: http://www.spiegel.de/international/germany/human-traffickIng-persists-despite-legality-of-prostitution-in-germany-a-902533.html [Accessed 22 October 2015].

Standing Committee on Justice and Human Rights & Subcommittee on Solicitation Laws. (2006) *The Challenges of Change: A Study of Canada's Criminal Prostitution Laws*, Ottawa: House of Commons Canada.

Staring, R. H. J. M. (2012) 'Human trafficking in the Netherlands: trends and recent developments', *International Review of Law, Computers & Technology,* 26(1), 59-72.

Stowe, H. B. & Douglas, A. (1981) *Uncle Tom's cabin : or, Life among the lowly,* New York, N.Y.: Penguin Books.

Sullivan, M. (2005) 'What Happens When Prostitution Becomes Work?: An Update on Legalisation of Prostitution in Australia' Available: http://www.turnofftheredlight.ie/wp-content/uploads/2011/02/What-happens-when-prostitution-becomes-work.pdf [Accessed 22 January 2012].

Swanberg, W. A. (1957) *First blood; the story of Fort Sumter,* New York: Scribner.

Swedish Institute. (2010) 'Selected extracts of the Swedish government report SOU 2010:49: "The Ban against the Purchase of Sexual Services. An evaluation 1999-2008"' Available: http://www.sweden.gov.se/download/96b1e019.pdf?major=1&minor=149231&cn=attachmentDuplicator_0_attachment [Accessed 8 August 2012].

Tan, L. (2010) 'NZ's sex-slave cases "slip under radar"' *New Zealand Herald* (4 Aug) Available: http://www.nzherald.co.nz/nz/news/article.cfm?c_id=1&objectid=10663446 [Accessed 19 August 2015].

The Coordination Office to Combat Trafficking in Persons. (2014) *Annual Report on the trend of Trafficking in Persons in Uganda 2013,* Kampala: Ministry of Internal Affairs.

The Economist. (2015) 'Bare branches, redundant males: The marriage squeeze in India and China' (18 Apr) Available: http://www.economist.com/news/asia/21648715-distorted-sex-ratios-birth-generation-ago-are-changing-marriage-and-damaging-societies-asias?fsrc=scn/tw/te/pe/ed/marriagesqueeze [Accessed 4 May 2015].

The Procurator General of the Supreme Court of the Netherlands. (2009) 'Ruling on the appeal in cassation against a judgment by the Court of Appeal of 's-Hertogenbosch of 30 January 2008, number 20/001124-07' (27 Oct) Available: http://ec.europa. eu/anti-trafficking/download.action;jsessionid=QyQPPlGbG QdKSTsXh6Bj61WdDBSkC0Gmzfs4zx2QLcclmPQHQHn8!5110 69867?nodeId=aef3940c-6f4a-41c4-99d4-06d624f8230b&fil eName=ENGELS+LJN+Hoge+Raad27Oct+2009.pdf [Accessed 13 July 2012].

The Victims of Trafficking and Violence Protection Act. Public Law 106-386, 114 Stat. 1464, Washington, DC: United States Government Printing Office.

The White House. (n.d.) 'The Constitution' Available: http://www. whitehouse.gov/our-government/the-constitution [Accessed 10 June 2014].

Thomson Reuters Foundation. (2014) 'Armed groups recruit 10,000 child soldiers in Central African Republic: NGO' *Reuters* (18 Dec) Available: http://www.reuters.com/article/2014/12/18/ us-centralafrica-children-fighters-idUSKBN0JW1PR20141218 [Accessed 9 March 2015].

Thucydides. (455? BC - 355BC) *The History of the Peloponnesian War,* Amazon Kindle Store [Online], Available: http://www.amazon. com/History-Peloponnesian-War-Thucydides-ebook/dp/ B0082Z8X2C/ref=sr_1_1?s=digital-text&ie=UTF8&qid=13972 22291&sr=1-1 [Accessed 11 April 2014].

TNN. (2013) ''Witch doctor' gets death penalty for beheading boy' *The Times of India* (17 Apr) Available: http://timesofindia. indiatimes.com/city/raipur/Witch-doctor-gets-death-penalty- for-beheading-boy/articleshow/19588624.cms [Accessed 20 March 2015].

Tordesillas, E. (2012) 'P100 million to combat human trafficking' *Malaya Business Insight* (2 July) Available: http://www.malaya. com.ph/index.php/column-of-the-day/7520-p100-million-to- combat-human-trafficking [Accessed 3 July 2012].

Turner, B. S. (1993) 'OUTLINE OF A THEORY OF HUMAN RIGHTS', *Sociology*, 27(3), 489-512.

U.S. Supreme Court. (1856) 'Dred Scott v Sandford' Available: http://caselaw.lp.findlaw.com/scripts/getcase.pl?navby=case&court=us&vol=60&page=393 [Accessed 6 June 2014].

UN General Assembly. (1948) 'The Universal Declaration of Human Rights' (217 A (III)) Available: http://www.unhcr.org/refworld/docid/3ae6b3712c.html [Accessed 20 June 2012].

UN General Assembly. (1956) 'Supplementary Convention on the Abolition of Slavery, the Slave Trade, and Institutions and Practices Similar to Slavery' (7 Sept) Available: http://www.ohchr.org/EN/ProfessionalInterest/Pages/SupplementaryConventionAbolitionOfSlavery.aspx [Accessed 13 March 2015].

UNAIDS. (2011) *The report of the UNAIDS Advisory Group on HIV and Sex Work*, Geneva.

UNAIDS. (2012) *UNAIDS guidance note on HIV and sex work*, Geneva.

United Nation. United Nations Office on Drugs and Crime (n.d.) *Human Trafficking* [Online], Available: http://www.unodc.org/unodc/en/human-trafficking/what-is-human-trafficking.html#What_is_Human_Trafficking [Accessed 20 June 2012].

United Nations. (2015) 'South Sudan: UN welcomes demobilization of child soldiers amid signs of peace' *UN News Centre* (27 Jan) Available: http://www.un.org/apps/news/story.asp?NewsID=49915#.VP7kA-GNCfl [Accessed 10 March 2015].

United Nations. Office of the High Commissioner for Human Rights. (2013) 'Ending Forced Marriage Worldwide' (21 Nov) Available: http://www.ohchr.org/EN/NewsEvents/Pages/EnforcedMarriages.aspx [Accessed 13 March 2015].

United Nations. UNICEF. (2008) 'Child Protection' Available: http://www.unicef.org/media/media_45451.html [Accessed 18 May 2015].

United Nations. UNICEF India. (n.d.) 'Changing lives in the brick kilns of West Bengal' Available: http://unicef.in/Story/896/Changing-lives-in-the-brick-kilns-of-West-Bengal [Accessed 24 March 2015].

United Nations. United Nations Global Initiative to Fight Human Trafficking. (n.d.) 'Trafficking for Organ Trade' Available: http://www.ungift.org/knowledgehub/en/about/trafficking-for-organ-trade.html [Accessed 27 October 2015].

United Nations. United Nations Office on Drugs and Crime. (2004) *United Nations Convention against Transnational Organized Crime and the protocols thereto*, New York: United Nations.

United Nations. United Nations Office on Drugs and Crime. (2010) 'Issue Paper: Organized crime involvement in trafficking in persons and smuggling of migrants' Available: http://www.unodc.org/documents/human-trafficking/FINAL_REPORT_06052010_1.pdf [Accessed 25 July 2012].

United Nations. United Nations Office on Drugs and Crime. (2014) *Global Report on Trafficking in Persons 2014*, New York: United Nations.

United States. (2008) *William Wilberforce Trafficking Victims Protection Reauthorization Act of 2008*, Washington, D.C.: U.S. G.P.O. : Supt. of Docs., U.S. G.P.O., distributor.

United States. Constitutional Convention (1787) & Farrand, M. (1911) *The records of the Federal convention of 1787*, New Haven: Yale University Press.

United States. Department of State. (2007) *Trafficking in Persons Report 2007*, Washington, DC: Department of State.

United States. Department of State. (2008) *Trafficking in Persons Report 2008*, Washington, DC: Department of State.

United States. Department of State. (2009) *Trafficking in Persons Report 2009*, Washington, DC: Department of State.

United States. Department of State. (2010) *Trafficking in Persons Report 2010*, Washington, DC: Department of State.

United States. Department of State. (2011a) *Trafficking in Persons Report 2011*, Washington, DC: Department of State.

United States. Department of State. (2011b) 'Trafficking Victims Protection Act: Minimum Standards for the Elimination of Trafficking in Persons' (19 Jun) Available: http://www.state.gov/j/tip/rls/tiprpt/2011/164236.htm [Accessed 2 March 2015].

United States. Department of State. (2012) *Trafficking in Persons Report 2012*, Washington, DC: Department of State.

United States. Department of State. (2014a) 'The Intersection Between Environmental Degradation and Human Trafficking' (20 Jun) Available: http://www.state.gov/j/tip/rls/fs/2014/227667.htm [Accessed 27 February 2015].

United States. Department of State. (2014b) *Trafficking in Persons Report 2014*, Washington, DC.

United States. Department of State. (2015) *Trafficking in Persons Report 2015*, Washington, DC.

United States. Department of State. (2020) 'Trafficking in Persons Report 2020' *Trafficking in Persons Report* Available: https://www.state.gov/wp-content/uploads/2020/06/2020-TIP-Report-Complete-062420-FINAL.pdf [Accessed 1 June 2021].

United States. Department of State. (2021) *Trafficking in Persons Report 2021,* [Online], Available: https://www.state.gov/reports/2021-trafficking-in-persons-report/ [Accessed 23 August 2021].

United States. Department of State. (n.d.) 'Trafficking in Persons Report' Available: http://www.state.gov/j/tip/rls/tiprpt/ [Accessed 17 June 2012].

Vandekerckhove, W., Pari, Z., Moens, B., Orfano, I., Hopkins, R., Nijboer, J., Vermeulen, G. & Bontinck, W. (n.d.) 'Research based on case studies of victims of trafficking in human beings in 3 EU Member States, i.e. Belgium, Italy and The Netherlands.' Available: http://ec.europa.eu/justice_home/daphnetoolkit/files/projects/2001_010/int_trafficking_case_studies_be_it_nl_hippokrates.pdf [Accessed 21 June 2012].

Viuhko, M. & Jokinen, A. (2009) *Trafficking for sexual exploitation and organised procuring in Finland,* 62, Helsinki: European Institute for Crime Prevention and Control, affiliated with the United Nations (HEUNI).

Walk Free Foundation. (2014) *The Global Slavery Index*, Australia.

Walk Free Foundation. (2018) *The Global Slavery Index*, Australia.

Walker-Rodriguez, A. & Hill, R. (2011) 'Human Sex Trafficking' *FBI Law Enforcement Bulletin* (March) Available: http://www.fbi.gov/stats-services/publications/law-enforcement-bulletin/march_2011/human_sex_trafficking [Accessed 23 July 2012].

War Child. (n.d.) 'Child Soldiers' Available: http://www.warchild.org.uk/issues/child-soldiers [Accessed 10 March 2015].

Weitzer, R. (2005) 'Flawed Theory and Method in Studies of Prostitution', *Violence Against Women,* 11(7), 934-949.

Weld, T. D. & American Anti-Slavery Society. (1839) *American slavery as it is; testimony of a thousand witnesses*, New York: American Anti-Slavery Society.

Wendyweneki (2015) 'Wendy's Story; Wendy Barnes Sex Trafficking', [Video Online], Available: https://www.youtube.com/watch?v=6VVHUP7TZbg [Accessed 19 November 2015].

Weston, G. M. (1857) *The progress of slavery in the United States*, Washington, D.C.: The Author.

Whewell, T. (2010) 'Witch-doctors reveal extent of child sacrifice in Uganda' *BBC New Online* (7 Jan) Available: http://news.bbc.co.uk/2/hi/8441813.stm [Accessed 19 March 2015].

Woodward, C. V. (1991) *The future of the past*, New York: Oxford University Press.

World Vision. (n.d.) 'Child Soldiers' Available: http://www.worldvision. org/about-us/media-center/child-soldiers [Accessed 10 March 2015].

WorldVision. (2012) 'Fact Sheet: Child Slavery & 3D Jobs' (Dec) Available:http://voices.worldvision.ca/wp-content/ uploads/2013/04/Fact-Sheet-for-HW-final-Dec-2012.pdf [Accessed 28 May 2015].

Appendix

Article 250*ter* became Article 250a.[1] The term "human trafficking" was deleted from the Article, which preferred instead to "penalise all forms of exploitation for prostitution and – from 1 October 2002 – other forms of sexual exploitation."[2] Dutch legislation did not fully comply with the *Palermo Protocol* until January 2005.[3] Hitherto legislative measures, under Article 250a, focused on sex trafficking, often at the expense of recognizing other forms of exploitation.[4] In time this too changed. Article 250a was replaced by Article 273a in 2005 and this article was itself renumbered as Article 273f in 2006.[5] The definition given in Article 273f of the Criminal Code is intended to be as compatible as is possible with Article 1 of the *Council Framework Decision of 19 July 2002 on Combating Trafficking in Human Beings*.[6] A summary of the framework decision specifically refers to the *United Nations Convention against Transnational Organised Crime* and the two protocols to the convention, signifying the implementation of the *Palermo Protocol* definition into European Law.[7] An earlier framework decision, Joint Action 97/154/JHA, which had used a different definition for human trafficking, was repealed under this newer version.[8] Further amendments were made to Article 273f in June 2009.[9]

A review of the descriptions of sex trafficking offered in article 250a, later in 273a, and again in Article 273f, reveals differences between them.[10] Although Article 250a predated Article 273a, which brought the Dutch definition into line with the *Palermo Protocol*, it shares many similarities with the definition given by the *Protocol*. Specifically, the acts given in 250a cover "any action which ... [an individual] knows or may reasonably be expected to know will result in ... [the victim] making him / herself available" for performing "sexual acts."[11] The only other item mentioned in Article 250a that can be reconciled as an act, under the *Palermo Protocol*, is recruitment.[12] The means detailed in Article 250a are "force," or "some other physical act," abduction, "threats of violence," "misuse of authority arising from the actual state of affairs," "deception" and "inducing ... [a] person to make him / herself available for performing sexual acts with or for a third party for remuneration."[13] The purpose of the exploitation is limited to "the performance of sexual acts ... for remuneration," a term that could be otherwise conveyed as forced commercial sexual exploitation.[14] Paragraph 1.2 of Article 250a deals with offences committed against children.[15] In an approach that can be likened to that of the *Palermo Protocol* no provision is made for means, as they become irrelevant where children are concerned.[16] There are differences too.[17] However, they do not present a significant stumbling block, as the changes that followed largely entail the recognition of other forms of exploitation, such as the removal of one's organs, and do not represent a significant amendment of the law with regard to exploitation *via* prostitution.[18] This is an important conclusion since it means a certain degree of homogeneity of the law, with regard to the definition of sex trafficking, can be presumed over the period of exploration. Of equal importance is the conclusion this homogeneity affords, specifically how sex trafficking as defined in Dutch law has largely been consistent with the *Palermo Protocol* since before 2005.

Notes

Chapter 1

1   Lebby, 1911, p.134.
2   Lincoln, 1863.
3   The White House, n.d.
4   Hatcher III, 2010.
5   Araujo, 2014, p.91.
6   Collins Jenkins, 2011.
7   Doubleday, 1876
8   Swanberg, 1957, p.15.
9   McClure, 2014.
10   Doubleday, 1876.
11   Jefferson, 1820.
12   *Ibid*.
13   *Ibid*.
14   *Ibid*.
15   Swanberg, 1957, p.329.
16   Encyclopaedia Britannica and Urofsky, 2014.
17   U.S. Supreme Court, 1856.
18   *Ibid*.
19   *Ibid*.
20   *Ibid*.
21   *Ibid*.
22   Hammond, 1866, p.115.
23   *Ibid*., p.126.
24   Harper, et al., 1853, p.6.
25   *Ibid*., p.6.
26   *Ibid*., p.6.
27   *Ibid*., p.6.
28   *Ibid*., p.10.

[29]   Ruffin, 1857?, pp.3-4.

[30]   Ibid., p.3.

[31]   Ibid., pp.3-4.

[32]   U.S. Supreme Court, 1856.

[33]   Singleton, 1922. Digitized and presented online by the University of North Carolina at Chapel Hill. Original book held by East Carolina University. Used with permission.

[34]   Northup, 2014, pp.90-91.

[35]   *Ibid.*, p.92.

[36]   Ibid., p.93. Racial slurs redacted.

[37]   Weld and American Anti-Slavery Society, 1839, p.169. Case lowered by the author for reasons of presentation.

[38]   Ibid., pp.169-170.

[39]   Jacobs and Child, 1861, p.64.

[40]   Ibid., pp.65-66.

[41]   *Ibid.*, p.66.

[42]   Stowe and Douglas, 1981.

[43]   *Ibid*.

[44]   Parker, 1848, p.15.

[45]   United States. Constitutional Convention (1787) and Farrand, 1911, p.211.

[46]   Parker, 1848, p.21.

[47]   U.S. Supreme Court, 1856.

[48]   *Ibid*.

[49]   Calhoun and Lence, 1992, p.321.

[50]   *Ibid.*, p.322.

[51]   Cooper, 1978, p.60.

[52]   Ibid. , p.70.

[53]   Weld and American Anti-Slavery Society, 1839, p.109.

[54]   Genovese, 1965, pp.33-34.

[55]   Calhoun and Lence, 1992, p.342.

[56]   *Ibid.*, p.314.

[57]   *Ibid.*, p.316.

[58]   *Ibid.*, p.315.

[59]   *Ibid.*, p.316.

[60]   *Ibid.*, p.316.

[61]   *Ibid.*, p.316.

62 *Ibid.*, p.316.
63 *Ibid.*, p.313.
64 *Ibid.*, p.314.
65 *Ibid.*, p.314.
66 *Ibid.*, p.314.
67 *Ibid.*, p.340.
68 *Ibid.*, p.323.
69 *Ibid.*, p.323.
70 Ibid., pp.320-326.
71 Cairnes, 1862.
72 *Ibid.*
73 Lincoln, 1858.
74 *Ibid.*
75 Jacobs and Child, 1861, p.38.
76 Lincoln, 1861.
77 Jefferson, 1853, p.154.

Chapter 2

1. Weld and American Anti-Slavery Society, 1839, pp.72-74.
2. *Ibid.*, p.74.
3. *Ibid.*, p.75.
4. Cairnes, 1862.
5. Douglass, 2014, Chapter VI. Racial slurs redacted.
6. Weld and American Anti-Slavery Society, 1839, p.20.
7. *Ibid.*, p.21.
8. *Ibid.*, p.20.
9. *Ibid.*, p.20.
10. Parker, 1848, p.34.
11. Weld and American Anti-Slavery Society, 1839, p.93.
12. *Ibid.*, p.93.
13. *Ibid.*, p.93.
14. *Ibid.*, p.94.
15. *Ibid.*, p.93.
16. *Ibid.*, p.109. Author's emphasis.
17. *Ibid.*, p.109.
18. Stowe and Douglas, 1981.

19. Jacobs and Child, 1861, p.78.
20. Weld and American Anti-Slavery Society, 1839, p.21.
21. Parker, 1848, p.36.
22. Jacobs and Child, 1861, p.38.
23. Stowe and Douglas, 1981.
24. Jacobs and Child, 1861, p.21.
25. *Ibid.*, p.46.
26. *Ibid.*, p.30.
27. Singleton, 1922.
28. Jacobs and Child, 1861, p.9.
29. *Ibid.*, p.29.
30. *Ibid.*, p.130.
31. *Ibid.*, p.44.
32. *Ibid.*, p.69.
33. Weld and American Anti-Slavery Society, 1839, p.128.
34. Ibid., p.128-129. Author's emphasis.
35. Jacobs and Child, 1861, p.123.
36. Olmsted, 1861, p.354.
37. Ruffin and African American Pamphlet Collection (Library of Congress), 1860.
38. *Ibid.*
39. Parker, 1848, p.40.
40. Weld and American Anti-Slavery Society, 1839, p.167. Author's emphasis and capitalization.
41. *Ibid.*, p.167.
42. Jacobs and Child, 1861, p.11.
43. *Ibid.*, p.30.
44. Weld and American Anti-Slavery Society, 1839, p.167.
45. Weston, 1857, p.147.
46. Northup, 2014, p.17.
47. Weston, 1857, p.148.
48. Weld and American Anti-Slavery Society, 1839, p.182. Author's emphasis.
49. Ibid., p.83. Author's emphasis.
50. *Ibid.*, p.73. Author's emphasis.
51. *Ibid.*, p.78.
52. *Ibid.*, p.74. Author's emphasis.
53. *Ibid.*, p.79. Author's emphasis.

54. *Ibid.*, p.79.
55. *Ibid.*, p.78.
56. *Ibid.*, p.78.
57. *Ibid.*, p.78.
58. Stowe and Douglas, 1981.
59. Jacobs and Child, 1861, p.32.
60. Weld and American Anti-Slavery Society, 1839, p.54.
61. Jacobs and Child, 1861, p.28.
62. Stowe and Douglas, 1981.
63. Northup, 2014, p.90.
64. Jacobs and Child, 1861, p.131.
65. Northup, 2014, p.90.
66. Douglass, 2014, Chapter VI.
67. Jacobs and Child, 1861, p.46.
68. Stowe and Douglas, 1981.
69. *Ibid.*
70. Parker, 1848, p.36.
71. Stowe and Douglas, 1981, p.303.
72. Singleton, 1922.
73. Cairnes, 1862.
74. Parker, 1848, p.32.
75. Jacobs and Child, 1861, p.49
76. Parker, 1848, p.30.
77. *Ibid.*, p.29.

Chapter 3

1. Weston, 1857, p.203.
2. Ruffin and African American Pamphlet Collection (Library of Congress), 1860.
3. *Ibid.*
4. Smith, 2012, p.1.
5. Cairnes, 1862.
6. *Ibid.*
7. Weston, 1857, p.232.
8. Burns, 1990.
9. Fogel and Engerman, 1989, p.91.
10. Weld and American Anti-Slavery Society, 1839, p.136. Author's Capitalization.

[11] Ibid., p.136. Author's Capitalization.

[12] Ibid., p.137. Author's Capitalization.

[13] *Ibid.*, p.136.

[14] Elliott, 1860, Chapter VII.

[15] Olmsted, 1861, p.89.

[16] Cairnes, 1862.

[17] Harper, et al., 1853, p.18.

[18] *Ibid.*, p.18.

[19] Cairnes, 1862.

[20] *Ibid.*

[21] *Ibid.*

[22] McDonald Beckles and UNESCO, 2002, p.60.

[23] *Ibid.*, p.60.

[24] Parker, 1848, pp.44-45.

[25] *Ibid.*, p.49.

[26] Olmsted, 1861, p.12.

[27] Genovese, 1965, p.97.

[28] Olmsted, 1861, p.342.

[29] Hergesheimer, 1861.

[30] Northup, 2014, p.58.

[31] *Ibid.*, p.104.

[32] Weston, 1857, p.62.

[33] *Ibid.*, p.62.

[34] Weld and American Anti-Slavery Society, 1839, p.167.

[35] Genovese, 1965, p.250.

[36] Weston, 1857, p.162.

[37] Johnston, 1853, p.17.

[38] *Ibid.*, p.17.

[39] *Ibid.*, p.18.

[40] Cooper, 1978.

[41] Howard, 1886.

[42] *Ibid.*

[43] Doty, 1956.

[44] Cooper, 1978.

[45] *Ibid.*

[46] Bordewich, 2011.

47   Finkelman, 2006, p.74.
48   Bordewich, 2011.
49   Cooper, 1978, p.311.
50   Lincoln, 1858.
51   Ruffin and African American Pamphlet Collection (Library of Congress), 1860, Section VII, Cairnes, 1862.
52   Lincoln, 1858.
53   Cairnes, 1862.
54   Lincoln, 1861.
55   *Ibid*.
56   *Ibid*.
57   *Ibid*.
58   *Ibid*.
59   Parker, 1848, p.49.
60   Calhoun and Lence, 1992, p.318.
61   Elliott, 1860, Chapter V.
62   *Ibid*., Table I.
63   Christy, 1856
64   Elliott, 1860, Table I.
65   Dickens, 1852, p.51.
66   *Ibid*., p.51.
67   *Ibid*., p.51.
68   *Ibid*., Volume 5, p.52.
69   Elliott, 1860, Chapter VI.
70   *Ibid*., Chapter VII.
71   *Ibid*., Chapter V.
72   *Ibid*., Chapter V.
73   *Ibid*., Chapter XIII.
74   *Ibid*., Chapter V.
75   *Ibid*., Chapter VI.
76   Weston, 1857, p.157.
77   Ruffin and African American Pamphlet Collection (Library of Congress), 1860, Section II.
78   *Ibid*., Section I.
79   *Ibid*., Section II.
80   *Ibid*., Section III.

81   Elliott, 1860, Chapter VI.

82   Johnston, 1853, pp.10-11.

83   Elliott, 1860, Chapter VII.

84   *Ibid.*, Chapter IX.

85   Calhoun and Lence, 1992, p.322.

86   *Ibid.*, p.322.

87   *Ibid.*, p.322.

88   Elliott, 1860, Chapter XII.

89   *Ibid.*, Chapter IX.

90   Ibid., Chapter XI. The journal is referred to as the London Economist and it is purportedly from the edition of June 9, 1855.

Chapter 4

1.   Harress, 2013.

2.   Olmsted, 1861, p.24.

3.   *Ibid.*, p.25.

4.   Cairnes, 1862.

5.   Olmsted, 1861, pp.25-26.

6.   Cairnes, 1862.

7.   *Ibid.*

8.   Conrad and Meyer, 1958, pp.121-122.

9.   Northup, 2014, p.58, Olmsted, 1861, pp.244-245, Weld and American Anti-Slavery Society, 1839, p.36.

10.   Olmsted, 1861 , p.325.

11.   Ibid. , p.326.

12.   Ibid., p.327.

13.   Ibid., p.325.

14.   Ibid., p.327.

15.   Northup, 2014, p.56.

16.   *Ibid.*, p.58.

17.   *Ibid.*, p.58.

18.   *Ibid.*, p.55.

19.   Olmsted, 1861, p.247.

20.   *Ibid.*, p.248.

21.   *Ibid.*, p.98.

22.   Ruffin, 1857?, p.4.

23. Ibid., p.4.
24. Helper, 1857, Chapter 1.
25. Cairnes, 1862.
26. Singleton, 1922.
27. Cairnes, 1862.
28. Northup, 2014, p.57.
29. Jacobs and Child, 1861, p.80.
30. *Ibid.*, p.84.
31. *Ibid.*, p.84.
32. Weld and American Anti-Slavery Society, 1839, p.29.
33. Olmsted, 1861, p.102.
34. *Ibid.*, p.245.
35. *Ibid.*, p.377.
36. Weston, 1857, p.77, Weld and American Anti-Slavery Society, 1839, p.95.
37. Northup, 2014, p.68.
38. Genovese, 1965, p.277.
39. Jones, 1827, p.12.
40. Olmsted, 1861, p.245.
41. Genovese, 1965, p.276.
42. Weld and American Anti-Slavery Society, 1839, p.45.
43. *Ibid.*, pp.44-45.
44. Genovese, 1965, p.276.
45. Weld and American Anti-Slavery Society, 1839, p.18.
46. *Ibid.*, p.138.
47. Jones, 1827, p.12.
48. Skinner, 1827, p.291.
49. *Ibid.*, p.291.
50. Weston, 1857, pp.229-230.
51. Fogel and Engerman, 1989, p.70.
52. *Ibid.*, p 93.
53. *Ibid.*, p.71.
54. Olmsted, 1861, p.319.
55. *Ibid.*, p.321.
56. Ibid., pp.321-322.
57. *Ibid.*, p.322.
58. *Ibid.*, p.322.

59. *Ibid.*, p.329.
60. *Ibid.*, p.239.
61. Ruffin, 1857?, p.4.
62. Hammond, 1897, p.452.
63. Olmsted, 1861, p.138.
64. Ruffin and African American Pamphlet Collection (Library of Congress), 1860, p.14.
65. Elliott, 1860, Chapter XII.
66. Ruffin and African American Pamphlet Collection (Library of Congress), 1860, p.10.
67. *Ibid.*, p.10.
68. *Ibid.*, p.10.
69. Ibid., p.6, Ruffin, 1857?, p.6.
70. Ruffin, 1857?, p.6.
71. Ruffin and African American Pamphlet Collection (Library of Congress), 1860, p.9.
72. Jones, 1827, p.8.
73. *Ibid.*, p.8.
74. Fogel and Engerman, 1989, pp.90-91.
75. Elliott, 1860, Conclusion.
76. *Ibid.*, Conclusion.
77. *Ibid.*, Conclusion.
78. *Ibid.*, Conclusion.
79. *Ibid.*, Conclusion.

Chapter 5

1. U.S. Supreme Court, 1856.
2. Northup, 2014, p.114.
3. *Ibid.*, p.108.
4. *Ibid.*, p.108.
5. Ibid., p.99. Racial slurs redacted.
6. *Ibid.*, p.108.
7. *Ibid.*, p.108.
8. Weston, 1857, p.188.
9. *Ibid.*, p.189.
10. Stowe and Douglas, 1981.

11. *Ibid*.
12. Weld and American Anti-Slavery Society, 1839, p.183.
13. Weston, 1857, p.185.
14. Olmsted, 1861, p.321.
15. Stowe and Douglas, 1981.
16. Singleton, 1922.
17. Stowe and Douglas, 1981.
18. Parker, 1848, p.31.
19. Stowe and Douglas, 1981.
20. *Ibid*.
21. *Ibid*.
22. Opala, 1987
23. Northup, 2014, p.99.
24. *Ibid*., p.56.
25. Moneyhon, 2012.
26. Stowe and Douglas, 1981.
27. Weld and American Anti-Slavery Society, 1839, p.167.
28. Olmsted, 1861, p.52.
29. *Ibid*., p.236.
30. Jacobs and Child, 1861, p.3.
31. *Ibid*., p.104.
32. *Ibid*., p.108.
33. *Ibid*., p.67.
34. Weld and American Anti-Slavery Society, 1839, p.18. Author's emphasis.
35. Jacobs and Child, 1861, pp.45-46.
36. Weld and American Anti-Slavery Society, 1839, p.140.
37. *Ibid*., p.140.
38. *Ibid*., p.139.
39. *Ibid*., p.139.
40. Woodward, 1991, p.151, Grenier, 1997.
41. Weld and American Anti-Slavery Society, 1839, p.139.
42. Fogel and Engerman, 1989, p.15.
43. Hammond, 1866, p.116.
44. *Ibid*., p.116.
45. *Ibid*., p.117.
46. Weld and American Anti-Slavery Society, 1839, p.139.

47. *Ibid.*, p.139.
48. Weston, 1857, p.141.
49. *Ibid.*, p.88.
50. Weld and American Anti-Slavery Society, 1839, p.39.
51. Ruffin, 1857?, p.8.
52. Northup, 2014, p.65.
53. Weston, 1857, p.133.
54. Fogel and Engerman, 1989, pp.35-36.
55. Weston, 1857, p.134.
56. Ibid., p.41.
57. Pogue, 2002, p.6.
58. *Ibid.*, p.6.
59. Opala, 1987
60. Weston, 1857, p.114.
61. Fogel and Engerman, 1989, p.47.
62. Weston, 1857, p.114.
63. *Ibid.*, p.114.
64. Ruffin, 1857?, pp.3-4.
65. Ibid., p.5.
66. Ibid., p.5.
67. Stowe and Douglas, 1981.
68. *Ibid.*
69. Fogel and Engerman, 1989, p.15.
70. *Ibid.*, p.16.
71. *Ibid.*, p.16.
72. Christy, 1856, p.261.
73. Ibid., p.27.
74. Weston, 1857, p.117.
75. *Ibid.*, pp.117-118. Author's emphasis.
76. Stowe and Douglas, 1981.

Chapter 6
1. United States. Department of State, 2012, p.7.
2. United Nation. United Nations Office on Drugs and Crime, n.d.
3. United Nations. United Nations Office on Drugs and Crime, 2004, p.42.
4. *Ibid.*, p.43.

5. *Ibid.*, p.43.
6. Interview given 24 October 2014.
7. United States Government, The Victims of Trafficking and Violence Protection Act, 2000, Division A, Section 105, Subsections (a), (b) & (c)
8. *Ibid.*, Division A, Sections 109 & 110.
9. *Ibid.*, Division A, Section 104, Subsection (a).
10. United States. Department of State, 2021, pp.52-53.
11. Ibid., p.56
12. United States. Department of State, 2014b, p.8.
13. CdeBaca, 2014.
14. Nielsen, 2012.
15. *Ibid.*
16. The Act was enacted as *Burma Act VI, 1907* but was dated January 1, 1908.
17. Walk Free Foundation, 2014, p.5.
18. *Ibid.*, p.6.
19. SlaveryFootprint.org, n.d.
20. Information provided by Made In A Free World.
21. United States. Department of State, 2014b, p.43.
22. The *2009 Coroner's Act* mentioned is the *Coroners and Justice Act 2009,* which the Ambassador contrasted to the *Modern Slavery Bill 2014-15*.
23. United States. Department of State, 2014b, p.30.
24. United States. Department of State, 2012, p.25.
25. *Ibid.*, p.25.
26. *Ibid.*, p.25.

Chapter 7

1. A *migrant* is a person who has made a conscious decision to leave their home in pursuit of a better life elsewhere; a refugee is a person for whom remaining in their home country is no longer possible owing to persecution or a well-founded fear of persecution; an *asylum seeker* is a person who has claimed asylum in a host country and who is presently awaiting a decision whether they are entitled to recognition as a refugee.
2. Hodal and Kelly, 2014.
3. Palmstrom, 2014.
4. *Ibid.*
5. Hodal, et al., 2014.

6. Hodal and Kelly, 2014.
7. Environmental Justice Foundation, 2015, p.5.
8. United States. Department of State, 2014a.
9. GlobalSecurity.org, n.d.
10. Agence France Presse, 2014.
11. GlobalSecurity.org, n.d.
12. United States. Department of State, 2014b, pp.38-39.
13. *Ibid.*, p.38.
14. War Child, n.d.
15. Ibid., World Vision, n.d.
16. Thomson Reuters Foundation, 2014.
17. United Nations, 2015.
18. Agence France Presse, 2015.
19. Obaji Jr., 2015.
20. DubaiCity, n.d.
21. Peachey, 2010.
22. Gluckman, n.d.
23. DubaiCity, n.d.
24. Asghar, et al., 2005, p.6.
25. Peachey, 2010.
26. Lewis, 2005.
27. Peachey, 2010.
28. Brook, 2015.
29. United States. Department of State, 2014b, p.99.
30. Ibid., pp.404-406.
31. *Ibid.*, p.73.
32. United States. Department of State, 2008, p.10.
33. United States. Department of State, 2014b, p.70.
34. La Strada International, 2008
35. ANSA, 2013.
36. Doherty and Whyte, 2014.
37. *Ibid.*
38. *Ibid.*
39. *Ibid.*
40. *Ibid.*
41. *Ibid.*

42. Kerry, 2015, International Labour Organization (ILO), 2014.
43. Walk Free Foundation, 2014, p.5.
44. United Nations. United Nations Office on Drugs and Crime, 2014, p.5.
45. *Ibid.*, p.12.
46. United States. Department of State, 2014b, p.397.
47. PolarisProject.org, 2014.
48. Hergesheimer, 1861.
49. UN General Assembly, 1956, Section 1, Article 1(c).
50. United Nations. Office of the High Commissioner for Human Rights, 2013.
51. *Ibid.*
52. *The Economist*, 2015.
53. *Ibid.*
54. Governor of Maharashtra, 2013.
55. Lancaster, 2003.
56. *Ibid.*
57. Agence France Presse, 2010.
58. Associated Press, 2012.
59. TNN, 2013.
60. Bunker, 2013a.
61. *Ibid.*
62. Bunker, 2013b.
63. Bunker, 2013a.
64. Albeit the reduction of cost is compatible with the making of profit.
65. Armstrong, 2014.
66. Phelan, 2014.
67. United States, 2008.
68. United States. Department of State, 2014b, p.203.
69. United States. Department of State, 2011a, p.7.
70. Hawksley, 2014.
71. *Ibid.*
72. Guérin, et al., 2007, p.601.
73. *Ibid.*, p.601.
74. *Ibid.*, p.601.
75. Kamyotra, 2015, p.6.
76. Interview given 13 January 2017.
77. Kamyotra, 2015, p.8.

78. Ibid., p.2.
79. Anti-Slavery International, 2015, pp.1-5.
80. Guérin, et al., 2007, p.604.
81. *Ibid.*, p.604.
82. United Nations. UNICEF India, n.d.
83. Hawksley, 2014.
84. Guérin, et al., 2007, p.600.
85. *Ibid.*, pp.601-604.
86. Hawksley, 2014.
87. Guérin, et al., 2007, p.603.
88. Samuel Hall Consulting, 2011, p.15.
89. Sinha, 2013.
90. United States. Department of State, 2010, p.332.
91. The Coordination Office to Combat Trafficking in Persons, 2014, p.5.
92. African Network for the Prevention and Protection against Child Abuse and Neglect, 2010.
93. Reuters, 2015.
94. *Ibid.*
95. Kabuye, et al., 2014, p.33.
96. Ibid., p.18, Whewell, 2010.
97. Whewell, 2010.
98. Rogers, 2011, Whewell, 2010.
99. Kabuye, et al., 2014, p.2.
100. *Ibid.*, p.19
101. Migiro, 2015.
102. *Ibid.*
103. Champaneria, et al., 2014, Nichter, et al., 1983.
104. Mayo Clinic Staff, 2015.
105. United States. Department of State, 2014b, p.32.
106. Campbell and Davison, 2012.
107. Haken, 2011, p.23.
108. Scalise, 1999.
109. *Ibid.*
110. Thucydides, 455? BC - 355BC.
111. Shimazono, 2007.
112. *Ibid.*

113. Havocscope, n.d.
114. United Nations. United Nations Global Initiative to Fight Human Trafficking, n.d.
115. Haken, 2011, p.22.
116. Pokharel, 2015.
117. Participants in the International Summit on Transplant Tourism and Organ Trafficking Convened by The Transplantation Society and International Society of Nephrology in Istanbul Turkey April 30 through May 2 2008, 2008.
118. Prabhakar and Raja, 2015.
119. United States. Department of State, 2011a, p.170.
120. Nigeria. National Agency For The Prohibition Of Trafficking In Persons, 2019, p.69.
121. Dugard, 2011. [Reprinted with permission of Simon & Schuster, Inc. from A STOLEN LIFE by Jaycee Dugard. Copyright © 2011 by Luna Lee, Inc. All Rights reserved.].
122. Ibid.. [Reprinted with permission of Simon & Schuster, Inc. from A STOLEN LIFE by Jaycee Dugard. Copyright © 2011 by Luna Lee, Inc. All Rights reserved.]
123. Interview given 19 November 2015.
124. Wendyweneki, 2015.

Chapter 8

1. National Human Trafficking Resource Center, 2014.
2. PolarisProject.org, n.d.
3. *Ibid.*
4. United Nations. UNICEF, 2008.
5. France24, 2012.
6. Kara, 2009.
7. Jakobsson and Kotsadam, 2011, p.4.
8. Ekberg, 2004, p.1189.
9. National Rapporteur on Trafficking in Human Beings, 2010, p.26.
10. Swedish Institute, 2010, p.3.
11. George W. Bush Administration, 2003.
12. Global Commission on HIV and the Law, 2012, p.39.
13. UNAIDS, 2011, p.16.
14. *Ibid.*, p.16.
15. *Ibid.*, p.18.
16. UNAIDS, 2012, p.15. Author's emphasis.

17. NSWP, 2014, p.74.
18. Global Commission on HIV and the Law, 2012, p.40.
19. Pedigo, 2013, Sattler, 2013, Hardaway, 2003, p.22.
20. UNAIDS, 2011, p.18.
21. Oxford Dictionaries, 2013.
22. Weitzer, 2005, pp.941-942.
23. United Nations. United Nations Office on Drugs and Crime, 2004, p.42.
24. United States. Department of State, 2011b.
25. UNAIDS, 2011, p.18.
26. Amnesty International, 2014, p.2.
27. Global Commission on HIV and the Law, 2012, p.39.
28. Mangel and Samaniego, 1984, p.259.
29. McRaney, 2013.
30. *Ibid.*
31. *Ibid.*
32. United States. Department of State, 2014b, p.30.
33. McRaney, 2013.
34. Calhoun and Lence, 1992, p.316.
35. *Ibid.*, p.316.
36. WorldVision, 2012.
37. DeWan and Lohan, 2012.
38. Organization for Security and Co-operation in Europe (OSCE), 2008, p.17.
39. Calhoun and Lence, 1992, p.316.
40. Lincoln, 1858.
41. Walk Free Foundation, 2014, p.11.
42. Aronowitz, et al., 2010, Aronowitz, 2009, Kara, 2009, Aronowitz, 2001.
43. Korvinus, et al., 2004, p.3.
44. Kerry, 2015.
45. *Ibid.*
46. National Rapporteur on Trafficking in Human Beings, 2002, p.5.
47. Some exceptions exist. These include the enslavement of persons for the purpose of sex (for example, pedophile networks) and for the purpose of human sacrifice, a crime that still persists today in some parts of South America, Africa and India.

48. Jakobsson and Kotsadam, 2011, p.2, United States. Department of State, 2010, p.45, Aronowitz, 2009, p.24, Kara, 2009, Vandekerckhove, et al., n.d., p.128. Some observers explicitly address the relationship between human trafficking and economics. Others implicitly do so through references to "cheap labor", "forced labour", other comparable terms and profit maximisation.

49. Aronowitz, et al., 2010, Aronowitz, 2009, Kara, 2009, Aronowitz, 2001.

50. AllAfrica, 2012, European Commission, 2012a, Marinova and James, 2012, p.2, Nielsen, 2012, Tordesillas, 2012, Ekberg and Wahlberg, 2011, Jakobsson and Kotsadam, 2011, p.2, Reformina, 2011, Walker-Rodriguez and Hill, 2011, Kloer, 2010, National Rapporteur on Trafficking in Human Beings, 2010, p.18, United States. Department of State, 2010, p.34, Biaudet, 2009, Kelly, et al., 2009, p.61, National Rapporteur on Trafficking in Human Beings, 2009, p.46, Siegel, 2009, p.6, Viuhko and Jokinen, 2009, Daalder, 2007, p.17, Polisen, 2006, p.24, Sullivan, 2005, p.4, Brants, 1998, p.627, Minister of Integration and Gender Equality Sweden, n.d., p.4, Vandekerckhove, et al., n.d., p.150.

51. Kara, 2009.

52. Jones, 1827, p.8.

53. UN General Assembly, 1948.

54. Council of Europe, 1950, Article 4.1.

55. United Nations. United Nations Office on Drugs and Crime, 2004, p.iv.

56. Nickel, 2007, pp.56.

57. Sandel, 2010, p.105.

58. Turner, 1993.

59. Nickel, 2010. Author's emphasis.

60. Nickel, 2007, p.35.

61. United States. Department of State, 2012, p.9.

62. United States. Department of State, 2009, p.32.

63. United States. Department of State, 2011b.

64. United Nations. United Nations Office on Drugs and Crime, 2004, p.46.

65. United States. Department of State, 2009, p.32.

Chapter 9

1. The Victims of Trafficking and Violence Protection Act, 2000, United States. Department of State, n.d.

2. The Procurator General of the Supreme Court of the Netherlands, 2009, Section 4.1.

3. European Commission, 2012a.
4. National Rapporteur on Trafficking in Human Beings, 2010, pp.10-11.
5. *Ibid.*, p.10.
6. *Ibid.*, p.10.
7. *Ibid.*, p.11.
8. *Ibid.*, p.11.
9. *Ibid.*, p.10.
10. United States. Department of State, 2015, p.259.
11. United States. Department of State, 2014b, p.289.
12. *Ibid.*, p.289
13. United States. Department of State, 2015, p.259.
14. Walk Free Foundation, 2018, p.180.
15. European Commission, 2012a.
16. National Rapporteur on Trafficking in Human Beings, 2002, p.2.
17. National Rapporteur on Trafficking in Human Beings and Sexual Violence against Children, 2013b, p.54.
18. Vandekerckhove, et al., n.d., p.262.
19. Siegel, 2009, p.6.
20. *Ibid.*, p.6.
21. *Ibid.*, p.6.
22. Staring, 2012, p.60. [reprinted by permission of the publisher (Taylor & Francis Ltd, http://www.tandfonline.com)].
23. Hindle, et al., 2008, p.16.
24. *Ibid.*, p.16.
25. Korvinus, et al., 2004, p.5.
26. *Ibid.*, p.14.
27. Brants, 1998, p.624.
28. *Ibid.*, p.624.
29. Ibid., p.625.
30. Ibid., p.625.
31. *Ibid.*, p.624.
32. Rade and Shah, 2010.
33. Kelly, et al., 2009, p.25.
34. National Rapporteur on Trafficking in Human Beings, 2002, p.9.
35. Brants, 1998, p.627.
36. *Ibid.*, p.627.

37. *Ibid.*, p.629.
38. National Rapporteur on Trafficking in Human Beings, 2010, p.26, Brants, 1998, pp.629-630.
39. Brants, 1998, p.632.
40. Hubbard, et al., 2008, p.142.
41. Ibid., p.142. [reprinted by permission of the publisher (Taylor & Francis Ltd, http://www.tandfonline.com)].
42. Brants, 1998, p.630.
43. Dettmeijer-Vermeulen, et al., 2007, p.4.
44. Staring, 2012, p.60, Hindle, et al., 2008, p.14, National Rapporteur on Trafficking in Human Beings, 2002, p.10.
45. Korvinus, et al., 2004, p.13.
46. Hindle, et al., 2008, p.14, Hubbard, et al., 2008, p.141.
47. National Rapporteur on Trafficking in Human Beings, 2002, p.10.
48. *Ibid.*, p.2.
49. *Ibid.*, p.2.
50. Staring, 2012, p.60, Hubbard, et al., 2008, p.141, Brants, 1998, p.623.
51. The Procurator General of the Supreme Court of the Netherlands, 2009, Section 4.1.
52. *Ibid.*, Section 4.1.
53. Schepers, 2011, Kelly, et al., 2009, p.23, The Procurator General of the Supreme Court of the Netherlands, 2009, Section 4.1, Hubbard, et al., 2008, p.142, Daalder, 2007, p.9, National Rapporteur on Trafficking in Human Beings, 2002, p.11, Vandekerckhove, et al., n.d., p.260.
54. Siegel, 2009, p.5.
55. National Rapporteur on Trafficking in Human Beings, 2002, pp. 23-26, Vandekerckhove, et al., n.d., p.264.
56. National Rapporteur on Trafficking in Human Beings, 2002, p.18.
57. Hindle, et al., 2008, p.16.
58. Bucken-Knapp, et al., 2012.
59. Hughes, 2005, p.37.
60. Bucken-Knapp, et al., 2012.
61. United States. Department of State, 2015, p.322.
62. *Ibid.*, p.322.
63. Walk Free Foundation, 2018, p.180.
64. European Commission, 2012b, Ekberg and Wahlberg, 2011.
65. Claude and Swedish Institute, 2010, p.6.

66. *Ibid.*, p.6.
67. Bucken-Knapp, et al., 2012.
68. Standing Committee on Justice and Human Rights and Subcommittee on Solicitation Laws, 2006, p.72.
69. *Ibid.*, p.71.
70. Ekberg, 2004, pp.1188-1189.
71. Sandel, 2010, pp.129-132, Nickel, 2007, pp.27-28.
72. Standing Committee on Justice and Human Rights and Subcommittee on Solicitation Laws, 2006, p.72.
73. Ekberg, 2004, p.1189.
74. Kelly, et al., 2009, p.31.
75. Hubbard, et al., 2008, p.142. [reprinted by permission of the publisher (Taylor & Francis Ltd, http://www.tandfonline.com)].
76. Ibid., pp.142-143.
77. *Ibid.*, p.143.
78. Ibid., p.143, Ekberg, 2004, p.1192.
79. Bucken-Knapp, et al., 2012, European Commission, 2012b, Marinova and James, 2012, p.7, Ekberg and Wahlberg, 2011, Claude and Swedish Institute, 2010, p.3, Swedish Institute, 2010, p.6, Englund, et al., 2008, p.23, Hubbard, et al., 2008, p.143, Standing Committee on Justice and Human Rights and Subcommittee on Solicitation Laws, 2006, p.71, Ekberg, 2004, p.1191, Minister of Integration and Gender Equality Sweden, n.d., p.5, Ruhama, n.d., p.2.
80. Bucken-Knapp, et al., 2012.
81. Ekberg, 2004, p.1192.
82. Ekberg and Wahlberg, 2011, Claude and Swedish Institute, 2010, p.6, Englund, et al., 2008, p.23, Munro, 2006, p.320, Minister of Integration and Gender Equality Sweden, n.d., p.5.
83. European Commission, 2012b.
84. Claude and Swedish Institute, 2010.
85. *Ibid.*, p.7.
86. *Ibid.*, p.9.
87. European Commission, 2012b. Acts of purchasing sexual services are dealt with under Chapter 6 of the Swedish Penal Code: Section 9 addresses the offence as it relates to children, Section 11 as it relates to adults.
88. Ibid., Ekberg and Wahlberg, 2011, Claude and Swedish Institute, 2010, p.7, Hubbard, et al., 2008, p.143, Standing Committee on Justice and Human Rights and Subcommittee on Solicitation Laws, 2006, p.73, Minister of Integration and Gender Equality Sweden, n.d., p.5.

89. Ekberg, 2004, p.1192.
90. Bucken-Knapp, et al., 2012, European Commission, 2012b, Englund, et al., 2008, p.22.
91. Claude and Swedish Institute, 2010, p.9, Minister of Integration and Gender Equality Sweden, n.d., p.5.
92. Polisen, 2010, p.29.
93. Englund, et al., 2008, p.22.
94. Bucken-Knapp, et al., 2012, European Commission, 2012b, Polisen, 2006, p.28.
95. Polisen, 2006, p.6.
96. *Ibid.*, p.8.
97. Polisen, 2011, p.32.
98. National Rapporteur on Trafficking in Human Beings and Sexual Violence against Children, 2013b, p.85.
99. Magnanti, 2012.
100. Amnesty International, 2015.
101. United States. Department of State, 2015, p.260.
102. *Ibid.*, p.260.
103. Walk Free Foundation, 2018, p.181.
104. New Zealand Government, 2003.
105. Prostitution Reform Act 2003, Part 2, Paragraph 18:1.
106. *Ibid.*, Part 2, Paragraph 18:2.
107. *Ibid.*, Part 2, Paragraph 17:2.
108. *Ibid.*, Part 1, Paragraph 3.
109. Interview given 12 November 2015.
110. Crimes Act 1961, Section 98D, Paragraph 1(a).
111. *Ibid.*, Section 98D, Paragraph 1(b).
112. United States. Department of State, 2014b, p.292.
113. United States. Department of State, 2015, p.261.
114. *Ibid.*, p.261.
115. *Ibid.*, p.261.
116. Glazebrook, 2010, p.17.
117. In November 2015 Section 98D of the *Crimes Act of 1961* was amended by the *Crimes Amendment Act 2015*. The amendment constituted a major overhaul of the previous provisions. A crime of human trafficking could now be committed within New Zealand's borders. These changes appear to bring the country's offense of human trafficking into line with international norms, especially with those of the *Palermo Protocol*.

118. United States. Department of State, 2020, p.372.
119. Ministry of Justice, 2002, p.5.
120. *Ibid.*, p.5.
121. *Ibid.*, p.13.
122. New Zealand. Parliamentary Library, 2012, p.8.
123. New Zealand Prostitutes Collective, n.d.-a, New Zealand Prostitutes Collective, n.d.-b
124. United States. Department of State, 2021, p.416
125. Ibid., p.416
126. Hagar International, 2015.
127. Tan, 2010.
128. *Ibid.*
129. *Ibid.*
130. United States. Department of State, 2007, p.158.
131. Ministry of Justice. Prostitution Law Review Committee, 2008, p.14.
132. *Ibid.*, p.56.
133. United States. Department of State, 2011a, p.274.
134. Carville, 2016.
135. Ibid..
136. Ibid..

Chapter 10

1. Brants, 1998, p.630.
2. Korvinus, et al., 2004, p.14.
3. Dettmeijer-Vermeulen, et al., 2007, p.76.
4. Schepers, 2011, Almelo District Court, 2008.
5. Schepers, 2011, Aronowitz, 2009, p.69, National Rapporteur on Trafficking in Human Beings, 2009, p.271, Siegel, 2009, p.9.
6. Aronowitz, et al., 2010, p.91.
7. Schepers, 2011.
8. Aronowitz, 2009, p.69.
9. The original members started to hire other personnel to fill positions, new positions emerged and promotion to higher level positions became possible. Eventually the network employed approximately 30 people. The operation was spread out over five Dutch cities and it collaborated with associates in Belgian and German cities (Schepers, 2011, Aronowitz, et al., 2010, p.91, Aronowitz, 2009, p.69).

10. Schepers, 2011, Aronowitz, et al., 2010, p.91.
11. Aronowitz, 2009, p.64.
12. Aronowitz, et al., 2010, p.91.
13. Schepers, 2011.
14. Aronowitz, 2009, p.69.
15. Schepers, 2011, National Rapporteur on Trafficking in Human Beings, 2009, p.299, Almelo District Court, 2008.
16. Almelo District Court, 2008.
17. *Ibid*.
18. Brants, 1998, p.630.
19. United States. Department of State, 2008, p.29.
20. National Rapporteur on Trafficking in Human Beings, 2009, p.256.
21. Pieters, 2015.
22. Persad, 2013.
23. National Rapporteur on Trafficking in Human Beings and Sexual Violence against Children, 2013b, p.67.
24. Interview given 10 September 2012.
25. National Rapporteur on Trafficking in Human Beings and Sexual Violence against Children, 2013b, p.306.
26. Agency Reporter, 2012, EUROPA, 2012, United Nations. United Nations Office on Drugs and Crime, 2010, p.44, National Rapporteur on Trafficking in Human Beings, 2009, p.364, Michaud, 2009.
27. European Commission, 2012a, United Nations. United Nations Office on Drugs and Crime, 2010, p.44, Agence France Presse, 2009, Dunne, 2009, Michaud, 2009.
28. EUROPA, 2012, National Rapporteur on Trafficking in Human Beings, 2009, p.364.
29. EUROPA, 2012, Agence France Presse, 2009.
30. Aronowitz, et al., 2010, p.91.
31. National Rapporteur on Trafficking in Human Beings, 2009, p.364.
32. Siegel, 2012, p.263, Biaudet, 2009, National Rapporteur on Trafficking in Human Beings, 2009, p.365.
33. EUROPA, 2012.
34. Agence France Presse, 2009.
35. Dunne, 2009.
36. Michaud, 2012.
37. Aronowitz, et al., 2010, p.92.

38. National Rapporteur on Trafficking in Human Beings and Sexual Violence against Children, 2013b, pp.13-14.
39. Brants, 1998, p.634.
40. Siegel, 2009, p.8.
41. Standing Committee on Justice and Human Rights and Subcommittee on Solicitation Laws, 2006, p.83.
42. Egizi, 2013, Ditmore, 2009.
43. DeWan and Lohan, 2012, pp.81-96.
44. National Rapporteur on Trafficking in Human Beings, 2009, p.280.
45. *Ibid.*, p.289.
46. National Rapporteur on Trafficking in Human Beings, 2010, p.59.
47. Dettmeijer-Vermeulen, et al., 2007, p.203.
48. Staring, 2012, p.68, Siegel, 2009, p.11, Dettmeijer-Vermeulen, et al., 2007, p.75.
49. National Rapporteur on Trafficking in Human Beings, 2010, p.59, Dettmeijer-Vermeulen, et al., 2007, p.77, Korvinus, et al., 2004, p.93.
50. Korvinus, et al., 2004, p.93.
51. National Rapporteur on Trafficking in Human Beings, 2010, p.59.
52. Dettmeijer-Vermeulen, et al., 2007, p.75.
53. Interview given 10 September 2012.
54. Hindle, et al., 2008, p.16.
55. This same conclusion was arrived at by a different route and at an earlier juncture. Daalder points to a situation that arose from the perception amongst licensed business operators that they were being inspected more often than their non-licensed counterparts (Daalder, 2007, p.11). Thus "a paradoxical situation can be said to have ensued: while the former prohibition of the exploitation of prostitution changed to a legalization, prostitutes and sex business owners now feel that the regulations have become stricter, whereas in practice it is a matter of a stricter enforcement" (ibid., p.12).
56. Daalder noted how a "large part of the available police capacity ... [remained] deployed for inspections in the licensed sector, thus limiting the capacity for monitoring and investigative tasks with regard to punishable forms of exploitation in the non-licensed sector" (ibid., p.11).
57. National Rapporteur on Trafficking in Human Beings, 2009, pp.30-31.
58. National Rapporteur on Trafficking in Human Beings, 2010, p.28.
59. *Ibid.*, p.28.
60. National Rapporteur on Trafficking in Human Beings, 2009, p.48.
61. Polisen, 2006, p.20.

62. Polisen, 2009b, p.6.
63. Swedish Institute, 2010, p.8.
64. *Ibid.*, p.8.
65. Polisen, 2006, p.20.
66. Claude and Swedish Institute, 2010, p.15, Swedish Institute, 2010, p.11.
67. Swedish Institute, 2010, p.10.
68. Claude and Swedish Institute, 2010, p.7.
69. Polisen, 2009a, p.10, Polisen, 2006, p.13.
70. This experience also likely provides an argument against those who advocate legalization and decriminalization on the basis that it would facilitate the interaction of those who sell sexual services with policing authorities. In Sweden there is no offence, thus there is no punishment. It is ubiquitous fear that prevents trafficked persons from presenting themselves and complying with law enforcement efforts.
71. Polisen, 2010, p.6.
72. Ekberg, 2004, p.1189.
73. Englund, et al., 2008, p.99.
74. *Ibid.*, p.116.
75. *Ibid.*, p.116.
76. Polisen, 2009b, p.19.
77. *Ibid.*, p.19.
78. Polisen, 2006, p.12.
79. *Ibid.*, p.12.
80. Claude and Swedish Institute, 2010, p.13
81. Interview given 15 June 2015.
82. Polisen, 2013, p.13. The report provides statistics for earlier years, but it provided statistics for trafficking and procuring only from 2003.
83. United States. Department of State, 2012, p.328.
84. National Rapporteur on Trafficking in Human Beings, 2002, p.49. STV data. Estimates from BNRM put the figure higher but the Rapporteur questions the data on several fronts.
85. National Rapporteur on Trafficking in Human Beings, 2010, p.167.
86. *Ibid.*, pp.174-175.
87. National Rapporteur on Trafficking in Human Beings and Sexual Violence against Children, 2014.
88. National Rapporteur on Trafficking in Human Beings and Sexual Violence against Children, 2013a, p.1.

89. *Ibid.*, p.1.
90. National Rapporteur on Trafficking in Human Beings and Sexual Violence against Children, 2013b, p.85.
91. *Ibid.*, p.19.
92. Prostitution Information Center, 2012.
93. National Rapporteur on Trafficking in Human Beings and Sexual Violence against Children, 2013b, p.70.
94. Brants, 1998, p.633.
95. National Rapporteur on Trafficking in Human Beings, 2009, p.277.
96. Drury, 2009.
97. SOAIDS, n.d.
98. National Rapporteur on Trafficking in Human Beings, 2009, p.254.
99. *Ibid.*, p.251.
100. DutchNews.nl, 2013.
101. Cruz and van Iterson, n.d.
102. Spiegel Staff, 2013.
103. Morris, 2013.
104. Cruz and van Iterson, n.d.
105. National Rapporteur on Trafficking in Human Beings, 2009, p.257
106. *Ibid.*, p.257.
107. Interview given 28 November 2013.
108. Interview given 19 November 2015.
109. Interview given 10 September 2012.
110. Cho, et al., 2013, p.75.
111. *Ibid.*, p.72.
112. *Ibid.*, p.68.
113. *Ibid.*, p.72.
114. *Ibid.*, p.75.
115. *Ibid.*, p.71.
116. *Ibid.*, p.72.
117. Dettmeijer-Vermeulen, et al., 2007, p.75.
118. Interview given 10 September 2012.
119. Interview given 10 September 2012.
120. Cruz and van Iterson, n.d.

Conclusions

1. Ruffin, 1857?, p.5.
2. United States. Department of State, 2009, p.32.
3. Interview given 24 October 2014.
4. Jefferson and Boyd, n.d.
5. Singleton, 1922.

Appendix

1. The Procurator General of the Supreme Court of the Netherlands, 2009, Section 4.1.
2. *Ibid.*, Section 4.1.
3. National Rapporteur on Trafficking in Human Beings, 2010, p.18, Kelly, et al., 2009, p.24.
4. National Rapporteur on Trafficking in Human Beings, 2010, p.19, Korvinus, et al., 2004, pp.17-18, National Rapporteur on Trafficking in Human Beings, 2002, p.2, Vandekerckhove, et al., n.d., p.260.
5. Staring, 2012, p.60, ECPAT International, 2011, p.9, The Procurator General of the Supreme Court of the Netherlands, 2009, Section 2.2.2, Dettmeijer-Vermeulen, et al., 2008, p.27, Daalder, 2007, p.11.
6. The Procurator General of the Supreme Court of the Netherlands, 2009, Section 2.2.2, Council Framework Decision 2002/629/JHA of 19 July 2002 on combating trafficking in human beings.
7. EUROPA, 2011.
8. *Ibid.*
9. The maximum fine that could be imposed upon human traffickers was increased to €74,000 and the maximum penalty for a human trafficking offence, one that brings about the death of person, was set at 18 years' imprisonment (National Rapporteur on Trafficking in Human Beings, 2009, p.46). Punishment for other human trafficking offences were also increased and, though they now carried lesser terms of imprisonment, these were significant nonetheless (ibid., p.46). Later that same year a parliamentary committee discussed further measures to centralize policy with regard to administrative measures, a responsibility that had originally been vested in the local municipalities (National Rapporteur on Trafficking in Human Beings, 2010, p.28). These measures were subsequently adopted (ECPAT International, 2011, p. 10).
10. International Organization for Migration, 2005, pp.87-89.
11. *Ibid.*, p.87.

12. *Ibid.*, p.87.
13. *Ibid.*, p.87.
14. *Ibid.*, p.87.
15. *Ibid.*, p.87.
16. Ibid., p.87, United Nations. United Nations Office on Drugs and Crime, 2004, p.43.
17. For example, some of the *means* listed in the *Palermo Protocol* are described as *acts* in Article 250a. When the article was amended human trafficking was no longer synonymous with sex trafficking. Other acts were now punishable, as acts of human trafficking, under the Dutch law. This was achieved by expanding on the *purpose* of the exploitation. The exploitation of persons for the purpose of forced commercial sexual exploitation remained in place but other forms of exploitation, such as the exploitation of persons for the purpose of removing their organs, were now recognized (National Rapporteur on Trafficking in Human Beings, 2010, p.19, National Rapporteur on Trafficking in Human Beings, 2002, p.2). Broadly speaking however Article 250a was more inclusive in relation to sex trafficking than Article 273a, the article that had succeeded it (Korvinus, et al., 2004, p.18). Any action could be deemed an *act*. The *means* given in Article 250a are, approximately, interchangeable with those given in the *Palermo Protocol*. The form of exploitation given in Article 250a is limited to that of forced commercial exploitation, a point that does not inhibit this work as this the practice being scrutinized.
18. Anti-Slavery International and International Trade Union Confederation, 2011, p.54, Konrad, 2005, p.2.